Dealing with the New Russia

Management Cultures in Collision

Nigel Holden
Copenhagen Business School

Cary Cooper
at UMIST, Manchester
and
Jennifer Carr

JOHN WILEY & SONS

Chichester • New York • Weinheim • Brisbane • Singapore • Toronto

National   01243 779777
International +(44) 1243 779777
e-mail (for order and customer service enquiries): cs-books@wiley.co.uk
Visit our Home Page on http://www.wiley.co.uk
                        or http://www.wiley.com

Other Wiley Editorial Offices

John Wiley & Sons, Inc., 605 Third Avenue,
New York, NY 10158-0012, USA

Weinheim • Brisbane • Singapore • Toronto

Library of Congress Cataloging-in-Publication Data
Holden, Nigel, 1945–
    Dealing with the New Russia : Management Cultures in Collision /
Nigel Holden, Cary Cooper, and Jennifer Carr
    p. cm.
Includes index.
ISBN 0-471-96456-5 (pbk.)
1. Corporate culture -- Russia (Federation)   2. Industrial
management -- Russia (Federation)   3. Post-communism -- Russia
(Federation) I. Cooper, Cary L. II. Carr, Jennifer. III. Title.
HD58.7.H644 1998   97–45613
302.3'5'0947—dc21   CIP

British Library Cataloguing in Publication Data
A catalogue record for this book is available from the British Library

ISBN 0-471-96456-5

Typeset in Palatino 11/13pt by Stephen Wright-Bouvier of the
Rainwater Consultancy, Longworth, Oxfordshire.
Printed and bound in Great Britain by Biddles Ltd, Guildford and King's Lynn.
Midsomer Norton, Somerset.
This book is printed on acid-free paper responsibly manufactured from sustainable forestry, in which at least two trees are planted for each one used.

Contents

List of Figures

List of Tables

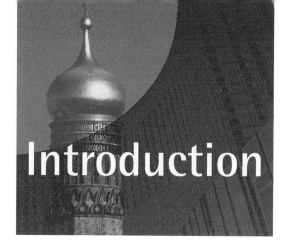

Introduction

Since the collapse of the Soviet Union, Russia and the CIS have become a hunting ground (but necessarily the proverbially happy one) for a group of people who might be called business and management adventurers: management consultants, educators, investors, economists and others, all of whom are involved, directly or indirectly, in the continued transformation of the former USSR into a modern democratic market economy. Working in Russia and collaborating with their Russian partners, westerners often face serious difficulties in understanding and communicating effectively, owing to differences in economic and political systems, infrastructures, national and business cultures, and managerial attitudes and habits. In this volume the word *gap* is used as a portmanteau term to express these difficulties.

This book is aimed especially at those business adventurers, who find dealing with Russians and coping with Russia new and unexpectedly trying experiences. For the manager and businessman who is specializing in the Russian/CIS market, there is no shortage of books giving advice on the market approach, investment opportunities, negotiating with Russians, not to mention personal safety. This book complements these offerings. Indeed, it draws on a good many of them, but the authors have sought to provide business adventurers with a book on Russia that differs markedly from others currently available.

We deal with a host of themes mentioned in a number of books on the Russian business environment, but that are, in our view, underdeveloped in them. The most notable theme is that of relationship building. It is common knowledge that Russian business people want a close relationship. But what does this mean in practice? What should foreign business people know about Russian expectations of close relationships? In what ways do interpreters sometimes inadvertently block relationship building? What role – and this is a highly pertinent question – does vodka play in all this? How does an appreciation of the Russian system of address help a foreign business person to adjust the level of closeness he wishes to attain with a business partner?

Two of the authors (Holden and Cooper) bring a particular advantage to the treatment of issues relating to the transformation of Russian management in the present phase of transition. They were both involved in devising and implementing management development programmes for the Russian construction sector from 1992 to 1995 under the EU Technical Assistance to the CIS (TACIS) programme. We have therefore been able to use first-hand information relating to management challenges in a branch of industry, in which the traditional (i.e. Soviet) management techniques were often slap-dash, given the pressures to complete projects against deadlines which were unrealistic in an economy short of supplies.

In this book we attach a good deal of importance to historical realities. Our conviction is that, in order to understand Russia today, you need to understand where Russia has come from. Therefore one of our major challenges as authors is to attempt to relate Soviet and even earlier periods of Russia's experience to the values, practices and philosophies of Russian managers decades and centuries later. It is customary in books about management systems in other countries to stress the value of gaining insights into their cultural dimensions. In the case of Russia – to make a crucial distinction – it is essential to understand the historical dimension, and there is a lot of history to digest. As Brian Moynahan, in his fine book *The Russian Century*, reminds us:

> History has flung itself at Russia this century, riding
> bareback and at the gallop . . . Its people have been killed
> by the million . . . It has produced cosmonauts, and can-
> nibals who flourished in starvation years . . . It put paid
> to old concepts – religious faith, private property, the
> rule of law – that are only now fitfully reappearing.

The point is that foreigners who are drawn (or sent) to Russia become part of its restless, unpredictable history. Mindful of that, this book has been designed to communicate what we believe to be important for management consultants, management educators and business representatives to understand about Russia, not just know about Russia.

As for structure, the book is effectively in two parts. The first six chapters are predominantly concerned with putting Russia and Russian managers into context, while Chapters 7 to 10 are more in the nature of explanations or unravellings with particular attention on issues of interpersonal communication. Chapter 1 is a scene-setting essay. It takes a compressed view of Russia's 20th century, highlighting recurring themes in Russian and Soviet experience which shape Russia's and the west's often distorted understanding of each other. In Chapter 2 we look directly at the findings of a workshop held near Moscow in December 1996, where Russian and western management experts tried to analyse the nature of the gap between each other's approaches to management challenges. Some observations may make unpleasant therapeutic reading for western management consultants and educators, whose efforts to illuminate the path to market economy thinking and behaviour often do not impress their Russian clientèle in the least. Thanks are extended to Kate Gilbert of Wolverhampton Business School who made notes at this workshop and assisted in the writing of this chapter.

Chapter 3 explores how management worked in the Soviet Union, arguing that Soviet managers cleaved to values that are strongly associated with traditional Russian concepts of collectivism and democracy. Chapters 4 and 5 are concerned with the transformation of the Soviet manager under *perestroika* and his emergence as 'the Russian manager', someone we call a 'deeply troubled man', for reasons that will be explained. In Chapter 5 we present material on current challenges facing Russian managers – some of it reproduced for the first time in English. The main point of Chapters 4 and 5 is to emphasize the structural and psychological impediments to management change in Russia since the mid-1980s with the launching of Gorbachev's *perestroika* programme.

Chapter 6 probes the issues of strain and malfunction in relationships between western and Russian business partners. The material is drawn from a survey of fourteen UK organizations with involvements in Russia ranging from the importing of high-tech products to management education. This chapter highlights awkward sticking points and areas of friction, many of which fall under the general heading of 'communication problems'. Chapters 7–9 examine these problematical issues in considerable depth. In Chapter 7 the broad theme of language will be taken up with a view to understanding of the subtleties of the way in which Russians use their language to regulate social distance and to share fellow feeling. You do not need to know a word of Russian to appreciate this chapter. You need merely to be motivated to understand the Russian communicative framework: because, when you deal with Russians, you are in it.

Chapter 8 will take on the big issue of 'language deficiency', which hinders the straightforward transfer of management terms and concepts into Russian – and therefore into Russian thinking. The aim of this chapter is to make clear how intimately the issue of language deficiency is bound up with the idea of the gap. This chapter should not be seen as a 'turn off' for those who find the formal presentation of language issues intensely boring. Anyone reading this chapter will never be casual in his choice of words with Russians again – and especially with interpreters, who are exasperating causes of communication breakdown. In Chapter 9 we discuss the social side of business, coping with Russian hospitality and understanding that toasting is not just a way of making vodka disappear dramatically, but a form of business interaction in its own right. In Chapter 10 we attempt to draw together the main themes which the book has addressed, highlighting implications for business practitioners, management educators and consultants, and policy makers.

If you have already flicked through the pages of this book, you will see that it is interspersed with *information panels*. These provide additional information on topics that are highlighted in bold, but which are given no further treatment in the main text. In many cases these are topics that you would expect to find more in a history or a travel book on Russia. But the logic is this: Russians strongly feel that western professionals, especially those who are in Russia to advise and instruct them, are disconcertingly ignorant of Russia and its culture. The information panels have been selected to augment what an otherwise educated management professional might already know about Russia (and the Soviet Union). Another source of quick reference is the glossary at the end of the book, which provides compressed information on historical terms, personalities and acronyms.

Russians appear to respect foreigners who know their history or have read (in most cases in translation, of course) the great works of Russian literature. Indeed, foreigners' appreciation of their literature seems to impress them more than a displayed knowledge of their history. But remember that Russians take a different view of their history. Gorbachev, lionized in the west even now, is often regarded as the man who weakened Russia and was therefore responsible for many of the present ills. Very few Russians seem to have anything good to say about him. But, most important of all remember, Russians do not take kindly to foreigners saying anything critical about their country. They are not naive, and they know that the west is better off materially, but they are hypersensitive to the point of deep offence if foreigners appear to mock Russia or the Soviet Union. As Solzhenitsyn wrote in *Rebuilding Russia*: 'God forbid that anyone should dare to offend or slight our nationality!'

One of the problems about a book on Russia and Russians is the very definition of these terms. We adopt an entirely pragmatic approach and address in the broadest sense the fate of nations and peoples who formed, first, the Russian Empire, then the Soviet Union, and who now belong to various countries, some of which are connected politically, others not; but all of them are geographically contiguous with the present Russian Federation and all of them experienced Russification (of which Sovietization was a particular kind). We shall always make clear when we mean the Soviet Union as opposed to Russia. Generally, when we speak of Russia now or in the past, we have in mind vast tracts of Eastern Europe and Asia, which are or were under Russian political and cultural hegemony. As for the term Russian, we certainly mean ethnic Russians, but it is inevitable that we shall be implying hundreds of thousands of ethnically non-Russians who live in Russia and regard Russia as their home. No disrespect is meant to them.

Another problem concerns the transliteration of Russian words, including names. Those with a knowledge of Russian will be familiar with the difficulties. Again, we are pragmatic and adopt a consistent transliteration scheme, but will use the conventional and most familiar form in English even if this is not the most 'efficient' rendering. For example, Peter the Great will be Peter not Pyotr, as his name becomes in Russian; *glasnost* will be written like this, and not as *glasnost'* the inverted comma signifying that it is followed in Russian by a sign which indicates that the *t* is softened).

Turn the page over. Russia beckons.

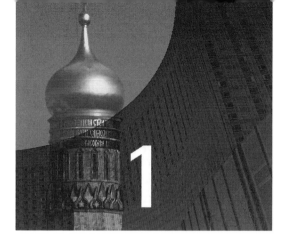

COPING WITH A NEW RUSSIA

A totalitarian system leaves behind it a minefield built into both the country's social structure and the individual psychology of its citizens.

— Sobchak, 1992

From the Uzbeks, Brezhnev wanted only cotton and, more important, wonderful cotton statistics.

— Remnick, 1994

Introduction

Russia has fascinated and perturbed other countries since the first western Europeans visited the country in the 16th century. Oxford scholar Ronald Hingley (1978) points out that these ambiguous, occasionally queasy feelings about Russia have 'derived less from its system of government than from the lure of the quaint, the bizarre, the incongruous'. These are not the most common adjectives that we associate with Russia. Normally our stereotypes are filtered through adjectives such as authoritarian, sentimental, turbulent, hard drinking and tragic (the last probably being the most common single word used to describe the course of Russian history). In a very real sense, this book will directly and indirectly highlight the quaint, the bizarre and the incongruous about Russian life and experience in ways which are crucially relevant to western managers operating in Russia or contemplating activities there. This chapter is in two parts: a brief survey of Russian history in the 20th century followed by discussion of some of the threads which are most important for outlining influences on the Russian mindset. Chapter 1 will therefore introduce many themes about Russia, the Russians, the Soviet experience and Russia's prickly, uneasy relationship with the west which will pervade this book. For western managers, for whom a clear understanding of the Russian mindset is a professional necessity, an awareness of the potency of these influences is truly essential knowledge.

Brief survey of Russia's 20th century

Russia's 20th century has been one of sorrow and slaughter, turmoil and tragedy; of ideals that went wrong and a vision that became perverted. The fatal war with Japan 1904–1905; the crippling participation in the Great War 1914–1918; the savage murder of the Tsar and his family in 1918; the bloody Civil War, 1918–1922, which followed the relatively bloodless 1917 October Revolution; the brutal collectivization of agriculture, 1928–1934; the great surge of industrialization in the 1930s, which depended so much on mass forced labour; the Great Terror of 1936–1938 and the Gulag which outlasted it (had not the dying Lenin had urged his cronies to ditch the odious Stalin); and the horrific war, 1941–1945, with Nazi Germany – all these momentous, numbing events created human suffering and sacrifice on a scale that is beyond imagination.

Yet in the 1930s Russia was being hailed as 'the second America': in less than two decades the socialist form of government seemingly proved to the outside world that a society, based on scientific (i.e. Marxist-Leninist) principles, developed on the back of Five Year Plans, and guided by the advanced thinking of the Communist Party, could represent a viable alternative to the old social orders of Europe and the USA. [**Five Year Plans**] Western apologists for socialism in the 1930s did not seem to appreciate that the Soviet variant only 'worked' because industrialization under Stalin was

Five Year Plans

By the mid-1920s it was becoming clear that the Soviet economy needed improved mechanisms for systematic control of production and distribution of key commodities, particularly metals. In 1927 the Council of People's Commissars called for 'a united all-union plan, which would . . . facilitate the maximum development of regions on the basis of their specialization'. This gave rise to the concept of the long-term, comprehensive national development plan; out of that arose the Five Year Plan, the first of which was implemented from 1928–1932 under the guidance of Gosplan, the State Planning Commission established in 1921. Not only did the first Five Year Plan provide an enduring structure and style of economic management, it also 'left conspicuous imbalances which would become more or less permanent features of the Soviet economy': the massive emphasis on heavy industrial sector at the expense of the chemicals sector, textiles, railways, housing and consumer goods and services.

The centralized planning system has been likened to one giant firm 'divided for administrative convenience into various industries, which were further subdivided within a planning-and-management hierarchy'. But this was a firm, whose main task was to make plan fulfilment in output terms a priority. 'Since the role of the state in the economy combined planning with management, both the future shape of the economy and the short-term assurance of goals and supplies for each productive enterprise had to be planned and integrated.' The plan therefore was 'a multiplicity of interdependent instructions, not only relating supplies and outputs, but also the value of sales, labour productivity and other 'plan indicators''.

The plans continued until the collapse of the Soviet era, but not seamlessly. For example, the third (1938-42) was interrupted by the war; the sixth, which was intended to cover 1956–1960 was scrapped in 1957, its last two years being added to a Seven Year Plan for 1959-65. By the time Gorbachev took power in 1985, it was clear that the centralized planning system had created conditions of shortage, sectoral imbalances and technological slowdown. The net effect was wide-spread bribery, hoarding, illicit production and selling of items in demand. Despite all attempts in the Soviet era to make the planning system more efficient (short of dismantling it altogether) through organizational restructuring, the fundamental problem, in Nove's neat (1990) encapsulation, was this: 'centralized decision-

> making could only encompass a portion of the multitude of decisions which, in an economy of the Stalin type, must be taken by the planner–administrators, and which, in the absence of any effective criteria other than plan-orders, logically cannot be taken elsewhere.'
>
> In the transition to the market economy, Russian management is deficient in four areas which had no place in the Soviet system:
>
> * marketing
> * human resource management
> * business strategy
> * financial management.
>
> Ironically, all these areas require good skills in planning.

characterized by 'the coexistence of volunteer and forced labour, of heroic self-sacrifice and violent coercion. It was a temporary and unstable dichotomy that could occur only in a society that was simultaneously undergoing a social revolution with substantial support from below while being enslaved from above' (Graham, 1996). Nor was it realized until much later that 'collectivisation was a social and economic disaster. Communist ideology, honed in the reading rooms of Western Europe, broke the spirit of the villages and turned the fields barren' (Moynahan, 1997).

The aura was further augmented by the fact that from the 1930s Soviet science was notching up conspicuous achievements, many eminent scientists working in the Gulag as 'prisoner specialists'. After World War II, the Soviet Union emerged as the west's great ideological adversary, its armies and commissars controlling an empire that extended westwards to the heart of Berlin. These tensions were not reduced with the death of Stalin in 1953. Indeed in less than ten years, by 1962, the Soviet Union and the USA were on the brink of nuclear war over Cuba. Between those years, in 1957, the USSR had launched the world's first artificial satellite. This 'electrifying event', as the veteran American journalist John Gunther termed it in 1965, propelled the west into the age of space wars – and into a new era of Russian and Soviet studies, for Russian was, momentarily, the language of the future. The standoff, alias the Cold War, would endure until the very collapse of the

Soviet system in 1991.

After the deprivations of the 1930s, 1940s and early 1950s (until Stalin's death) the Soviet people were at last able to partake of some of the promised benefits of the socialist way of life – free education, free healthcare, cheap housing and transport. If you were a member of the Communist Party, you had all this and much more. The standard of living improved (not in comparison with the west, but certainly in comparison with the past), so that today there are those who look upon the last years of the Brezhnev era (1964–1982) as socialism's halcyon days, cursing Gorbachev for ruining everything for which so many people had sacrificed so much. One reason why the standard of living rose is that many basic items, either as imports or as illegally produced goods, became increasingly available to the general public. This illegal or semi-legal business was massive. It constituted more than one third of the Soviet Union's entire GDP; and, unless gross corruption was involved or political scandal could no longer be concealed, the Communist authorities turned a blind eye. In many cases, they were heavily involved as instigators as well as being direct beneficiaries of the trade.

During this period, the resources of the state were pumped into upgrading military capability, the prestigious space programme, and large-scale and ultimately ecologically disastrous projects, such as the Chernobyl nuclear plant. The state planning system was such that it took less time to approve and put up a blast furnace than a barber's shop. It did nothing for agriculture (nearly half of agricultural produce destined for Moscow rotted on the way) and totally failed to supply basic consumer goods, such as soap, tampons and toothpaste, on a consistent basis.

As for the invasion of Czechoslovakia in 1968, the mood of ordinary people was: 'The Party obviously knows what it is doing. Just pray that it is not your son who is being sent abroad to defend socialism.' There was, until the Gorbachev era, little freedom as understood in the west. Soviet citizens were issued with internal passports, and you had to present yourself at a police station if you were away from your home for more than 48 hours. Travel to other socialist countries needed official approval, which could take months. For most Soviet citizens, travel to the west was an impossible dream until the late 1980s. Despite Khrushchev's thaw in the

1960s, censorship was tight and the KGB was vigilant in stamping out imports of unwanted literature from abroad as well as stifling home-grown talent. [KGB] Solzhenitsyn was too well known in the west; he was persecuted and then unceremoniously kicked out of the Soviet Union in 1974.

KGB

The first Tsarist secret police, known as the Third Department, was established by Tsar Nicholas I (1796–1855). Later colloquially called the *Okhrana* (defence), it was abolished in February 1917 by the provisional government. The first Soviet secret police was the Cheka (Extraordinary Commission (1917–1922)), set up by Lenin and headed by Felix Dzerzhinsky. This was followed by OGPU (1922–1934), NKVD (1934–43), NKGB (1943–1946), MGB (1946–1953), MVD (1953) and KGB (1953–1991). KGB are the initials of the Russian words for State Commission for Security.

The activities of these organizations included counter-espionage, disinformation at home and abroad, internal state security, protection of borders, execution of deemed enemies of the state, running the Gulag, and harassment of political undesirables (such as Solzhenitsyn and Sakharov). It employed about half a million people. In 1991 the KGB was broken up and a residual security service was formed under various names, originally employing a mere 35,000–40,000 staff.

Perhaps Russia's most odious secret policeman was Stalin's henchman, Lavrentii Beria (1899–1953), who was in charge of state security from 1938 until his death. Executed on the orders of Stalin's successors, Beria is said to have been 'shot while gagged, for fear he would compromise Khrushchev and his fellow-conspirators in front of the army firing squad'. The only General Secretary of the Communist Party to have risen from the pinnacle of the security service was Yuri Andropov, who was in charge of the KGB from 1967–1982. In 1991 angry crowds pulled down the statue of Dzerzhinsky outside the notorious Lubyanka prison. It was a far cry from the 1930s when Stalin was told that 'the people love the secret police'.

Although the Brezhnev years were good by Soviet standards, except for those who courageously or idiosyncratically brought the wrath of the state upon themselves, they were, in reality, years of economic decline and mismanagement. Since the death of Stalin there had been countless experiments of economic management, but these had become nothing more than tinkerings with the levers. Anything that smacked of debunking the sacred principles of Marxist-Leninism was considered heretical. The Brezhnev years became known as 'stagnation' (*zastoi*) and when the car-crazy General Secretary died in 1984, the Soviet Union was reduced to a state of virtual collapse.

When he took up power in 1985, Gorbachev referred coyly to 'a pre-crisis situation'. The Soviet Union had, in effect, been living on borrowed time. The system had to be changed. Gorbachev, the best educated of all Soviet supreme leaders, set about the task, using his famous catch-words *perestroika* and *glasnost*. His reign was full of reforms and resistance to reforms, and he knew that the biggest challenge lay in changing people's attitudes.

By 1991 *perestroika* (literally, restructuring) had failed; *glasnost* had fared better. Gorbachev, the darling of the west for 'liberating' eastern Europe and defusing the Cold War, was toppled from power and with him went the Communist Party and its monopoly of power. Overnight (or so it seems now) Russia – no longer the Soviet Union – was swept into transition. Russia, which for 70 years had suspended the normal laws of supply and demand, was suddenly transformed into a grand bazaar. In cities, lines of people stood holding items for sale: pairs of shoes, puppies, vases, photograph frames, ancient-looking cameras, even bottles of vodka. Soon the more enterprising set up kiosks, selling everything from chewing gum to cognacs of dubious origin. This, for millions, was the start of the long walk from communism, with all its terrible certainties, to the market economy and the great feared unknown.

For foreigners, it is easy or at least uncomplicated to see Russia as having thrown off the shackles of communism and now embarking on a quest to introduce a new way of life based on market economy principles. We now go on to review aspects of this epochal transition. As foreigners we find the deep sense of anger and impotence that many Russians feel about their country's fate in the 20th century hard to comprehend. The great writer Alexander Solzhenitsyn is as powerful a voice as any, articulating both a great anguish for the past and an anxiety for the future. [**Alexander Solzhenitsyn**] This mood is reflected in his

Rebuilding Russia (1991):

> For seventy years in laboured pursuit of a purblind
> and malignant Marxist-Leninist utopia, we have lost a
> full third of our population . . . We have forfeited our
> earlier abundance, destroyed the peasant class togeth-
> er with its settlements, deprived the raising of crops
> of its whole purpose and the soil of its ability to yield
> a harvest, while flooding the land with man-made seas
> and swamps. The environs of our cities are befouled
> by the effluents of our primitive industry, we have poi-
> soned our rivers, lakes, and fish, and today we are
> obliterating our last resources of clean water, air and
> soil, speeding the process by the addition of nuclear
> death, further supplemented by the storage of Western
> radioactive waste for money. Depleting our natural
> wealth for the sake of grandiose future conquests
> under a crazed leadership, we have cut down our lux-
> uriant forests and plundered our earth of its incompa-
> rable riches – the irreplaceable inheritance of our
> great-grandchildren – in order to sell them abroad
> with uncaring hand. We have saddled our women
> with backbreaking, impossibly burdensome labour,
> torn them from our children, and have abandoned the
> children themselves to disease, brutishness, and a
> semblance of education. Our healthcare is utterly
> neglected, there are no medicines, and we have for-
> gotten the meaning of a proper diet. Millions lack
> housing, and a helplessness bred of an absence of per-
> sonal rights permeates the whole country.

Themes

Geography, climate, work

No discussion of Russian life past or present can preclude mention, on the one hand, of 'the brutally harsh climatic and economic conditions of Russia' (Vlachoutsicos and Lawrence, 1996), and,
on the other, of the mind-boggling vastness of Russian territory.
For it is in this 'unpatrollable eternity' (Fallowell, 1994), in this
'ungraspable formlessness' in which 'everything falls apart, is

Alexander Solzhenitsyn

In November 1962 the literary magazine *Novy Mir* caused a sensation with the publication of a semi-autobiographical account of conditions in a labour camp. The story was called *One Day in the Life of Ivan Denisovich*, and its author was Alexander Solzhenitsyn. It was not an anti-communist polemic, but compellingly conveyed the dreary fruitlessness of labour camp life through the power of understatement. Its author came to world attention. Solzhenitsyn (b. 1918) had been an artillery officer during World War II. In 1945 he was arrested as a result of politically suspect statements in an intercepted letter. The next ten years were spent in labour camps, including one where scientific research was being conducted (*First Circle*, published in 1968), and in exile in Kazakhstan, where he survived cancer (*Cancer Ward*, 1968).

Following the publication of *Ivan Denisovich*, Solzhenitsyn was in almost constant confrontation with the political and literary authorities. He was expelled from the 'politically correct' Writers' Union in 1969, but the next year was awarded the Nobel Prize for Literature, to the acute embarrassment of his Soviet detractors. He was unceremoniously expelled from the USSR in 1974. This was the year in which he wrote his *Letter to Soviet Leaders*, where he articulated three concerns for the fate of the Soviet Union/Russia. The country had suffered from 'superindustrialisation', officially sponsored atheism, and over-involvement in international affairs.

Exiled, but not muzzled, Solzhenitsyn took up residence in Vermont and did not return to his native Russia until 1994. During 1973 and 1975 he published *The Gulag Archipelago*, which records the fate of the millions who fell victim to that terrible system. In the USA Solzhenitsyn wrote other works chronicling Russia's history in the 20th century (*August 1914*, 1971; and a project known as *The Red Wheel*, 1991). Before the collapse of the Soviet Union there were many who saw Solzhenitsyn as a great moral force prevailing against the iniquities of life. As such he was compared with Tolstoy. After 1991 he became associated with ideas for a national revival in Russia based on Christian ethics and Russian values (*Rebuilding Russia*, 1991). But it seems that the new Russia (all his works have been available there since 1990) is not very interested.

diluted, drowned' (Kapuściński, 1994) that we perhaps find the most potent influences on the Russian mind and temper. The very size of the country may help explain gigantomania in architecture, a penchant for meandering, and what Hingley (1978) calls an 'obsession with untrammelled spaciousness'. On this last point we may mention the Russian preference for open landscapes, sweeping vistas – and high ceilings. Another illustration may be that many urban Russians view their small flats as a necessary evil to be escaped from whenever climatic conditions allow, going to great lengths to spend all summer in a primitive *dacha* in the countryside, even commuting to their workplace in the city. [**Climate and geography**] One of the great paradoxes of Russian geography is, as Kapuściński (1994) brilliantly observed, that the poverty of the soil undermines the people, while the vast riches underneath are a great source of power to the regime.

Geography and climate have not only conspired to keep Russia out of step first with Europe and then with 'the west', but these influences have also shaped the Russian value system, with its emphasis on the primacy of the collective for sheer survival. In these traditions, we find two consistent traits of Russian life, which were by no means diminished in the Soviet era: first, the governance of the collective by tough leadership; second, the performance of work in energetic bursts.

The rigours of the climate meant that, traditionally, Russians could work only for limited periods – in late spring and summer. For the rest of the time they were indolent. But, when the work could be done, it was done with a vengeance. The industrialization of life in the Soviet period inevitably disrupted the traditional seasonal pattern of work: in the 1930s it took place not only against the background of new Five Year Plans with their output hysteria, but also in the grim shadow of Stalin's Great Terror which decimated the high command of the armed forces, created a slave labour force of several millions, imprisoned 7000 of the country's 35,000 trained engineers (Graham, 1996), and gave the world the word Gulag (Conquest, 1990). [**Stalin**]

But the greatest disruption and yet ultimate spur to industrialization was Hitler's nearly successful masterplan for the subjugation of the Soviet Union. By the end of 1941, less than six months

Climate and geography

It has been argued that geography and climate are the two key formative influences on Russians, accounting for their tenacity, group survival instinct, carefree exuberance, not to mention predilection for the vast and spacious which expresses itself in bouts of gigantomania. Be that as it may, 90% of Russia's land area is closer to the North Pole than to the Equator. The proximity to the Arctic means that Russia gets virtually no benefit from the Gulf Stream, so the climate gets colder the further east you travel. The coldest place in Russia is Omyakon in Siberia, where the winter temperature can reach almost -70°C. Extraordinarily enough, this region is not much further north than Oslo or the Shetland Isles. Indeed, much of Siberia lies on the same latitude as the British Isles. Yet nearly half of Russia's land is permafrost (perennially frozen ground.) Here is Polish writer Ryszard Kapuściński (1994) on the overwhelming power of the Siberian winter, marvellously capturing in a few words the almost obscene size of Russia:

> Outside the window everything appears stiff from cold, even the firs, pines, and spruces look like great, petrified icicles, dark green stalagmites sticking out of the snow. The immobility, the immobility of this landscape, as if the train were standing still, as if it too were part of this region – also immobile.
>
> And the whiteness – whiteness everywhere, blinding, unfathomable, absolute. A whiteness that draws one in, if someone lets himself be seduced by it, lets himself be caught in the trap and walks further, deep into the whiteness – he will perish. The whiteness destroys all who approach it, who try to decipher its mystery . . . There is something in this January Siberian landscape that overpowers, oppresses, stuns. Above all, it is its enormity, its boundlessness, its oceanic limitlessness. Man is not created for such measurelessness . . . Man is created for the kind of space that he can traverse at one try, with a single effort.

after the Nazi onslaught, 1360 large war plants and 17 million people were transferred from ravaged European Russia to the Urals, Kazakhstan, Central Asia and Siberia (Moynahan, 1997). The new factories were built in sub-zero temperatures, explosives dislodg-

Stalin

Josif Djugashvili, later the Marxist revolutionary Koba, then known as Stalin 'the man of steel', was born in Georgia in 1879. Later referred to simply as 'the boss' (*khozyain*) by his closest associates, Stalin was 'the most accomplished totalitarian ruler of modern times.' His name is linked to the brutal collectivization of agriculture, the development of the Soviet economy on the basis of Five Year Plans, the Great Terror, the show trials, the creation of the Gulag, the promulgation of atheism, the mass deportations of entire nationalities, the notorious non-aggression pact with Hitler, the triumph of the Red Army over Nazi Germany, the extension of Soviet rule over the postwar satellites states of east and central Europe, the imposition of the Iron Curtain and the instigation of the Cold War. With his vice-like grip on the Soviet people and his merciless use of coercion and mass terror, no wonder Khrushchev declared of his old master: 'When Stalin says dance, a wise man dances.'

Norman Davies (1996) notes that Stalinist ideology, which developed in the 1930s, 'involved the adoption of numerous official fictions which were then enforced as the absolute and incontrovertible truth'. These fictions included: 'the role of Stalin as the "best disciple" of Lenin; the role of communists as the chosen leaders of the people; the role of the Great Russians as "elder brothers" of the Soviet nationalities; the status of the Soviet Union as the crowning achievement of "all patriotic and progressive forces"; the function of the Constitution as a democratic power; the unity of the Soviet people and their love for the Communist system; the "capitalist encirclement" of the USSR; the equitable distribution of wealth; the joyous freedom of learning and art; the emancipation of women; the solidarity of workers and peasants; the justness of "the people's wrath" against their enemies.'

When in 1953 Stalin lay dying from a stroke, his housekeeper 'wailed like a peasant'; the doctors quaked; Beria, head of the secret police, behaved like a crown prince coming into his kingdom, while other leading comrades plotted Beria's execution. Stalin's daughter, Svetlana, said that 'he died a difficult and terrible death' – if not so terrible, as Robert Conquest (1993) observed, 'as many of the millions he had himself procured, or was still planning.' Unlike Nazism, which in effect died with Hitler in 1945, Stalinism outlasted its creator until the collapse of the Soviet Union. It has yet to be fully dismantled, even though Stalin's heirs started to ignore his precepts within hours of his death.

ing the frozen ground which bent and broke pickaxes. The perpetually undernourished workers lived in dug-outs and bivouacs near the vast building sites. Yet within two years Russian plants were turning out 2000 tanks a month. It was a supreme, heart-breaking effort. The Nazi enemy was eventually evicted, costing an estimated 26–27 million Soviet lives (Volkogonov, 1991). [**The Great Patriotic War**]

Even after the death of Stalin in 1953 the centralized planning system never really evened out the balance between periods of slackness and those of intense activity. The latter were frequently associated with bursts of energy towards the end of an official planning period, the most important such deadline marking the end of a five year plan. Interspersed were the periods of slackness, when men and machines were idle: there was variously skiving, waiting around for supplies and producing things in a lackadaisical fashion (and sometimes for the black market). Under this 'tradition of mechanistic growthmanship' (Dyker, 1992) a consequence was that many projects were never completed by the official deadlines through chronic supply inefficiencies. By the late 1980s, for example, about one third of capital investment in construction was being poured into projects which would remain uncompleted (Dyker, 1992).

Both the traditional Russian and the Soviet way of working in intensive bursts has been widely noted. Hingley (1978) discusses this in detail:

> Are the Russians energetic or lazy? Abundant evidence can be quoted to show them as both. Where one observer stresses their 'dynamic energy' and 'enthusiasm for work', another says that they cannot bear to exert themselves.
>
> That the Russian tends at any moment to be a prodigy of laziness or of energy – that he works, if at all, in spasms of momentary enthusiasm – is a common observation. This pattern is often linked to the peasant psychology of a nation largely consisting until recent years of farm labourers accustomed to toil in a northern latitude where field work is concentrated with a short period, thus demanding greater efforts than milder climes

Great Patriotic War

Known to Russians as the Great Patriotic War, it is more aptly termed the German-Soviet War. This most horrific of conflicts, known as Operation Barbarossa, was launched by Hitler on 21 June 1941 and achieved complete strategic surprise. According to Volkogonov, the attack was 'a paralysing shock' – all the more so since Stalin had not expected it so soon, despite warnings from his brilliant agent in Japan, Richard Sorge and Churchill. *The Oxford Companion to the Second World War* describes the conflict in these words:

> The German-Soviet War . . . ranks as the greatest armed conflict ever fought on a single front. Statistically and strategically, it dominates the Second World War. For most of four years, on average, more than 9 million troops were continuously engaged. The German forces, with Finnish, Hungarian, Italian and Romanian support, advanced 2,000 km. (1,240 mi.) into Soviet territory; and Soviet forces counter-marched 2,500 km. (1,550 mi.) to Berlin. Germany at no time had less than 55% of its divisions committed. The cost in lives was horrifying. The accepted figures have been 5.5 million German and 20 million Soviet military and civilian dead, which together account for half the total for the Second World War. Of those, 13.6 million Soviet and 3 million German dead in the military category alone account for over two-thirds of the world total. However, researchers in the former USSR have projected losses in the range of 26 or 27 million.

In addition, the war destroyed 70% of housing and industry in European USSR and left 25 million people homeless throughout the country. No Soviet family was spared the horror of war. Events such as the 900-days' siege of Leningrad and the Battle of Stalingrad stand out as particularly heroic achievements, showing Russian spirit at its most redoubtable. Although Stalin, as supreme commander of Soviet forces, motivated his people through patriotic appeals rather than narrow communist propaganda, memory of the great sacrifice has been tinged owing to wider knowledge about the Nazi–Soviet Pact and the secret protocols about the division of Poland and the annexation of the Baltic States. It is accepted that the Soviet Union's great military commander was Marshall Georgiy Zhukov, whom the jealous Stalin demoted after the war. Zhukov holds the rare distinction of brooking no interference from Stalin and surviving – just.

impose. To this brief, violent spurt of annual labour the Russian peasant long ago gave the name *strada* (etymologically, 'suffering'). It is from the *strada*, according to the historian Klyuchevsky, that the people derives its talent for 'short, concentrated bursts of excessive exertion. Hence the routine of brisk, frenzied, effective toil followed by the autumn's and winter's enforced idleness. No other nation in Europe can put forward such concentrated spasms of labour as the Russian.

Are the Russians energetic or lazy? Are they European or Asiatic? Are they for us or against us? According to the great Russian Christian philosopher, Nikolai Berdyayev (1874–1948), Russia has the capacity to intrigue the world with its inner mysteries and repel it in equal measure for its sheer barbarity (Berdyayev, 1918). Ever since her first contacts with western Europe in the 16th century, Russia has bemused and perturbed visitors with its bizarre combination of the familiar and unfamiliar; indeed early travellers 'did not know how to interpret' the mysterious Muscovites, as Russians were then known (Hingley, 1978). Or, as Winston Churchill famously described Russia in a speech of 1939: 'a riddle wrapped in a mystery inside an enigma'. Post-Soviet Russia continues to bemuse and perturb us, but the late 20th-century scenario has enhanced both the familiar and unfamiliar with many a deadly twist.

An ancestral suspicion

To those without much knowledge of the country and its people, Russia's not infrequent anti-western swipes and postures are a particular source of bafflement. Was not Russia supposed to be getting visibly pro-western after the country had been liberated from the shackles of communism? So how is it that Alexander Rutskoi, a former vice-president of the Russian Federation, could dismiss western aid – millions of dollars, ecus and yen – as nothing more than 'free cheese in a mouse trap' (in Steele, 1994)? Are there really Russians in high places who believe that the main work of western organizations based in Moscow, including the Ford Foundation, the Soros Foundation and US Peace Corps is 'to thwart Russia as a state'. The Federal Counter-Espionage Agency, the successor to the KGB, thinks so (*Financial Times*, 1995). Is there really a strong Russian conviction that the EU TACIS programme, accounting for about 70 per cent of technical aid to the former Soviet Union, is being used by European companies 'as a stepping-stone to the "exploitation" of the Russian economy' (*The Economist*, 1993)? Did a former Russian ambassador to Washington really describe his country's foreign policy in the so-called post-communist honeymoon period as 'infantile pro-Americanism' (*The Economist*, 1995a)?

For those with a knowledge of Russian history much of this is uncomfortably redolent of Russia's deep-seated wariness of the west: the conviction that western aid and investment, as well western-sponsored management training initiatives in Russia, are a ploy to weaken still further the Russian economy and keep Russia in a state of semi-colonial tutelage to the west. Russians seem to forget that western businessmen see only ruin for their investment if the Russian economy were actually to buckle under, and are western management educators to be seen as purveyors of a lethal anti-Russia preparation codenamed 'management knowhow'?

The fact is that every person professionally involved with Russia needs to be fully aware of the vigour, occasional zaniness and sometimes the actual justice of Russian perceptions about the motives of western governments and companies. A 1993 issue of *The Economist* referred to Russia's 'ancestral suspicion' of the west. Russians look into their history and all too often see betrayal and abandonment. Today in Russia then, there is more than a passing feeling that the west cannot be trusted. This mood is not restricted merely to politicians and bureaucrats. The following vignette quoted by Wilson and Donaldson (1996) speaks volumes about prejudices lying just below the surface:

> The foreign boss of a growing company told a Russian sales representative that profit would go toward sorely needed equipment purchases, then later to salary hikes. 'I know what you're doing,' she protested. 'I've read Marx. You're an exploiter.'

Every foreigner who seeks insights into developing relationships with Russian counterparts needs to be very clear on the potency of this ancestral suspicion. It is against this background of ancestral suspicion and the corresponding deep-seated western wari-

ness of Russia that western professionals wi
develop their business relationships. Solzhei
the mood. Western capital, he warns his fellc
be lured in on terms that are advantageous
us, in come-and-rule-over-us style'.

Whither Russia?

Russians now live in a country, which 'does not correspond to any
previous "Russia" in history' (Applebaum, 1995). This new Russia
is the product of what Yergin and Gustafson (1994) term Russia's
'triple transition' which followed the disintegration of the Soviet
Union in December 1991. The three transition processes are:

- from dictatorship to democracy

- from centralized economy to free market

- from four-century-old empire to nation state.

The awesome scale of Russia's transformation and the very swiftness
with which the Communist Party lost its grip still astound us today.

No-one knows where the new Russia is heading. After the disintegration of the Soviet Union in 1991 experts were only too quick to
suggest that Russia, true to its past, would be unreformable and that
its leaders would be incapable of transforming the wreckage of communism into viable companies and market institutions. In the words
of *The Economist* (1995b), at the tail end of the Gorbachev era:

> The overwhelming consensus among Soviet econo-
> mists and foreign Sovietologists then was that the
> Russians were different: they lacked entrepreneurial
> ability, they harboured an unusually strong suspicion
> of wealth, and they had no interest to become rich.
> Homo Sovieticus was only distantly related to eco-
> nomic man.

When the Soviet Union collapsed in 1991, most forms of private
business activity were illegal. By 1997 Russia had some 2500
licensed commercial banks, 600 investment funds and 40 million

olders. The liberalization of prices and privatization of some medium-sized and large enterprises within 18 months have eated a private sector market which accounts for more than 60 per cent of GDP. To put that in another way: 'Proportionately, Russia's state-owned sector is now smaller than Italy's.'

This is a remarkable transformation, even though there is a long way to go to the sustained deindustrialization of the Russian economy, without which a true market economy cannot come into being. The battle for deindustrialization means:

- breaking down gargantuan enterprises into smaller productive units, which specialize in the manufacture and marketing of products that people want to buy

- creating a diverse service sector

- spread of consumer markets

- creation of conditions attractive to investors.

See Sachs (1994) for an admirably lucid discussion of these issues.

This complex act of rebalancing resources and priorities can only take place satisfactorily in a politically stable environment (which Russia both is and is not) and against a background of continued infrastructural improvement. Fortunately, and this is easily overlooked, Russia's legacy from the Soviet period has not been too bad in the latter respect. Russia, in comparison with other former socialist countries, has a serviceable national electricity grid, national and regional road and rail networks, a country-wide system of airports and – vital for business development – a national telephone system, which people are no longer afraid of using.

This last point is but one highly significant indicator of how life has changed almost beyond recognition for the peoples of Russia. But the big question is: will the advance to a market economy be worth it all in the end? The dilemma is well posed by Mikheyev (1996):

> Everything has changed: how people earn a living, buy things, address each other, choose their homes and vacations, educate themselves, seek medical assistance, and socialize. The changes have been greater for some than for others. Social status, living

standards, and quality of life are now defined differ-
ently: different social problems, ills, and fears now
preoccupy people. But have these changes been for
better or worse? A great debate rages on this issue.

Within five years Russia has created a business culture comprising
two dominant, but opposing tendencies, if we are to believe Wilson
and Donaldson (1996). On the one hand, there are those who hanker after the old days of socialism with all its mapped-out security
and its lumbering centralized economy, and who presumably miss
the dreary, empty stores and the 9 *billion* queuing hours a year
(Skurski, 1983). These people are attached to the old style of doing
things and often work in the generally unreconstructed realms of
officialdom. While disapproving of Russia's 'descent into capitalism', they rapidly gain from it, making handsome sales from foreign and Russian businessmen alike, out of their insider knowledge
of the oppressive bureaucracy to get a document legalized *now*.

On the other hand, there are the new movers and shakers of
Russian society: the new entrepreneurs, who may be revamped
Soviet bosses, or the young thrusting yuppie class, which is buying up portentous residences and cruising around the cities in
Mercedes and Jeeps. Of course, not everyone belongs either to one
group or to the other. Where, for example, do we place those PhD
biochemists who are now vastly over-qualified car salesmen, bar-
men and bouncers, whose 'highly trained minds are now roaring
round the rim of despair?' (Fallowell, 1995).

Another way of looking at this polarization is to say that one
part of Russia is cautious, conservative and suspicious of the west,
which is merely continuing its policy, well established in the Cold
War, of trying to unhinge Russia; while another part of Russia
wants change and looks upon the west as an essentially positive
support and source of ideas. But have not we been here before?
Are we not seeing the late 20th-century version of the 19th-cen-
tury division of Russians into the modernising westerners (*zapad-
niki*) and the 'Russia-is-special' Slavophiles? Alas, for the rest of
the world, not to mention Russia, the 1917 Revolution failed to
resolve this dilemma about Russia's special direction. The dramatic collapse of the USSR in 1991 has merely exposed afresh the
Russian 'love–hate hysteria about the West' (Hingley, 1978).

A bad fit

What are we to make of all this? After all, since the demise of Soviet power, Russia has lost her empire, her international political influence has shrivelled, she is no longer the great counterpoise to the western way of life, no longer a beacon for the world non-aligned movement. The short answer is that Russia is experiencing a severe identity crisis. Russians are hypersensitive about their status with those whom they formerly regarded as equals in terms of world power and prestige, and they are feeling vulnerable now that for the first time in nearly 500 years Russia's borders have shrunk. In other words, Russia is reappraising its place in the world. The point not to overlook here is that these processes of reappraisal and readjustment are not just political: they have a transcendental dimension, focusing on a deep-seated Russian sense of special mission.

Perhaps the first inkling in the west of this Russian sense of special mission became noticeable after the Napoleonic wars, when Russia established itself as a 'mercurial and meddlesome' ally (Kissinger, 1994) of Great Britain and Austria. This political recognition by the two other great imperial nations of Europe not only whetted the Russian appetite for territory, but also intensified Russian awareness of its special, Eurasian destiny.

Russia's non-conforming outsider specialness was articulated by Pyotr Chaadayev, a leading 19th-century philosopher: 'We do not belong to any of the great families of mankind, neither to the East nor to the West' (quoted in *The Economist*, 1996). The theme was taken up by the Russian translator of John Stuart Mill and Karl Marx, who argued that 'Russia can lay down a new historical path from that taken by Europe' (quoted in *The Economist*, 1996). Both Tolstoy and Dostoyevsky were of the same persuasion. (Was it not Dostoyevsky who described the Russia of his day as 'sublime chaos'?) But perhaps the most eloquent and certainly most mystical advocate of the 'Russia-is-special' school was the philosopher Berdyayev, who wrote in 1918 that 'from earliest times there has been a premonition that Russia is predestined to something great, that Russia is a special country, unlike any other.'

In the Soviet era this thinking took on new garb: the USSR (i.e. the Sovietized successor to the Russian Empire) was 'the world's

first socialist state', the single-handed slayer of Hitlerism with minimum support from its western allies, and the bulwark against
world capitalism. Consider the matter of the Allies' support for
the USSR to repel the Nazi hordes. It is worth quoting informed
journalist Brian Moynahan (1997) at some length. He tells us that
by 1944, when the great Soviet counter-offensive was in full swing,
two thirds of Red Army trucks were American. He goes on:

> Aid started even before the US entered the war [in
> December 1941]; the agreement was celebrated with thir-
> ty-one vodka and champagne toasts in the marble and
> gold Catherine Room of the Kremlin in October 1941.
> [**Kremlin**] Arctic convoys ran the gauntlet of U-boots
> and bombers amid ice-floes, drifting fog and heavy seas.
> The Russians provided no naval or air support. In the
> summer of 1942, the outbound convoy PQ 16 lost a
> quarter of its tonnage and an American freighter, *City
> of Joliet*, was attacked eight times by torpedo and eigh-
> teen times by dive bombers in a day. The crews were
> not welcome; the dock labourers were prisoners under
> NKVD guards [NKVD being the forerunner of the
> KGB]. The effort was immense. The Americans largely
> clothed, shod, fed and transported the Red Army.
> Enough cloth was sent for 54 million uniforms, togeth-
> er with 1.5 million dollars' worth of buttons to do them
> up. Red soldiers marched on 14.5 million pairs of US
> boots. They ate a quarter of a million tons of Tushonka
> canned pork produced to a Russian formula by
> Midwestern packers. Red Army cooks used Ford corn
> oil from Cedar Rapids and Pillsbury flour from
> Minneapolis. As well as the trucks – 405,526 of
> them – the Russians were supplied with tens of thou-
> sands of Wilys jeeps . . . Freighters supplied enough
> railroad equipment for a new trans-Siberian. Russian
> mobility, which so terrified increasingly horsebound
> German units, was American-engined.

> There was little Soviet gratitude. The Americans, the
> Russians had it, bought the German defeat with
> Russian blood and paid in Spam . . . 'The Russian
> authorities seem to want to cover the fact that they are
> receiving outside help,' US Ambassador Standley, an

Kremlin

What sojourner to Moscow will ever forget that first eyeful of the convex expanse of Red Square and the ruddy battlements of the Kremlin?

Colton (1995)

No other building in Russia exerts such awe as Moscow's resplendent and brooding acropolis, the Kremlin. To Mikhail Gorbachev it was 'more than a beautiful sight: it evoked a very special feeling'. All the time that the Kremlin was his official residence the Soviet leader was never indifferent to its majesty and lowering splendour. Maurice Paléologue, who was French ambassador to Russia during World War I, captures something of this special feeling:

> This curious conglomeration of palaces, towers, churches, monasteries, chapels, barracks, arsenals and bastions . . . this complex functions as a fortress, sanctuary, seraglio, harem, necropolis and prison, this violent contrast of the crudest materialism and the most lofty spirituality – are they not the whole history of Russia, the whole epic of the Russian nation, the whole inward drama of the Russian soul?

Another Frenchman, the Marquis de Custine, who travelled in Russia in the 1830s, wrote this about the Kremlin, almost as if anticipating events under its terrible master, the dictator Joseph Stalin, exactly one hundred years later: 'To inhabit a place like the Kremlin is not to reside, it is to protect oneself. Oppression creates revolt, revolt obliges precautions, precautions increase dangers, and this long series of actions and reactions engenders a monster.'

Before World War II, under conditions of impenetrable secrecy, the Communist Party constructed a vast subterranean network of bunkers and passageways radiating from the Kremlin. Towards the end of the war Stalin ordered the building of the ultra-secret Metro-2, a subway line linking the Kremlin to his exclusive residence at Volynskoye, in case of an American nuclear attack, not to mention Kremlin coup. Construction work ceased on Stalin's death in 1953. It would appear that Mr Yeltsin has not only acquired the Kremlin but also at least some of its escape routes.

admiral, said bitterly at a Moscow press conference. 'Apparently they want their people to believe that the Red Army is fighting this war alone.

It was the same Soviet Union that had paid handsomely for US engineering and technical expertise to help build two of the great industrial 'mega-projects' of the 1930s: the Great Dnieper Dam and the steel city of Magnitogorsk (Graham, 1996; Moynahan, 1997). These were 'wonders' of socialist achievement, coinciding with 'capitalism's greatest crisis . . . when the unemployed lined up in the soup kitchens of Detroit, Manchester and Pittsburgh' (Graham, 1996). Yet the mere need for foreign help could always be construed in such a way as to highlight Russian inferiority and failure: better to play down the significance of outside assistance especially from an ideological adversary. From the time that Peter the Great shaved off the beards of his nobility, the boyars, to Europeanize them, Russians have, with varying degrees of intensity, rejected or accepted and then minimized the value of foreign contributions in architecture, military affairs, and science and technology. Little wonder that in the Soviet era party hacks habitually propped up legitimate indigenous scientific and technological achievement with improbable boasts about Russians being the first to invent the incandescent lamp, the telegraph, radio and penicillin (Moynahan, 1996).

Whatever else it was, the Soviet Union was always an alternative. Present-day Russia, which is steadily showing signs of nonconformity with western aspirations, is continuing the tradition of being a mettlesome outsider nation. In his much acclaimed study of the history of Europe, Norman Davies (1996) has written:

> For more than five hundred years the cardinal problem in defining Europe has centred on the inclusion or exclusion of Russia. Throughout modern history, an Orthodox, autocratic, economically backward but expanding Russia has been a bad fit.

The term 'bad fit' is excellent shorthand for describing the peculiar dilemma of Russia's place in the world. In the Soviet era the description 'bad fit' would have had plenty of ideological overtones. It would have been seen overwhelmingly in terms of cold war political relations and military posturing. In today's world, her internal politics and foreign policy are causing Russia to be called 'an especially awkward customer' (*The Economist*, 1993), by western governments, and the west's intelligence community is haunted afresh by cold war rhetoric with 'an awful sense of déjà-vu' (*Financial Times*, 1996a).

Being a bad fit, Russia has also been not so much behind and backward as out of phase with the countries and societies with whom she has traditionally measured herself. This is surely the price that Russia has paid for being bypassed by the great shaping influences of 'the Reformation, the Enlightenment, the Age of Discovery; and modern market economics' (Kissinger, 1994). But Russia has paid another price, if we accept the potent argument of leading historian Geoffrey Hosking (1997). According to him, the centuries-long expansion of its empire has impeded Russia flowering into a nation with complementary civic and ethnic traditions. These explanations may help to account for the fact that no small number of observers – even Russian ones – are describing Russia as a *pre-modern* society.

At first glance the suggestion that Russia is pre-modern seems pejorative, almost insulting, but how else are we to consider this country? Has not Solzhenitsyn (1991) written that Russia 'has cruelly forfeited the entire 20th century', while other writers emphasize that Russia has lost its way as a result of the trauma of the collapse of the USSR from superpower to bankruptcy and virtual third world economy? Russia today is 'a pre-democracy' (Yergin and Gustafson, 1994). According to a Russian historian, quoted in Remnick (1994) 'a medieval mind-set has lasted until very recently ... We are leaving the Middle Ages.' Consistent with that, one western authority on Russian history describes Stalin's last years as 'the Dark Ages' (Keep, 1996). Even Richard Poe (1993), a vastly enthusiastic 'Russia-preneur', to use his own idiosyncratic self-designation, concedes that Russia 'never left the Middle Ages'.

Pre-modernness is admittedly a tricky concept; the modern western mind finds it difficult to handle; we will not find any reference to it in the current literature on international management (you will find more discussion of *post*-modernism). But we believe it to be a vitally important heuristic for understanding the Russian mindset. Pre-modernness is in fact part of the bad fit: it jars with the western world, which Russia both admires and envies; it is a major factor creating clashes with foreign business counterparts. It is an element of what Vlachoutsicos (1995) terms 'the inner logic' of Russian managerial thinking and behaviour; for this inner logic, which operates like 'an obstructive fist' in the transformation of the Russian economy, is a still potent expression of the Russian collective value system, whose origins can be clearly traced back the Kievan state (1054-1238). The important theme of the persistence of deep-seated values and their influence on post-communist management systems is discussed later.

These days it is not just governments that are experiencing Russia as a kind of unreconstructed bad fit. Western management educators, consultants and investors are constantly reminded of Russia's reluctance, inability or unwillingness to develop structures and practices that coincide with those of actual or potential business partners' organizations. Western experiences with Russian counterparts often speak of clashes of opinion, mutual misperceptions of motives, abortive discussions and so forth. No small literature is being built up on 'chilling tales of failure and frustration' (Dunayeva and Vipperman, 1995).

Consider these instances and observations. Management training programmes for Russians have been described as 'a cross-cultural mine-field' (*Financial Times*, 1993). German companies 'are getting the impression that they are being treated like criminals intending to buy up Russia cheap' (Kravchenko, 1995). Richardson (1995) has observed that 'every negotiation is an occasion for Machiavellian intrigues, maneuvring and posturing.' Russians and westerners do not share a common language of business and management – literally and metaphorically: literally, because the Russian language has not developed the necessary concepts and terminology (Holden, 1995, 1996). This in turn may help to explain why business negotiations between Americans and Russians have been likened to 'a dialogue of the deaf' (Dunayeva and Vipperman, 1995).

Conclusion

In the light of everything discussed so far we can safely draw one major conclusion of crucial importance to every foreign professional operating in Russia or planning to do so. Unless one can cope with Russia, he or she will not be able to manage relationships with Russians. Russia always was, and is likely to remain for the foreseeable future and beyond, 'a test of wits and endurance' (*Financial Times*, 1996c). Therefore, the most important relationship that a foreigner has, or ever will have, is the one with Russia itself.

We are now in a position to move from the broad sweep of Russian history to try to account for these crosscultural minefields and dialogues of the deaf.

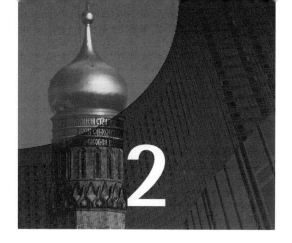

MANAGEMENT CULTURES IN COLLISION

Peter the Great (1672–1725) to his ministers:

> *You yourselves know that anything that is new, even if it is good and necessary, our people will not do without being compelled.*

> — *Massie, 1992*

> *Resist giving unsolicited advice and instruction. Russians know things are bad – and they're trying to cope. Russians are also a proud people, highly sensitive to outsiders' critical opinions and instruction. It's unbearable for them to watch foreign business people arrive believing they are emissaries of light, bringing modern ideas to the natives living in the dark forest.*

> — *Wilson and Donaldson, 1996*

Introduction

So there we have it: interactions with Russian management counterparts land western professionals in cross-cultural minefields, expose them to Machiavellian intrigues, subject them to suspicion about their motives, and plunge them into a twilight world of semi-communication, if not outright non-communication. From such hand-wringing indictments two themes emerge. First, we in the west do know little about Russian management and how it is evolving in the rapidly marketizing conditions in Russia. Second, these verdicts – and they can be supported by any number of comments to the same effect – suggest that there exist serious misconceptions between western and Russian managers as to each other's behaviour, attitudes and motivations. From this it follows that, if we understand more clearly the nature of these misconceptions, we should be in a better position to deal with them and therefore make interactions with Russian partners more productive.

This chapter and the next three are overwhelmingly concerned with the challenge of understanding Russian management, its aspirations, constraints on its development as well as reactions to involvements with western managers as consultants, educators or investors. This 'tour' will also take in a view of management as it was in the Soviet period, of the impact of deep-seated traditional values, of its evolution in the Gorbachev era (1985-1991) and its sudden totally unequipped exposure to the literally mysterious workings of the market economy and all its ways. [**Gorbachev**] In this chapter we address the issue of differences – the gap, as we termed it – in western and Russian approaches to management by focusing on reactions to each other.

The National Training Foundation

The main source of information is material presented at a workshop held in Moscow in December 1996, sponsored by the National Training Foundation.[1] [**Moscow**] Much of this material is presented to a wider western readership for the first time. This was perhaps the first attempt to bring together western and Russian management experts on Russian soil to discuss the dimensions of this gap in order to gain a clearer understanding of the complex factors that are seriously inhibiting the smooth transfer of market economy management and business know-how to Russia. The workshop was implemented as consistent with the central mission of the National Training Foundation: to promote the transfer and full utilization of best management and business expertise – western or otherwise – for the benefit of Russian managers and their enterprises. In this chapter we examine information that was presented at the December workshop.

Gorbachev

From each according to his abilities, to each according to his needs.

— Karl Marx

[taken from *The Oxford Dictionary of Quotations* (1985)]

In his memoirs Gorbachev summed up his achievements thus:

> After leaving the Kremlin – and the circumstances surrounding my departure were most uncivilized, in the worst inherited traditions – I faced the question: what to do next. Naturally, the first days were emotional for me and my family. I had to get used to a new situation; I did not go anywhere, and hardly met anyone. Nevertheless desperation and hopelessness never overcame me. And my conscience was clear. The promise I had made to the people when I started the process of *perestroika* was kept: I gave them freedom. This was reflected in quite specific things: *glasnost*, freedom of speech, the ending of ideological persecution, the right to live anywhere one wanted, the removal of the monopoly on property and power, the creation of the foundations of a genuine parliamentary system, the end of the nightmare threat of nuclear war, and openness to the world, which responded with understanding and support for our desire to become a normal democratic state.

> *Perestroika* did not give the people prosperity, something they expected of me as head of state, based on an ingrained, traditional feeling of dependence. But I did not promise that. I urged people to use this new-found freedom to create prosperity, with own hands and minds, according to the abilities of each.

Intriguing that Gorbachev should use such a redolently Marxian phrase to sum up his hope for the future of his people. Or maybe not so intriguing.

The event brought together a group of Russian consultants, academics, industrialists and trainers and a number of western participants including consultants, management educators and representatives of international agencies. The process was novel for many of the participants in that it was led largely by Russian, rather than western experts. The overall aim of the workshop was to find methodologies and conceptual tools for analysing, developing and applying new and much needed approaches for upgrading the competencies of western consultants who need to know both the Russian and western systems in order to explain each to specific clients in and outside Russia. Objectives of the workshop were to:

- provide insights into the transformation of management in Russia from a Russian perspective

- eliminate stereotypes about the background and operations of Russian management

- develop, with participants, conceptual tools for aligning western training and consultancy activities with Russian expectations and values

- supply high-quality learning materials on all the major themes developed in the workshop

- involve participants in the preparation of guidelines for improving business and management interactions with Russia.

One major aim of the workshop was to present the Russian perspective; another was to synthesize the knowledge of key presenters with the practical experience of the participants. The thrust of the workshop was to:

- isolate the stumbling blocks which impede interaction between foreign professional and their Russian counterparts

- unravel the inner logic of Russian management practices

- develop guidelines significantly to reduce mutual misconceptions in business exchange and know-how transfer.

In this chapter we present information first, on Russian percep-

Moscow

Moscow has approximately 9 million inhabitants. It is as such Russia's most populous city (next is St Petersburg with a population of 5 million), and the fourth biggest incorporated city after Tokyo, Bombay and São Paulo. With 11 million people in Greater Moscow, it is the world's ninth largest conurbation. In his fascinating history of this remarkable city (1995), Harvard scholar Timothy Colton writes that Moscow 'comingles not only the antique and the modern but the Occident and the Orient, the sacred and the profane, the picturesque and the squalid, the regimented and the chaotic'. Two hundred years earlier, the English historian William Coxe (1747–1828) noted that he had never before seen 'a city so irregular, so uncommon, so extraordinary, and so contrasted'. He summed up what he saw, and it sounds astonishingly similar to the Moscow of today: 'In a word, some parts of this vast city have the appearance of a sequestered desert, other quarters of a populous town; some of a contemptible village, others of a great capital.' For this reason, as *The Rough Guide* to Moscow points out, this 'huge, surreal and apocalyptic' city is all things to all men with its inseparable beauty and ugliness, its cynical political culture and intellectually sophisticated private life, its casual brutality and cheerful sentimentality. If before the Russian Revolution in 1917 Moscow was a city of revels, under the communists it became more puritanical. It was architecturally transformed to suit the new era i.e. to express the 'genius' of Stalin and reflect his vulgar taste for the imposing and pretentious. Possibly the supreme example of this 'high Stalinist opulence' (*The Rough Guide*) is the Moscow Metro. Today Moscow is a city of moody decadence, regionalized by mafias. Its citizens have never been quite reconciled to the fact that 'Mother Moscow' is no longer the hub of an empire, no longer a place of political homage. Muscovites feel, above all, mocked and disillusioned. In the socialist era they accepted the phoney propaganda about their great city being the envy of all the world. It now grieves and mystifies them when they learn that a western executive may be earning around $100,000 a year for the privilege of being in Moscow with its worldrenowned cultural attractions.

tions of western consultants and then counterpoise this with the perceptions of western consultants of their experiences with Russian clients. Next we shall perform a similar exercise, focusing on mutual perceptions about experiences of management training. Following this we record information supplied by the Economic Development Institute of the World Bank (EDI). Since 1992, the Moscow office of the EDI has been running training courses throughout the former Soviet Union, using Russian trainers. It is particularly valuable – and unusual – to be able to secure this particular perspective, as it gives a certain independent credence to highly complex issues, which westerners can never really appreciate from an insider standpoint.

How Russians see western consultants

'I have been both a consultant and a victim of consultants,' declared one of the Russian presenters at the workshop. From this one can safely deduce that as a rule western consultants are respected in Russia neither for their professional competence nor for the lifestyle they are able to enjoy there. Not only are they outlandishly well paid in comparison with Russian personnel working for them, who – to add insult to injury – are rarely given much opportunity to develop their own careers, western consultants, the Russians claim, do not really understand the Russian economic environment and the wider social and cultural framework which supports it. Resentment, discrimination and incompetence seem to be the key words associated with Russian reactions. We look at these reactions under the general categories of how western firms (including consultancy firms) conduct themselves as consultants, how westerners behave as expatriates in Russia, and their attitudes and general level of knowledge about Russian management and business.

A director of Inkombank, one of Russia's leading commercial banks, did not mince his words on these issues. According to him, Russians are made to feel like aboriginals in their own country who should be grateful for what the foreign firms care to pay them. What makes things even more galling is the fact that the western businessmen are on nice, big expatriate salaries. Where now a Russian manager might be earning $35,000 a year (a very good salary in Russia) the expatriate manager with a western company in Moscow would be on $100,000. He would be living in a luxury flat, going to the best restaurants, going to the Bolshoi and, if that were not already enough, the fat salary would be topped up with a hardship allowance. 'They want the benefits of the European lifestyle that Moscow and St Petersburg offer, and get paid hardship money as well.'

Western executives in Moscow do not give the same importance to the quality of life of their Russian employees, if their employment practices are anything to go by. To emphasize his point further, the director referred to an Italian company in Moscow that sought a PA for the company president. This person would have to speak fluent Italian and English, work 11 hours a day for 6 days a week and be prepared to travel abroad. The salary offered was $38.00 a week. But the appointed person would not be permitted to eat lunch in the office, as the boss did not like the smell of food. This was not employment; it was exploitation. Western companies want their Russian employees to come to them fully skilled and prepared for the tasks that will be required of them, and are unwilling to invest in training for them. For example, they are unwilling to consider Russians taking MBAs who might need time off for study. Why pay for your workers to do MBAs if you have no intention of ever promoting them or using those skills? Russians at the workshop cited other examples of unreasonable expectations on the part of western employers, which seemed to betray an assumption that Russians will fall over themselves, and one another, for the chance to work for a western firm. That might have been the case soon after the Soviet collapse, but now it is pretty wide of the mark. 'Some Russian 30–35 year-olds, working for western firms, with good experience feel like monkeys snatching chestnuts from the fire. These Russians are now seeking more independent employment. Some foreign companies do not give Russian employees any opportunities to grow.' There was even a suggestion that western companies are overly suspicious of prospective and actual employees' possible underworld connections. Given the combination of poor prospects, poor working conditions, pay differentials and suspicion, it is small wonder that those talented young Russians who cannot secure equality of treatment with their western colleagues are leaving for Russian firms.

It is probable, however, that the huge wage differentials and poor prospects would be more acceptable if western consultants were professionally competent to operate effectively in Russia. The Moscow representative of the World Bank, a keynote speaker at the workshop, was all too aware of this. He articulated the Russian attitude as follows: 'Why is this western manager being paid ten times more than me, when he doesn't know anything?' What kind of things do the consultants not know about? According to the Russian Privatization Center, the consultants are generally ill informed about:

1 The specific nature of the Russian business environment in its transitional dimensions.

2 The Russian style of enterprise management and the diffusion of different interests within management teams.

3 The strong sense of enterprise responsibility to the local community.

Consequently, western consultants are regarded as ignorant, lacking 'a Russia perspective', and inclined to find economic solutions to problems which Russians see as economic and social and cultural. They assume too readily that privatized enterprises are now concerned to 'increase shareholder value'. This does not figure so much in Russian managerial thinking. Hence, Russian clients feel that the consultants are using economic criteria and rationales, which might be fine in a western market economy, but which patently do not work in Russia, especially now. This was seen as high-handedness and it went hand-in-hand with a western reluctance to recognize that there had been industrial achievement during the Soviet period.

By the same token, it is important that western companies send to enterprises teams that the Russian top managers could respect, particularly westerners with a recognized international background and a firm grasp of the industry in question. 'We are looking not just at the name [of the firm] but also at what kind of team a company can put together. It is very important advice to western firms – the inclusion in the team of someone with international experience and background, not Russians with no experience.'

There were two other problems about the consultants. First, because they were often seen as incapable of assisting a Russian enterprise, they must have an ulterior motive. They were obviously spies paid for by foreign governments (foreign governments, note, not companies) to identify juicy takeover targets. Second, consultants had a tendency to make some things appear more complicated than they were and another to make Russians look stupid for not understanding simple things. In the first case everything was wrapped up in high-flown terminology; in the second, explanations were kept 'at a basic level', as if Russians could not cope with anything more demanding. Western management catch phrases, such as KISS ('Keep it simple, stupid'), are guaranteed to go down like a lead balloon with Russian top managers who not only know that their own situation is anything but simple, but also expect western consultants to bring with them a complex and challenging intellectual toolkit.

The representative of the Russian Privatisation Center, which employs both Russian and western consultants, did emphasize that Russian managers did not always quite understand the challenges facing consultants, and we discuss those points later. But his general remarks about Russian wariness of consultants was borne out by other contributors. For example, one Russian management scientist specializing in conflict resolution had made a comparative study of how a Russian consultancy and a Dutch consultancy had offered advice to a paper company employing 2500 people which was facing 'multilevel conflict': problems over the running and manning of new Finnish equipment, pressure from local and regional authorities which were beginning to exercise their shareholder power negatively, a tussle between a new general manager who had been hired to take over from the old-style boss, but who was still with the company, and a kind of 'hostile bid' from a spinoff joint venture that wanted to take over the company. And there was one more tricky factor in the equation: the company had also retained 'a typically Soviet responsibility' for agricultural production – and 500 agricultural workers – in a former collective farm.

What was interesting to the Russian management specialist was not so much the outcome of the involvement with the Dutch consultancy team, but more its approach to the problem. He conceded that the internal and external problems facing the paper plant were extremely complicated, 'too complicated for the Dutch people'. The complex web of relationships and mutual dependencies both internal and external to the enterprise were beyond their comprehension. He found that the Russian consultants identified far more markedly with the human issues; in other words, the welfare of employees who might be made redundant. 'The Russian consultants included group dynamics and philosophy of the enterprise as dimensions in their analysis of the enterprise: the Dutch included neither of these.'

The Dutch, it seems, were out of their depth. They did not seem capable of making any urgent decisions for the company management (presumably the Russian consultants were swifter). Their approach was very focused. They used a three-man team which attempted to get to the heart of all the issues. But, if the complexity of the problems was beyond them, they made a professional misjudgment. They came to advise and they did that as best they could. But they did not come to learn anything. The Dutch consultants did at least visit the company, and spent some time there. According to another informant at the workshop, some western consultants did not even bother to visit their industrial clients. Others would spend half a day on site, and expect the top man to drop everything to see them. But nothing can substitute for spending time, methodically and patiently gathering and sifting information, and, importantly, listening:

> As a consultant you need hard facts; but you need to combine the right hard facts with a soft approach – I mean being company-centred. You need the hard facts because top management will challenge consultants' understanding of the business. For example, in Sameko it took six weeks to develop a model of the costs. So you have to push to get the information you need . . . But after that, you're better off if you don't push too hard. Give them the model and let management talk.

Too often top managers have been subjected to long-winded and patronizing presentations by western consultants who did not seem to consider the possibility of management's contributing something to the process.

How western consultants see Russian enterprises and managers

Consultants have two publics in Russia: their own locally appointed staff and their clients. We have already noted some negative attitudes characterizing Russians in the employ of foreign firms. As for attitudes to clients, the Russian Privatization Center, which itself has a mixed Russian-western team, noted that western consultants are strongly conditioned by the following convictions.

1 Russian managers do not know how to work hard; they leave at 5pm 'just when there is a crisis'.

2 Business problems in Russia are pretty simple compared to those in the west.

3 It is fundamentally impossible to institute change in Russia.

4 Russian management lacks both the experience and know-how to transform an enterprise into a viable concern.

5 The only way for a Russian enterprise to improve itself is to follow the consultant's advice: 'Don't think about it, just do it.'

6 Russian managers base their decisions on intuition; this approach seriously conflicts with the western approach which emphasizes the gathering and analysis of hard facts.

7 Russian managers do not understand that the role of consultants is to provide the best possible advice based on information given by a client and their understanding of his needs. Specifically they do not appreciate that consultants help to clarify problems, but not to supply decisions. That, of course, is the prerogative of the Russian client.

These seven points disclose much about western prejudice and, probably, bad experiences, and there can be little doubt that the implied attitudes are revealed in behaviour which reinforces Russian perceptions of western arrogance and *'know-all-ism'*. They also reveal serious contradictions in the situation of the western 'expert' trying both to make sense of a fiendishly complex and novel situation (the 'Russian reality'), while simultaneously trying to make it fit their own expertise and experience. However, consultants do face genuinely severe challenges in the application of their expertise to Russian conditions. These challenges include:

- The fact that Russian enterprise management is rarely a team; there is a boss, inclined to take all big decisions and delegate authority and to take it back at will.

- The Russian tendency (point 6 in our earlier list) to make decisions based on intuition; the western quest for hard facts cannot only seem unnecessary and time consuming, but could be interpreted as probing for secret information (hence, consultants are 'spies').

- The problem of transforming an organization, while retaining a specific strength (such as production skills) and creating not just a structure, but also an internal environment to foster market economy skills redundant under socialist management (such as marketing).

- The emergence of a generation gap between older managers (especially those accustomed to Soviet-style authority) and younger employees (who may be well educated and more open to new (western) ideas.

- The problems of coping with two strongly culture-specific practices: (a) Russians' extreme aversion to creating redundancies as an answer to business problems and (b) the persistence of the Soviet tradition of enterprises being 'guardians' of social and cultural facilities in their localities or (as noted earlier) running 'unrelated' activities such as agricultural production.

Already we can see some major elements in the creation of the gap dividing Russian and western management motivations, attitudes and practices. In the following chapters we attempt to account for the ways of Russian management, an amalgam of experiences tempered under 70 years of socialism and traditional Russian values, which include the long-established tendencies to trust in one leader figure through thick and thin (and hope for the best) and to create alternative practices which do not appear to be dependent for their implementation on foreign (i.e. western) ideas.

There was evidence at the workshop that some western consultants are becoming more aware of these challenges themselves. Participants who had worked in and with Russian enterprises gave examples from their own experience of difficulties in understanding what is going on under the surface of Russian organizational life, and in fathoming out the complexities of relationships and motivations. Knowledge of the Russian language was not necessarily the key: one participant suggested that a good many consultants who were fluent Russian speakers had unfortunately turned out to be mediocre in the field, and in general the combination of an excellent consultant and a good professional interpreter might be better. Yet there was a strong feeling among some participants, on both sides, that anyone serious about working in Russia should at least be acquainted with the language. In the case of the Dutch consultancy team, the use of Russian consultants as interpreters caused understandable resentment: 'Some of our Dutch colleagues only want to work through interpreters, who are actually good consultants themselves and who are not asked for their ideas. So Russians are being exploited to develop business for our foreign colleagues.'

There was, however, a general consensus that there is no substitute for knowing the reality from the inside, and evidence for this was the fact that the 'big seven' international consultancy companies are now scaling down their expatriate presence in Russia to about 15–20 per cent of the workforce. Yet, it was stated, not without irony, that the Russian consultancy profession cannot be said to have come of age until we see Russians heading up consultancy teams in other countries.

How Russians view western management educators and trainers

Western management educators did not escape sharp criticism either. They failed in four main ways by:

1 not making their teaching material suitable for Russian conditions

2 not knowing how to teach Russians

3 not appreciating how much Russian society is changing

4 disappointing the expectations of their clients as a result.

A business psychologist explained the Russian approach to training (i.e. to being trained): there were two things that western educators and trainers should avoid at all costs. First, Russians do not like western educators who say 'We are here to help' . This sounds patronizing and supercilious. When educators add that they see their role as facilitators and as such are not or do not have to be experts, this is likewise damning in Russian eyes. The distinction a western trainer would make between being a process expert and being a content expert is lost on them. 'They wonder what you are doing there if you are not an expert', said a Russian participant. A further complication is that the concept of facilitation, as understood in training, is virtually impossible to convey succinctly in Russian. Russians do not want merely to respect their teachers; they want to be impressed by them. 'The trainer is expected to provide a model of behaviour. Russians like to give you credibility on the basis of your qualifications, experience and travelling experience. Trainers have to be impressive.'

When a trainer or educator is presented to Russians as very well qualified and having extensive professional experience, a considerable head of steam of expectation builds up. Russians know perfectly well that some educators may be genuinely modest about their expertise. But possession of the expertise is what the Russians want to see demonstrated. One contributor supplied an anecdote which neatly highlights the Russian attitude. It happened that an American professor had come to Russia to give a training course about conflict resolution in international affairs. His Russian audience told him that they had already been on a course on this topic, so would he please talk about the history of conflict resolution in the USA, giving more insight into the theory. He was thrown into confusion and could not respond to the request. Either could not or would not, the outcome was inevitable. He totally lost the respect of his listeners.

This anecdote threw into relief the distinctions between the western concept of training and the Russian concept of being taught.

Western course participants on various kinds of management skills and personal development courses, are used to being 'thrown in at the deep end', and plunging into practical activities which illustrate or simulate problem situations. Trainers are expected to have a repertoire of experiential techniques at their disposal. Often these activities include the use of toys or play equipment, such as building structures out of Lego, which are supposed to be fun (the assumption being that people who are having fun learn better), to model real-life processes and, through subsequent discussion and reflection, to generate ideas and observations which can be generalized back to the workplace. This is so commonplace in western training as to be almost taken for granted. But, the business psychologist warned, using such techniques with Russian groups can be a big mistake. Russians see a toy as a toy, and though not averse to sophisticated and complex 'business games', are likely to feel insulted if asked to engage with anything that seems childish.

Hence, it was emphasized that Russians do not like to feel that they are being taught anything which is a simplification. To Russians simplification is tantamount to trivialization. Thus, the KISS acronym mentioned earlier does not suit the Russia learning style. Russians like intellectual exertion and therefore some theoretical input. This is what they tend to expect when they attend western-sponsored management courses especially when the tutors are university lecturers and professors. All in all there is a gulf between the western philosophy of management training and Russian anticipations. One experienced Russian trainer was particularly adamant about placing theoretical inputs at the beginning of training programmes; these could be used to 'intrigue' participants, whereas a participatory group activity might be more likely to alienate them. He appreciated that a standard western approach is to begin a session with such an activity, designed to stimulate experiential learning, and to follow this up with a theoretical input which builds on that experience (an approach advocated by a western participant), but felt strongly that the value of the experiential activity would not be compromised by putting the formal theoretical input first. It simply requires a different style from the trainer in handling the group – a style more suited to the Russians expectations in putting the emphasis on the knowledge and expertise of the trainer. A further problem is that Russian has no word to convey the concept of training (see Chapter 8 for a discussion of this). It was recommended, therefore, that western trainers should explain at the outset what they understand by training.

Various contributors to the workshop noted that Russians bring different attitudes to training programmes. For example, younger Russians will have a more open view of the value of western training than older ones, who are more sceptical or simply too old to be coaxed into a different way of looking at things. Young western trainers often have problems with mature Russian groups because they are perceived as being not old enough to train older people. Unremarkably perhaps, Russian contributors were suggesting that there existed a specific incompatibility between western course philosophies and Russian expectations. A major factor here was the clash between teaching style and learning style. First, the open, participatory style of teaching does not suit Russians. Under this approach the teacher is really a facilitator, and Russians want to be taught by teachers who are demonstrably experts. In other words, Russians do not appreciate, indeed do not even detect, the intellectual flexibility which is the hallmark of a good facilitator.

The open style, which encourages participants to introduce their own ideas and experiences, does not work well for several reasons. First, it appears to lack rigour and is therefore intellectually non-taxing. Second, the concept of participants learning from one another is largely alien (after all, they have come to hear the foreign expert). Third, in group learning situations it takes Russians some time to 'unfreeze', so they may not feel confident about participating actively until the second day. Efforts to relax participants into disclosing personal information can misfire drastically, as in the case of an American trainer who asked a group of young women about their boyfriends. This was considered rude and an invasion of privacy, and he lost the trust of half the group at one stroke. He was confused because he had not experienced this reaction in the USA. Similarly, Russian groups prefer to be observers, and it can be a big issue to them who is selected to present the results of small group work to the larger group. Volunteering to do this may be seen as pushing oneself forward. In many groups, especially for women, personal modesty is the norm. In a group situation nobody wants to be individually singled out for praise from the instructor, and for many this will be embarrassing rather than gratifying.

Fourth, despite all the talk about participation and sharing of experience, in the end it was observed that the western teachers would impose their views and rarely listen. The example was given of an American cosmetics company which imported its standard staff training package complete with young American trainers. When the Russian co-trainer suggested changes to the programme to meet Russian needs and expectations, the rhetoric about flexibility of training approach evaporated. No changes to the programme would be acceptable. No deviations from the set package could be considered. The Russian trainer concluded that this said a lot about the lack of confidence of the young American expatriate trainers, as well as about the lipservice paid to flexible and responsive ways of running training programmes. Fifth, if the western teacher finds his group unresponsive and challenges them about it, this will be interpreted negatively: he has failed, and, in effect, has lost face with the group. Finally, this way of learning may be successful elsewhere, but may not necessarily work in Russia.

How western management educators view Russians

The western reactions to the Russian experiences were variable. Frustration was vented both about Russian partners in training ventures, and about the actual process of working with groups of Russian participants. There were stories of the western university representative going to a pre-arranged meeting to discuss training needs only to find that the key person was unavailable or had made other plans. When training was discussed with a senior manager, it was often seen as benefiting individuals and not the company as a whole.

In the case of western training institutions working with Russian universities or colleges, a particular problem was that there was either a high level of turnover of key staff, or they were involved in other (i.e. money-making) activities which prevented their sustained association with specific training programmes. Sometimes both happened at once. Often academics would be managing complex 'portfolio careers' of part-time jobs in different institutes and business schools, and might at any time leave to take up a more lucrative or full-time position elsewhere. Hence, many western trainers, having invested considerable time and resources in training their Russian colleagues, had the experience of having to reinvent the wheel, going through the whole process again with new people. In general this problem was more prevalent in Moscow and St Petersburg than in provincial cities, because of the plethora of institutes and training organizations offering alternative openings.

A further frustration was that Russian companies were often mystified by requests to supply information on themselves so that trainers could gain an appreciation of their problems. In this respect the concept of training needs analysis is not yet well understood. Development of materials was a perennial problem, as it demanded close collaborative working between the western and Russian trainers, for which the necessary time and money were not always available. The most critical issue, however, was that many Russians continued to give the impression that, as far as they were concerned, western management knowhow and practices were, in the final analysis, non-transferable. There was a strong sense that for many Russians the idea that they are a unique people with unique characteristics and a special place in the world is an important part of their identity, and they actually want to think themselves different.

There was also evidence of some Russians, particularly at staff and clerical levels, being resentful of being sent on courses. Some did not take to the participatory way of learning. Others felt that their boss, far from investing in their skills, was actually trying to get rid of them, and giving them a coded message that they would not last long in the job. They would not believe that the boss wanting them to learn something new did not mean that he thought badly of them. Then there were some who would not attend punctually. It was mentioned that participants leave early, sometimes apparently to return to their office, sometimes to go home to their families. However, it was often assumed that the western trainers would 'understand'. These perceptions were, perhaps surprisingly, strongly endorsed by the Russian trainers, who experience the same reactions.

Not all the experiences were negative. In fact several participants stressed that collaborative training ventures can be successful, especially where Russians and westerners work together as co-trainers, and pay careful attention to expectations, their own as well as their participants', and share the tasks involved to play to their mutual strengths. There was a consensus between Russian and western participants that, by and large, incompany forms of management training are more effective than sending Russian employees on 'off-the-peg' short courses. One Russian banker stated that 'the majority of new entrepreneurs favour incompany training and it seems to work better'. Some Russian companies, allowing employees to follow MBA programmes, are solving the problem of obtaining a return on their investment by getting them to sign loyalty contracts in which they undertake to stay with the company for two or three years after completing their MBA. If they do leave, they must pay back their training expenses.

For western participants in the workshop who had been involved in training and consultancy projects funded by external agencies, such as TACIS and the British Government Knowhow Fund, a crucial issue was their need to manage both the expectations of the Russian beneficiaries of their projects and the expectations of the funder. Often terms of reference were worked out long before the organization or consortium winning the tender embarked on the project. In the rapidly changing Russian environment, this meant, more often than not, that project activities, even basic aims and objectives, had to be reworked from scratch. Some western participants had felt aggrieved at observing contracts being given to consultants and training providers with dubious credentials, for commercial criteria only. Sometimes they felt that the tensions involved in managing the multiple agendas and matching perceptions gave the Russians the impression that the westerners were dragging their feet. Ideally, they believed, consultants and trainers should be able to build up local networks and relationships on which projects could be based. As both sides develop more experience in working together, this way of working may well become better established. One western participant clarified the perspective of his organization:

We believe that simply reacting to calls for interest in a project proposal with the terms of reference already decided is not enough to keep control over the process of management development in Russia. So organizations willing to be proactive in this field have to be willing to build a strong local network, to monitor the evolution of the relevant issues and to be able to go to the donors with project ideas well supported locally. In this respect local associations for management development could play a crucial role.

The experiences of the Economic Development Institute of the World Bank

The aim of the EDI is to promote economic and social development in member countries. The programmes cover such activities as:

- preservation of the environment and natural resources

- combatting poverty

- regulatory reform

- private sector development

- macro-economic management

- social policy reform.

The programmes range from seminars and short courses to longer term projects (such as training of trainers in 'emerging economies') and multiyear projects. In the 1995/96 financial year one third of the entire EDI budget was allocated for development projects in the former socialist countries of east/central Europe and the former USSR. The Moscow representation on the EDI is responsible for activities in the former USSR, the emphasis being on customizing new programmes on:

- fiscal policy reform

- decentralization: investment decision making and public management for subnationals

- environmental economics and policy

- securities' market development for policy makers

- turnaround management and reorganization of policies on bankruptcy

- rural finance system development

- social policy in transition.

The guiding objectives are to:

1 create human and institutional networks

2 share best world experience and knowledge

3 maximize exposure to market economy concepts.

Between 1990 and 1995 the EDI Moscow office (hereafter EDIMO) has run nearly 350 courses throughout the former USSR. So far 2150 trainers have been trained and courses run with or for some 200 partner institutions, involving 10,000 participants. These efforts required the commissioning of new training materials including textbooks, glossaries and case studies with increasing use being made of computer-based distance learning methods, including electronic networking of partner institutions.

The EDIMO teaching approach and evaluation is revealing, because it has been developed by Russian consultants for countries which were republics of the former Soviet Union. A typical programme cycle has the following components:

- identification of a fundamental, significant development issue

- elucidation of the characteristics and attributes of the issue

- awareness raising regarding importance of the issue, popularizing it, and placing it squarely on the development agenda

- the teaching of analytical skills and theory necessary to understand the issue

- explorations of alternative solutions to the issue

- selection of a solution to the issue within a specific social, political and economic context

- follow up with support to participants as they apply the selected solution

- evaluation of the impact of EDI's involvement.

EDIMO's evaluations suggest a high success rate with their training programmes (averaging about 4.8 on a six-point scale): 90 percent of participants claim to use the EDI know-how 'fully' or 'a lot' and about the same proportion make wide use of EDI teaching materials. Significantly, in 1995 53 percent of the courses were fully recoverable from participants or their institutions; in 1996 this proportion had risen to 78 percent.

One of the impressive aspects of the EDIMO approach is that it tries to learn from experience as a matter of policy. Concerning 'problems and stumbling blocks' EDIMO had encountered several which will be familiar to western trainers and they were classified into four groups: business environment; trainers; trainees; targeted audiences. Under business environment, EDIMO had identified serious imbalances between demand for management knowhow and its supply as well as differences in the ability and willingness to pay for training programmes. This situation was not helped by the 'low capacity of universities' to satisfy the demand and the 'embryonic state' of the training market, which created a monopoly for providers who did not really have to improve their offering in order to sell it. This was especially the case in the provinces, where, in the absence of competition, there was even less incentive. It was recognized that 'active and participatory modes of training for practitioners' were needed to explain the principles and working of the market economy system. Such modes might include the use of case studies, self-appraisal by participants and involvement in projects and role plays. All of these methods were largely unfamiliar in Russia and there was resistance to them, among both prospective trainers and participants. Under the heading of environment EDIMO had also entered the word mentality: to change this mentality was 'a must'.

With respect to EDIMO 'graduates' (i.e. trainers trained by EDIMO), there were several stumbling blocks here. These largely concerned their selection in the first place and their development into a professionally reliable force. It was exceptionally difficult to monitor performance, as they were not affiliated to a major national body such as the National Training Foundation or the Ministry of Economics. There was also disconcerting news to the effect that the EDIMO graduates were not competently managing their own training programmes, being either unable or unwilling to market their new skills, and were not bothering to make post-programme evaluations. A further problem was that many of the graduates had not really assimilated or understood the terminology associated with market economics, finance and accountancy.

When it came to trainees (i.e. potentially eligible participants on EDIMO programmes), the stumbling blocks were, broadly speaking, institutional by nature. First, there was no national institutional framework for supporting training initiatives. For certain programmes to be implemented it was necessary to go through 'a complexity of official approvals' from the *Duma* in Moscow to regional administrations. Companies often gave 'low priority to staff training compared to alternative capital expenditure' (not exactly an exclusively Russian problem). Even when people came on training programmes, it was not clear why they were participating: they had 'vague responsibilities and accountabilities'. The 'imperfections' in the tax system did not help: there was no logic to the tax breaks available, or not, for staff training. Interestingly, EDIMO had identified that it needed to influence politicians and the media about its activities.

Especially illuminating were problems and stumbling blocks associated with two kinds of targeted audiences. One audience was 'high-level officials', who were in effect largely unreconstructed communists; the other was so-called 'mid-level officials'. The high-level officials still suffered from a 'Soviet mentality'. For such people training should be entirely paid for by the sponsor so that what they are getting is what they have come to expect: 'free lunches' and 'everything for nothing'. High-level officials want courses that 'concentrate on current, urgent operational problems', that open doors to 'permanent business'; the courses should for preference take place abroad (especially in the USA); they should provide fun; should not include subordinates under any circumstances (subordinates are not worth training, anyway); and avoid concepts and theories, because in the end there was nothing really wrong with the well-tested forms of administrative management (which would still be in place today were it not for that reformist Gorbachev).

The mid-level officials, being younger and probably better educated, will become tomorrow's high-level officials and do not suffer so badly from the Soviet mindset. They do, nevertheless, have a need for special skills for operating in a new system with different forms of accountability. They lack know-how for analyzing problems. In this regard EDIMO has discovered that training for the new breed of government administrator can beneficially include the use of business games and simulations, which enable problems to be presented as they really are and not as they appear to the blinkered bureaucratic eye.

Towards new insights for understanding the gap

These western and Russian views on the role of management educators and consultants identified a series of stumbling blocks. It is possible to isolate four major problem areas which seriously impede communication and cooperation:

1 Mutual mistrust and suspicion.

2 Lack of appreciation and understanding of each other's way of working (including teamworking), thinking and goal setting.

3 Lack of knowledge of each other's management methods, procedures and decision-making processes.

4 Lack of understanding of the particular pressures on, and special priorities of, Russian managers.

The first three are mutual, but even concerning the fourth point, the workshop contributors were arguing that Russian companies are not always forthcoming about themselves.

Analysis: Russian perceptions, western perceptions

Having examined in depth these mutual perceptions (and misconceptions), we can now offer an analysis of them.

Russian perceptions

Russian reactions are consistent with the spirit of the times (the post-communist era as well as the post-honeymoon-with-the-west era). Western management behaviour often makes Russians feel discriminated against in their own country. They perceive that:

- Foreign firms are not really interested in developing and using Russians' capabilities; there are no career paths for them; they are not consulted before decisions are made, but merely directed to carry out instructions.

- Foreigners are overpaid; Russians are paid 'a colonial rate'.

- Russians in the employ of foreign firms do not receive adequate explanations as to those firm's procedures, thereby excluding Russians from full participation, and hence their potential intellectual contribution is ignored.

- Russians expect employment with a foreign firm to mean an opportunity directly to familiarize themselves with western management practices and the market economy in general.

- Consultants are often not sufficiently briefed or trained about Russia before assignments; they do not understand 'the Russian mentality' (i.e. 'Russians can work for an idea'; 'Russians make decisions based on intuition', etc.) nor the particular pressures on enterprise managers in Russia today; consultants' prescriptions often do not take account of the Russian sense of social responsibility (i.e. to supply scarce goods and services to employees).

- Consultants tend to magnify the complexity of problems; as a result, clients are unnecessarily confused.

- Russian clients have unrealistic expectations of western consultants to solve their problems. Consultants may enter Russia with professional authority; but they have to win Russian respect , and their ability and willingness to adapt are highly rated. Consultants who fail to meet Russian expectations are, in effect, held in contempt.

- Russians are not being adequately briefed on the logic and procedures of western management, e.g. the balancing of long-term and short-term goals, the use of 'soft' approach (non-coercive methods) to get things implemented, the nature of delegation of authority, and concepts of teamwork.

Western perceptions

One helpful aspect of the workshop is that most of the western participants were already knowledgeable, experienced and informed about Russia, albeit in varying degrees. There was broad consensus about perceptions:

- There are serious problems about effective interaction and they are extremely complicated owing mainly to (a) Russia's evolution as a Eurasian country forcibly secluded from traditions that powerfully shaped the western world (i.e. the Renaissance, Reformation, Enlightenment, etc.) and to (b) the Soviet experience which represented an alternative path to social and economic development.

- There is recognition that Russians are well educated with high standards of literacy and numeracy.

- The west lacks informed understanding of Russia in ways that are no longer so true of other important non-western countries such as China, Japan and the Arab world.

- There is severe lack of experience of working with one another (but plenty of experience of confrontation and antagonistic cooperation).

- Western experts misunderstand what Russians expect of them as employees, partners, clients, colleagues, trainees and even as advisors representing official bodies.

- Russian clients and partners tend to have unrealistic expectations of what westerners can offer, especially when western consultants and trainers are working to a set of terms of reference drawn up by a third-party organization, such as a major funder.

The lessons to draw – counting the cost

A central insight to emerge from the workshop is that 'the west' has generally not been successful in managing effective relationships with Russian counterparts because westerners have failed to understand Russian expectations and align them with their own. Management educators do this repeatedly by failing to build Russian expectations into their training needs analysis and therefore into the actual programmes. Western firms seldom accommodate Russian expectations of being taught about western management methods and business principles. Russian staff feel very strongly that they are both undervalued and underutilized; as such they are deprived of making a significant intellectual contribution to the western firm that employs them. Consultants do this by hiring otherwise talented Russians, but using them mainly as mere facilitators to progress the company business.

The atmosphere of working relationships is antagonized and negatively reinforced by perceptions that consultants and trainers do not have much interest in understanding the 'Russian mentality' and by the wide disparities in remuneration. The relative severity of the gap is determined by Russian and western partners' respective understanding of each other's frame of reference as well as by more elusive factors such as personal affinity and professional competence as intercultural communicators. Not only is there a gap between western and Russian managers, but also between managers who operated within the Soviet system and younger managers who have a greater stake in their country's transition to the market economy.

By now it is perfectly clear what kind of factors – both attitudinal and institutional – put so many management consultancy and training assignments on a collision course with Russian clients. And we are not talking about one or two projects going off the rails. One of the keynote speakers at the December 1996 workshop was the Moscow representative of the World Bank. The World Bank started its activities in Russia in 1992. Of the original allocation of US$6.5bn, about $2bn had been disbursed by 1996. Commenting that the Bank's relationship with Russia had been 'intensive and difficult', the official added this comment:

> The efficiency of foreign consultants here is unacceptably low. It is my estimate that as many as 40 per cent of western assignments fail. This is especially unacceptable because western consultants are so expensive.

In terms of the World Bank's operations in Russia, this suggests that US$800mn (40 per cent of $2bn) have not been well spent. If we take the World Bank's 40 per cent as a benchmark and apply to other major donors of technical aid to Russia, the sums of money which may have been inadvertently misused through the clash of expectations and power of perceptual mismatch become truly enormous. For example, the EU which accounts for about 70 per cent of the world's technical aid to Russia/CIS, supported 2000 projects between 1991 and 1994 to the value of ECU1870mn (European Commission, 1994). Assuming that EU consultants fare no better than those appointed by the World Bank, then a 40 per cent drain on that allocation becomes ECU740mn. Other major donors include US Aid, the European Bank for Reconstruction and Development, the Soros Foundation, the Ford Foundation, the Finnish Ministry of Foreign Affairs, the British Government Know-how Fund, not to mention countless other donors representing governments, academic institutions, and charities. Yet, it may be that 40 per cent of these vast sums of western, Japanese and Middle Eastern money (the destination of the last is the former Islamic republics of the USSR) is 'doomed'.

Conclusion

This is a sorry state of affairs. There can be no doubt that a major factor in this saga is that the west – donor organizations, policy makers, and the actual providers of consultancy expertise and management knowhow – do not really understand the motivations of Russian management, its priorities and constraints.

Note

1. The National Training Foundation was established in 1994 with a $40mn loan from the World Bank and a grant of 1.4mn Swiss francs from the Swiss government. The NFT is a non-governmental, non-profit organization with the aim of developing effective, long-term management training programmes appropriate to the market economy. The headquarters is in Moscow, but there are regional offices in St Petersburg and Nizhny Novgorod.

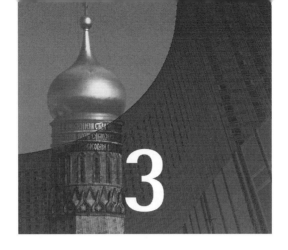

TECHNOCRATS AND TIGERS

*As to liberty, strikes were illegal, trade unions were Party mouth-
pieces – and a Stalin aide, Lazar Kaganovich, said that a factory
should quake when the Director walked through it.*

— Moynahan, 1994

*When first built in the 1930s, Magnitogorsk was hailed as one of
the most modern steel plants on the world. No more. 'We had
some Japanese here', said Vadim, a rolling-mill worker, to a
visiting American journalist in the summer of 1988.
'We said, "Tell us, how far behind are we?"
They said, "Forever. You're behind us forever."'*

— Kotkin, 1991

Introduction

As Chapters 1 and 2 clearly demonstrate, western managers having
professional involvements with Russian counterparts need to understand how the past contributes to the mindset of the Russian manager at the end of the 20th century. As, slowly but surely, younger
managers with a modern outlook replace the older bosses who were
tempered in the hard school of socialism, some of these influences
from the past will begin to wane. Eventually the Soviet mindset will

disappear, irrelevant in a market economy. But the values to do with the immensely powerful instinct for survival and collectivism will no doubt become great, shaping forces of the future. In fact these forces are already at work. [**Russian collective value system**]

Russian collective value system

The Russian collective value system has been described in these terms by Dr Charalambos Vlachoutsicos (1996):

> A unique and apparently contradictory combination of suppression of the individual, on the one hand, and considerable freedom of self-expression, on the other, is deeply rooted in Russian culture. It is expected of members of any organization to articulate their interests and opinions. They are, however, obliged, once a decision has been reached, to abide by it. As a rule, Russians respect authority but are not intimidated by it. They regard themselves as coequal with others and are not shy about speaking up in public or asserting themselves in meetings. Nor are they hesitant about forcefully demanding things that they believe are rightly theirs. Far from Western notions of grassroots participation in decision-making, the medieval Russian village, which was the foundation of the culture, was admirably suited to society's need to survive under conditions of extreme hardship due to the severe climate, perennial shortage, and constant threats from conquerors and adversaries.
>
> Russian collectivism and its ethic of egalitarianism are an intrinsic component of the inner logic of managerial values. The movements of the 'invisible hand' of the nascent market economy are still being thwarted by the 'invisible fist' of the stubborn collectivism as shown by attitudes, ethics and actions of workers, managers and the whole community. In fact, managers of state enterprises have neither the institutional authority nor the effective power to implement changes against the workers' will.
>
> While a new class of Russian managers with a stake in a market economy is now emerging, essential aspects of traditional social values still determine tangible and intangible rewards and penalties. Consequently, they play a vitally important part in the

> Russian manager's thinking, and therefore persist as important elements of Russian management practices. Thus, whenever ignored or antagonized, the collectivist mentality can indeed thwart change. However, if it is understood and properly acknowledged by Westerners, it can paradoxically act as a potent force for transformation.
>
> In addition to whatever self-serving career agendas and aspirations Russian managers might nurture, preserving the jobs of the members of their enterprise's workers' collective still remains one of their main priorities. This fact must be taken into serious consideration by Western consultants and investors in their elaboration of proposals to Russian enterprises. If mass redundancies are required, their proposals should provide concrete suggestions on how the particular enterprise can ensure that redundant workers are provided with jobs or other incentives to leave on their own (early retirement plans, loans, retraining, etc.). Investments proposed should be increased by the costs involved.

But, for the foreseeable future, Russian managers must cope with the aftermath of the Soviet period: the thinking that went with it, the wrecked economy, the gargantuan factories, and the cynicism ('We pretend to work; they pretend to pay us.') Therefore anyone dealing with Russia now is to some extent also involved with this most complicated past-in-the-present situation. For that reason, it is important for western management professionals to appreciate how management operated in the centralized economy and why the associated mindset appears to have remained so forbiddingly entrenched. The aim of this chapter is to present first an overview of the Soviet manager as a vital cog in the plan fulfilment machine.

Before leaving this introduction, we need to make some qualifying remarks about two important topics which will receive attention in the chapter. These topics concern the treatment of the Soviet economy and the Soviet manager respectively. As connoisseurs of the USSR know only too well, the Soviet economy was continually being subjected to reorganization, not least because various general secretaries had pet schemes which usually caused chaos, or overstabilization, necessitating yet another reorganization. In fact, economic historians divide the evolution of the Soviet economy into various periods. A typical seven-point periodization is as follows (based on Brown, Kaser and Smith, 1994): the immediate post-revolution years, called War Communism (see later), 1918–1921; the New Economic Policy, 1921–1928; the pre-war Five Year Plans (1928–1941); planning in wartime and post-war reconstruction (1941–1953); the Khrushchev era (1953–1964); the Brezhnev and (to a lesser extent) Kosygin eras (1964–1982); reform attempts and *perestroika* (1982–1991). [**Brezhnev**] No attempt will be made in this book to account for change and evolution in the Soviet economy using this or any other periodization. We shall merely supply an all-purpose description which should provide sufficient background for studying the Soviet manager.

As for the Soviet manager, we encounter various problems of description and classification, which we will deal with later. In this chapter we will regard the Soviet manager as the 'industrial boss' who wielded executive power, albeit within prescribed domains, to ensure that the state met (and possibly exceeded) its output targets. This will distinguish him from other kinds of functionaries, such as 'bureaucracy cleaving apparatchiks' who were to all intents and purposes administrators.

The Soviet economy

The centralization of the Soviet economy began in 1918, within 8 months of the 1917 Revolution which swept the Bolsheviks under Lenin into power. It was not until the early 1930s, when Stalin was in unassailable command of the Soviet Union, that the country finally operated under a centrally planned economy. The transformation of life in those years has been described by Brown, Kaser and Smith in the *Cambridge Encyclopedia of Russia* (1994) as follows:

> A hectic process of state-building took place, in which much of the familiar in the Soviet scene was born. Large-scale ministries and collective farms were formed, vast construction sites started to cover the countryside with towns and industry, and the repressive organs extended outwards, including their major manifestation: the growing Gulag empire of concentration camps, forced labour camps and transit pris-

Brezhnev

Leonid Ilyich Brezhnev (1906–82) became the de facto leader of the Communist Party and therefore of the USSR following the ousting of Khrushchev in 1964. He wielded power neither as individually as his predecessor nor as ruthlessly as Stalin, but he did succeed in surrounding himself with a string of protégés and cronies. With their connivance he acquired an array of important political posts, which had the effect of elevating him above the people who had put him there. As a result, these supporters did, as they say, very well for themselves and it is hardly surprising that he received all manner of honours for his 'exemplary devotion to the cause of Lenin'. These include: the Lenin Peace Prize (1973), Marshall of the Soviet Union (1976), the Order of Victory (the highest military decoration) (1978) and the Lenin Prize for Literature (1979). This last award he received for his ghost-written memoirs. At the conferment ceremony, the president of the Writers' Union (who had had all that trouble with Solzhenitsyn), declared: 'For their popularity and their educative influence on the mass of readers, the books of Leonid Ilyich are unrivalled.'

In between launching the Warsaw Pact assault on Czechoslovakia in 1968, condoning the psychiatric abuse of dissidents, allowing the USSR to be entangled with Afghanistan, and letting the economy cruise into a state of stagnation, Brezhnev found time to indulge his passion for stabling and driving classy western cars, including a somewhat dilapidated Rolls-Royce. As he grew older and more remote from ordinary life, Brezhnev became the butt of countless political jokes and these still cause a chuckle among Russians today. The fact that Brezhnev shared the same patronymic, Ilyich, with Lenin, is exploited in many jokes. Here is an example of one, slightly modified to facilitate translation, poking fun at the bumbling potentate:

> Brezhnev visits the famous Tretyakov Art Museum in Moscow. The guide explains the exhibits. 'That's a painting by Savrasov, the landscapist.' Brezhnev: 'S-s-savrasov.' Guide: 'Yes, it's called "The Rooks". A splendid composition.' Brezhnev: 'S-s-splendid c-c-composition.' Guide: 'Here we have "The Demon". Brezhnev: 'D-d-demon.' Guide: 'It's a truly magnificent painting. Obviously a Vroubel.' Brezhnev: 'A rouble! Is that all?'

ons. [**Gulag**] All levels of society changed places: peasants became workers, millions of whom migrated annually to the towns (until stopped by the restoration of the internal passport), workers poured into offices and the swelling ranks of lower administration, and the top echelons coalesced into an amorphous and privileged élite.

Gulag

Gulag is the abbreviation of the Russian for 'chief administration of camps', which was in charge of some 6000 corrective labour camps and colonies that existed from 1934 to 1960 in some of the least accessible and inhospitable regions of the USSR. The word Gulag has come to refer to the camps themselves. It has been estimated that at least 10 million and perhaps as many as 17 million Soviet citizens (and representatives of other non-Soviet nationalities) were held in the camps under Stalin's rule. About 10% of all inmates perished through starvation, trauma, extreme hardship, beatings or execution. The average life expectancy was just one winter. All the major construction projects of the 1930s were carried out largely by forced labour. The standard sentence was 10 years.

Most prisoners were charged under the notorious Article 58 of the Soviet criminal code, which 'covered all forms of remotely political crime'. Under the Gulag system work was regulated by Five Year Plans exactly as in civilian economy. In 1939 it was the biggest employer in Europe. Special camps were built for scientific research. Illustrious inmates include Andrei Tupolev, the aircraft designer, and Sergei Korolev, the father of the Soviet space programme. In 1941, after the Nazi onslaught on the USSR, thousands of prisoners were released to join the Soviet forces. Many were high-ranking officers who had been incarcerated during the Great Terror. After Stalin's death in 1953 the camp system began to wind down through a series of rehabilitations. The Chief Administration itself was abolished in 1960. In 1987 Mikhail Gorbachev declared an amnesty to all political and religious prisoners.

So it was, against this background, that the centralized economy began to acquire the essential features which were largely to endure until the very end of the Soviet regime. These features, to summarize the leading economic historian Alec Nove (1990), were as follows:

1 State enterprises were directly responsible to the appropriate ministry, and each enterprise director was subject to the ministry on all matters. The centre allocated and regulated, directly or indirectly, the output and activities of the enterprise.

2 Plans had the force of a binding order given by a hierarchical superior. Depending on the industry, these plans covered such questions as quantity and assortment of output, purchases of inputs (from where and in what quantities), the delivery obligations of the enterprise, prices, wages, staff establishments, costs. All these planned objectives were subordinate to the supreme, the gross output indicator.

3 Plans were devised by the ministries for enterprises in their competence and were subject to the authority of the party and government, who laid down the general policy objectives and key targets. Gosplan, the state planning commission, coordinated and reconciled the national planning activity.

4 Gosplan's main methodological method was the system of so-called material balances, whereby the planners drew up a entire balance sheet of inputs in quantitative terms needed by Soviet industry to meet its output targets within a given timescale. The main normal planning period (with certain exceptions) was five years (hence the Five Year Plan). Any changes to the balances, which were frequent owing to conditions of perpetual supply shortage and the imposition of new (i.e. unplanned) priorities by government and party (and the latter could include a major structural reorganization), resulted in 'rewriting' the allocations for entire enterprises and even industries.

5 The overriding criterion at all levels was the plan, which expressed the economic will of the party and government. The plan was based on political priorities and not on considerations of profit and loss. As the role of prices was kept to a minimum, the prices seldom bore any relationship to costs.

6 Although they were encouraged to make efficient use of resources allocated to them, enterprises had no influence over

what should be produced or even with what materials.

7 In order for the entire system of material balances to be reconciled with targets for Soviet industry, each enterprise was provided with detailed production and output plans.

Accordingly, under this method of economic management:

> The conventional laws of supply and demand, taken
> for granted in the West, did not apply . . . the result of
> a political struggle in which property rights were
> taken away from social classes and vested in the state
> . . . Private ownership of productive assets (stores,
> workshops, farms, tools, factories) was abolished, to
> the maximum feasible extent. All such assets became
> the property of the state, managed by directors who
> were answerable to the industrial ministries based in
> Moscow, and to the network of political monitoring
> agencies (the party and the secret police) which
> spread down into every factory.
>
> (Rutland, 1994)

The structure which superintended the day-to-day management of the economy existed to maintain all economic activities under its control and to subordinate them to the state and, through the state, to the dictates of the Communist Party. By the 1930s this structure had the principal features that were to persist until the disintegration of the USSR in 1991. At the apex of the structure stood the State Planning Commission, Gosplan, which received from the Communist Party output targets for specific industries. The task of Gosplan was to '[match] the flow of available inputs (labour, capital, and raw materials) with these desired outputs. Beneath Gosplan were some 60 economic ministries, supervising 120,000 factories, farms and other units in industry, construction, commerce and agriculture' (Rutland, 1994). In addition to the ministries there were some 20 state committees which had responsibility for functional aspects, such as pricing and labour. Beneath the central ministries came the republican ministries, other analogous agencies, and the regional soviets which had some control over local industry.

The planning frame for all the nation's economic activity was the Five Year Plan, but the industrial ministries issued output targets to enterprises on an annual basis. This annual plan was 'the operational document', as the Five Year Plan 'was altered so frequently that it was little more than a forecasting exercise' (Rutland, 1994). Enterprises would frequently fret at the output demands made of them and specified their input requirements to another important central organization, the State Commission on Supplies, Gossnab, which was facetiously described as 'a kind of civilian Ordnance Corps for putting suppliers in touch with clients' (Wilson and Bachkatov, 1992). As Dyker (1992), points out, 'the hierarchy of Soviet planning developed into a fairly neat, three-tiered system, running Gosplan → sectoral ministry → enterprise', but it was 'in no way a multilevel planning system'. Gosplan issued the targets which would extend 'right down to the level of individual commodities'; it was then up to the ministries to give Gosplan's targets an organizational dimension, by translating them into specific targets.

It does not take much imagination to appreciate that, in a country the size of the USSR, such a top-heavy centralized system of economic management, especially one that was 'shadowed' by party machinery level for level, was 'incredibly complicated and difficult to manage' (Rutland, 1994). Kotkin (1991) decribes how things worked practice between Gossnab and the steel industry:

> Soviet firms are not allowed to purchase steel from other firms. Instead, they put in 'bids' for metal to the State Supply Commission (Gossnab). Because a firm knows that it will receive less than it requests, the firm logically asks for more than it might otherwise need, secure in the understanding that it will not suffer for higher costs because an enterprise does not need to make a profit to stay in business. Gossnab tries to anticipate this upward bidding and almost invariably allocates less than requested, but without the lever furnished by cost, the commission invariably finds the task of disciplining enterprises impossible.

In the end, of course, the system did prove impossible to manage. But even by the late 1970s the Soviet economic system faced serious problems. Economic historian Alec Nove (1990) describes the mess which Gorbachev would attempt to reform – an attempt that would fail. It was a system that is 'much more attuned to quantity than to quality, poor at relating production to consumer demand, and, above, increasingly overwhelmed by its own complexity'. He goes on:

> Inefficiency and waste, the slow diffusion of technical progress, imbalances and bottlenecks, continue to plague the economy . . . Production continued to adapt itself not to user demand but to the 'success indicators', i.e. to plan fulfilment statistics in roubles, tons, square metres . . . New products or new machines are required to be approved by numerous bureaucratic instances, and then fitted into planned target figures, and the allocated material inputs frequently fail to match requirements. Information flows remain distorted by the interest of information providers in being given an easy plan to fulfil. Unreliability of supplies encourages hoarding and over-application for input allocations; frequent changes of plan encourage hoarding of labour too.

The 'distorters' of information could be central ministries and other central economic organizations, research institutes and scientific bodies; their counterparts at republican and then regional level. At every level there was a special interest to promote, a special interest to protect, and, as Dyker (1992) has it, there were additionally 'so many good departmental reasons for doing "bad" things'. Furthermore, 'there were so many "priorities" in force that the centre lost the ability to make any impact' (Rutland, 1994). For example, in the regions party bosses could override local economic authorities and use their political clout in 'forcing through a local construction project, helping a factory acquire scarce supplies, persuading factory workers to help with the harvest and so forth' (Rutland, 1994).

Even after Gorbachev's attempts at reform, the system still retained what Dyker (1992) calls its 'classic shortcomings'. As he explains:

The insensitivity of the system to quality, to technology, to cost-effectiveness, to what the customer really wants – these are the classic shortcomings of the system dedicated to extensive development, the shortcomings which have produced surpluses of things that no one wants, shortages of the most essential commodities, both consumer and industrial, and a structural rigor mortis which has defied the best attempts of Moscow planners to breathe into the body the life of industrial adjustment.

We do not need to extend this brief sketch of the Soviet economy nor do we need to account for its collapse. But we have outlined enough of the framework within which the Soviet manager operated. We can turn to this remarkable figure, whose job it was to do the impossible for those whom the system served: not the people, but its bureaucratic masters (Campbell, 1991).

Soviet management

Earlier in this chapter we supplied a seven-point periodization of the evolution of the Soviet economy. Here we introduce a five -stage periodization, depicted in Figure 3.1. In fact this second scheme maps fairly easily on the first, the essential difference between them

1918–1921	War Communism
1921–1928	New Economic Policy
1928–mid-1960s	'Classical' Stalinist management
1957–1988	Technocratic management
1988–1991	Management under *perestroika*

Figure 3.1 Five main systems of Soviet management
Source: Based on Lawrence and Vlachoutsicos, 1990

being that we are positing only two main kinds of Soviet management in the period after Stalin, where we have identified four clear phases of economic evolution and reform. We now characterize management in each of these five phases, concentrating on technocratic management and management under *perestroika*.

War Communism

War Communism is the name for the Bolshevik Government's social and economic policy from 1918 to 1921, when civil war was raging between the Reds and the Whites. The policy had two aims: to support the Bolshevik effort during the civil war and to accomplish the transition to conditions of communism (Utechin, 1961). In practice War Communism meant:

- the nationalization of virtually all industry, combined with a central allocation of resources

- the state monopolization of trade

- a collapse of monetary policy (for some Bolsheviks money was to have no place in a socialist society)

- requisitioning of agricultural produce (Hosking, 1992).

It was a time of chaos, anarchy and dislocation, when 'sleepless, leather-jacketed commissars [worked] round the clock in a vain effort to replace the market economy' (Nove, quoted in Hosking, 1992), and 'commanding became the only management method' (Lawrence and Vlachoutsicos, 1990.)

New Economic Policy

As soon as it became apparent that the rigours of War Communism could be relaxed, the Bolsheviks introduced a new and generally successful policy 'with the aims of restoring the economy by making concessions to private enterprise, in agriculture, trade and industry, and of neutralising the peasants practically' (Utechin, 1961). By 1923, 76 percent of the retail trade was in private hands (Brown, Kaser and Smith, 1994), but the government kept a firm control over banking, foreign trade and notably heavy industry, the ideological heartland of the proletariat. During the NEP period, the status of management increased, and there was recognition that the well-being of the workers was 'not just an ethical principle but a requirement for efficient production' (Graham, 1993). Even some party officials received management training and many 'bourgeois specialists' were employed in the task of regeneration. It would be 60 years, under *perestroika*, before Soviet managers would be able to act and take decisions so independently.

'Classical' Stalinist management

Soviet industrial development in the 1930s took place against a background of mayhem, terror and, although perhaps easy to over-look or minimize, idealism and belief in the new way of life. Industrialization proceeded despite the fact that collectivization of agriculture directly and miserably affected the lives of 75 percent of the entire Soviet population (Channon and Hudson, 1995); that millions – many of them the incarcerated victims of Stalin's terror machine – were employed in conditions of unspeakable hardship on the great prestige projects of the 1930s and the creation of the heavy industrial base (see Conquest, 1994; Moynahan, 1994; Volkonogov, 1991); that 7000 of the country's engineers were imprisoned by 1931 for being 'bourgeois'; that failure to achieve 'norms' was disruptive, and therefore indictable; that tools and implements were in short supply as were precision instruments; that the overloaded railroad system almost collapsed in 1933 (Moynahan, 1994). [**The Great Terror**]

In this hectic period, society was gripped with a terrifying fren-zy of plan fulfilment. For the heroic task of constructing the foun-dations of the world's first socialist state in the 1930s and to protect the achievements of the Communist Party, the NEP-type manager was then an anachronism. Thus, the 1930s saw the emergence of the 'Red directors', dynamic and ideologically committed man-agers, who highly mobile, applying their skills in several industrial sectors, and able to pursue 'substantial promotional opportunities' (Granick, 1972). Indeed, industrialization proceeded so smoothly that well-disposed foreign commentators were extolling the USSR as 'the second America' in terms of economic might, adding that

The Great Terror

The Great Terror, alias the Great Purge, convulsed the USSR in 1936-1938, when some 10 million Soviet citizens were arrested on various charges of sabotage, treason, terrorism, espionage, etc., and declared 'enemies of the people'. Arrest frequently followed denunciation ('A woman in Kiev is believed to have denounced 8000 people, most of whom died . . . the sidewalks emptied as she walked through the city.') Upon confession, often extracted by deceit, intimidation or torture, victims were summarily executed or sentenced to the long periods of imprisonment in the Gulag. The wave of terror began in 1934 with the assassination of Sergei Kirov, the party boss in Leningrad, which was almost certainly perpetrated on Stalin's orders. Gradually Stalin widened his noose, doing away first with all imaginable political rivals, then all manner of 'unreliable' persons: higher officials, national minorities, figures in arts, sports, science and culture and the armed forces. Indeed Stalin's decimation and subsequent demoralization of the Soviet high command are known to have been factors convincing Hitler that a Nazi attack on the USSR would be impossible to withstand.

With his internal security chief, Nikolai Yezhov, Stalin would sometimes work for four or five hours a day scrutinizing lists of victims who were senior figures in Soviet life. Stalin is known to have approved 383 lists containing 44,000 names. Junior officials dealt with the millions of other cases. At the height of the terror it was said that 'nobody could afford not to love Stalin.' But the truly extraordinary fact is that the great mass of people, believing in the propaganda about the benevolence of Stalin – in other words, falling for the cult of personality – did not know that it was the great and wise leader himself who had unleashed the terror machine and was keeping it running at full throttle. 'If only Stalin knew' was their anguished hope.

When the purges abated in 1938, Stalin instigated an investigation into the internal security services and, lo and behold, they were shown to be infiltrated with enemies of the people, too. Yezhov, the leader's principal henchman, was duly unmasked and demoted to Commissar for Water Transport. In 1939 'he was shot but – like many thousands of his victims – when and where and on what basis has not been established.' Stalin's connivance in the Great Terror only became known to the Soviet people in Khrushchev's so-called secret speech to the 20th Party Congress in 1956. That was quickly followed by the release of millions of inmates from the camps.

socialist society was more advanced than the capitalist countries. According to Granick (1972), the Red directors 'were largely swept away in the purges of 1936–1938'. They were succeeded by younger managers who were not as technically qualified, but whose political convictions were not in doubt. Of these managers Granick (1972) writes:

> Only one-quarter of enterprise managers had attended normal higher educational institutions, the rest of those with higher education having been sent to the industrial academies for the brief and inferior education there.

Nevertheless, these were the men who drove the Soviet war economy to its absolute limit, restored Soviet industry in the post-war reconstruction and retained the top industrial jobs until the mid-1960s. Their task was to execute to the letter the directives of higher authorities and deliver more and more output for Stalin, the wise and benevolent leader, whose 'portrait was on every shop floor, his slogans on every lip' (Moynahan, 1994). Nor should we forget that these men were also called upon to exercise a paternalistic concern for their workers, to protect the *kollektiv*, no matter how much they cajoled and taunted it. Accordingly, enterprise managers were 'in varying degrees, involved with feeding, clothing and housing of employees' (Hickson and Pugh, 1995). In the case of major industrial facilities, such as huge steelworks or truck plants, which dominated life in a city or region, their managers would have ultimate responsibility for the upkeep of accommodation, running of shops, theatres, polyclinics, swimming pools and the local newspaper, not to mention organizing summer camp for the children of employees and having to manage agricultural enterprises (see Kotkin, 1991).

It is only too easy to denigrate the Stalinist manager (and his successors) through ignorance and prejudice. Yet we should not forget the extraordinary achievements that were performed by him. It is he who may be credited with the dubbing of the USSR as 'the second America' in the 1930s; with the creation of the second most powerful industrial economy; and with the development of a fully fledged economic system which presented, especially to non-aligned countries in the Cold War era, a radical alternative to western systems of economic management. But the real triumph of the Stalinist manager is that he achieved anything at all in a society where the bureaucracy was oppressive and secrecy universal and endemic. Under Stalin 'failure' could readily be interpreted as a political crime, which in turn meant a sham of a trial, trumped-up charges, and years of penal servitude or execution. Under Stalin's successors the fate was gentler, but still humiliating: a disgraced manager would have to accept possible ostracism for oneself and his family, stripping of privileges such as access to special shops (if, as was likely, he was a party member), or relocation to a remote place.

Technocratic management

From the early 1960s, the Soviet manager is a technocrat: that is, he is somebody who belonged to the USSR's 'technical intelligentsia' or 'technocracy', that is 'rule by people well educated in technical areas' (Graham, 1993). [*Intelligentsia*] The technocrat emerged in the 1960s, when the USSR was urged on by competition with the USA (Mikheyev, 1996). It would be inconceivable to describe the USSR under Stalin as a technocracy, no matter how considerable the technological achievement, no matter how important technology was to the feat of industrialization during the 1930s and to the development of weapons for repelling the Nazis during World War II. Indeed, as noted earlier, the Stalinist manager from the end of the 1930s to the mid-1960s was generally less technically qualified than his predecessors in the great age of industrialization.

However, with the launch of Sputnik in 1957 and increasing scientific and technological competition between east and west, the Soviet Union, as destined to spend its last decades, was clearly a technocracy in the sense described above. [**Sputnik**] Accordingly, as of the mid-1960s, if not earlier, there was an urgent need for a new kind of educated Soviet manager: the technocrat. In this book, the 'technocratic manager' is important because he represents, as it were, the highest stage of development of his species under socialism before the collapse of the USSR despite the decentralizing reforms of Mikhail Gorbachev. Henceforth, the term Soviet manag-

Intelligentsia

To professional connoisseurs of Russian and Soviet history, the word *intelligentsia* 'is one of the vaguest and most difficult to define in the whole social science vocabulary' (Hosking, 1997). In the west the word has negative connotations: it is often readily associated with those among the idle rich who aspire to independent thinking by virtue of having had a good education. The image of slightly shop-soiled intellectuals is well removed from the concept of the *intelligentsia*, as it developed in 19th-century Russia and became a kind of pillar of Soviet society. To be a member of the *intelligentsia* – to be an intelligent – largely was, and is seen positively by the rest of society. Broadly speaking, the word *intelligentsia* refers to people of different social backgrounds who have a shared interest in culture. Their outlook may embrace what we call 'social conscience', but does not necessarily have to. In Russia the word culture is seen as a totality of achievements across a wide range of human endeavour, which enrich society. It is not, as in Britain, narrowly identified, often dismissively, with 'the arts'. Members of the *intelligentsia* should not be seen as a specific class united in protecting or promoting a similar set of political ideals or economic interests. Until the collapse of the USSR in 1991 and the advent of the market economy, such people had 'a superb indifference to money' (Wilson and Bachkatov, 1992). Precisely because members of the *intelligentsia*, in pre-revolutionary Russia, as in the USSR, could readily be accused of criticizing or subverting the prevailing political system, adherents were inclined, and indeed still are, to use creative literature as a medium for disseminating ideas. Ronald Hingley notes that in the last century *intelligenty* were often powerhouses of cerebral activity, who engaged in far too much frenzied verbalizing, and generally failed to register any solid achievement in any field. Thus Dostoyevsky and Tolstoy 'could not rate as members of the *intelligentsia* . . . due to the monumental size of their achievement'. Be that as it may, it is useful to appreciate that every other Russian is in reality an *intelligent* manqué.

er will refer to the technocratic manager prior to, and during, *perestroika*. In order to understand the Russian manager of today, we must understand the functions, attitudes and priorities of the Soviet technocratic manager. It is no exaggeration to say that at the time of the collapse of the Soviet Union, the absolute majority of Russian (i.e. immediately post-Soviet) managers were largely unreconstructed, even after three years of the Gorbachev reforms from 1988 on.

Although the manager in the USSR had an important task in the Soviet economy, enterprise management per se did not enjoy a great deal of social prestige. According to Boycko, Shleifer and Vishny (1995), the ambition of an enterprise manager was 'to become a minister or a high-level party official . . . so that he could give orders to other managers'. With this vision of Soviet-style upward mobility, it is not surprising that, according to the same authors, 'playing the system was one of the most important managerial skills'. It was precisely the same skills that were needed to get output targets modified because the haggling, the pleading, the cajoling, the fixing and attendant sycophancy involved the self-same sets of bureaucrats and party officials. In a highly centralized economy the size of the USSR, with conditions of perpetual shortage and chronic supply breakdown, while demanding ever increased output, it was often only through machinations that non-existent supplies would suddenly materialize and bottlenecks would became unblocked.

Although he was but a cog in the cumbersome state machinery responsible for running the command economy, the Soviet manager was not insignificant. He was a crucially important implementer of the Communist Party's masterplan for the country. His job was not to query why 'it needed 20 signatures in Moscow to produce cakes in Vladivostok' (Zaitsev, 1996); to challenge party thinking on its plans for improving cotton production around the Aral Sea, which would eventually lead to one of the world's largest inland seas becoming a desert (Feshbach and Friendly, 1992); to question how it was that in the USSR it was possible to continue building a nuclear power station (Chernobyl) without adequate construction plans (Read, 1993). His job was not ask questions; it was to implement. In the words of Lawrence and Vlachoutsicos (1990):

> Management practice was essentially paternalistic . . . demanding the punctual, absolute, selfless execution of each directive. Sparing no effort, working all the

Sputnik

On 4 October 1957 the world's first artificial satellite was launched, and the Russian word *sputnik*, (companion or fellow traveller) became known throughout the world. Weighing 83.6kg and orbiting the earth in 96 minutes, Sputnik I was 'little more than a radio transmitter encased in an aluminium sphere from which long "whip" aerials extended, but the regular "bleep-bleep" of its transmitter picked up all around the world signalled the dawn of a new age' (Brown, Kaser and Smith, 1994). Coinciding with the celebrations for the 40th anniversary of the 1917 Revolution, Sputnik I was not only a stunning propaganda coup for the Kremlin, but it also created a great surge of national morale. Any American who happened to be on the streets of Moscow would be greeted with a triumphant 'bleep-bleep' by grinning Russians. News of this stunning event caused many people to think that the Soviet Union had taken a dramatic lead over the west, not only in space exploration, but in science and technology generally. It was a spectacular, if short-lived victory over the USA with its much more powerful technological base.

Within a month, and to the west's greater consternation, Soviet space scientists launched Sputnik II, carrying a large dog, Laika, for experimental purposes. Laika did not survive her space odyssey: the oxygen ran out. In 1959 a Soviet space probe reached and circumnavigated the moon. Then in 1961 came the world's first manned space flight, and all the world knew the name of Yuri Gagarin. In 1966 the USSR made the first successful landing of a space capsule on the moon. Behind all these sensational achievements was the brilliant Sergei Korolev (1906–1966), father of the Soviet space programme, who between 1938 and 1944 had been imprisoned for allegedly selling blueprints of aircraft designs to the Germans. He worked on rocket technology in a special prison laboratory of the type described by Solzhenitsyn in *The First Circle* until he was rescued from the Gulag by the famous aircraft designer Tupolev. He was the driving force behind the development of the Soviet intercontinental ballistic missiles.

In the early 1960s it looked to many Soviet citizens as if their country really was poised to lead the world. With hindsight it is clear that the USSR could never match the energy, will and resources of the USA and it exhausted itself – actually wrecked itself – in the very pursuit. It is more than a passing irony that, when the USSR disintegrated in December 1991, a Soviet cosmonaut, Sergei Krikalev, was 500 kilometres above the earth in the Mir space station. He had been there since May and was asked to stay up 'until further notice', because of shortage of funds for the space programme. When he returned to earth after 310 days in the space station, the country that had initiated the space age no longer existed.

harder, the director kept the operation on its toes. But such a system discouraged innovation and creativity. Even in the best-run enterprise, detailed and petty rules from above made the manager merely an implementer.

Under this regime, managers 'quickly discovered that with a captive market the easiest way to cut costs is to skimp on materials and quality' (Dyker, 1992). So it was by no means surprising to find reports in the 1970s commenting on the problem of defective work. According to Dyker's (1992) sources, in Azerbaidzhan 'completed' schools were left without running water or window glass, with unpainted walls and unfinished classrooms. 'New houses in Lithuania lacked proper insulation, and the removal of a light switch could leave a hole right through to the next house' (Dyker, 1992). Things did not improve in the 1980s, as the Chernobyl disaster underlined. Quite apart from factors to do with the management and control of such a potentially lethal facility, the plant had been constructed with all the worst features of Stalinism: 'the complete absence of a safety culture' and 'a tradition of driving a worker on to such superhuman accomplishments as breaking production records or exceeding the norms, which encourage him to improvise and cut corners' (Read, 1993).

Catastrophes great and small were readily attributable to supply uncertainty, an endemic characteristic of the over-centralized Soviet planning system, which affected the construction industry particularly acutely (Dyker 1992). In 1979, holdups in deliveries affected 1293 projects, with an estimated value of 58 billion roubles (nearly half the value of annual investment) in 1979 (Dyker, 1992). Not that supplyside failure should be seen mainly in terms of materials and equipment. As Dyker (1992) also notes, the general 'bureaucratic maladroitness' of construction industry planners frequently resulted in 'chronic lateness in the delivery of [design] documentation'.

Supply uncertainty was to some extent alleviated by the activities of 'semi-legal supply agents called "pushers" (*tolchaki*)', whose task was to identify sources of urgently needed materials and equipment for the completion of projects (Dyker 1992). The role of these 'pushers' was so extensive, Dyker suggests, that enterprise managers were often in collusion with the 'unofficial pusher network to filch supplies from centralized investment'. Indeed, these larcenies were so prolific that 'entire warehouses of construction materials and equipment' sprang up everywhere (Smith, 1991). Not only was it possible to engage in 'construction projects . . . outside the official plan, using materials and men earmarked for planned projects', in 1971 no fewer than 880 such projects were in operation (Dyker, 1992).

It would be quite false, however, to assume that the Stalinist manager was so obsessed with meeting his output targets that he had no scope for initiative. One of his key roles, in fact, was to try to secure a modification to the state directives cascaded from Gosplan, down through the chain of industrial ministries and administrations. As we saw when we examined technocratic management, petitioning for a relaxation of quotas often involved the use of semi-legal, if not downright illegal inducements to those in positions of influence in the *nomenklatura*, the higher realms of the Soviet establishment. [**Nomenklatura**] The most important modification would generally be a reduction of the production goals, but there might be other concerns: the reluctance to carry out work in a part of the USSR with an untried production team or to avoid commitment to targets that depended on the delivery of production equipment, if the enterprise could have no influence over the delivery date. In such circumstances, the enterprise manager would activate his party and ministry networks to achieve the modification so as to '[avert] the danger of underfulfilling quotas'. Lawrence and Vlachoutsicos (1990).

The life of the Soviet manager was dominated by achieving his output targets, while fretting over bottlenecks which prevented his supplies reaching him. He had no interest in costs or pricing, and he did not have to think about customers or product innovation.

Nomenklatura

The *nomenklatura* system is the communist version of jobs for the boys. The leading British historian Norman Davies has provided an excellent description of the workings of the system in his history of Poland published in 1986. The following is an abridged extract:

> It is an axiom of Soviet practice that every position of authority in every sphere of public life must be held by persons dependent on the grace and favour of the ruling Party. All state and Party officials are subject to rigorous hierarchical discipline, akin to that of an army. Their higher ranks form a closed élite enjoying monopoly power together with sole access to the fixed list of the most influential and remunerative appointments – the *nomenklatura*. State and Party organs at the regional, city and district level follow the same procedures as their seniors in central government . . . All posts are filled by the Party's nominees, trained in the Party's own academies, and kept in check by the security services and by the threat of periodic purges. It involves a network of political patronage on a scale unthinkable in pluralist societies. In theory at least, no one capable of making a decision which might be hostile to the communist Establishment can ever reach a position to make it. It follows that enterprising, imaginative, or eccentric personalities are disadvantaged from the start.

Thus, the socialist state is nothing more than the administrative branch of the ruling communist party. However, it would be mistaken to regard the nomenklatura as a magic circle of top bosses. There is not a cleaning supervisor or a park keeper in the land whose job, directly or indirectly, does not fall within its purview. Membership of the magic circle carries important privileges – higher salaries, preferential pensions, special identity cards, access to education, private party clinics, holiday homes, cars, luxurious family housing, foreign travel with currency, and most lucratively, the ability to exact favours with impunity. Many of these privileges were invested not just in the incumbents themselves, but in their spouses and relatives.

In short, he was a very different managerial animal from his western counterparts. But in what ways exactly? This is an important question, of direct relevance to our understanding of the so-called gap which still prevents Russian and western managers easily finding common ground years after the collapse of the command economy system.

Before attempting to answer the question it is necessary to say a few words about two factors which so strongly condition Russian attitudes they can help us to understand the mindset of the Soviet manager and the logic of his behaviour. First, be aware that for centuries Russians have seen themselves as working for and in some kind of collective. They may work themselves to death in these collectives, but paradoxically that does not seem to matter! One of the west's leading historians of Russia has noted that 'when Russians try to define their national character . . . they feel themselves to be warm, humane, informal, chaotic but able to get things done by community spirit' (Hosking, 1997). This community spirit, once roused, has shown itself capable of collective triumph, as in the defeat of Napoleon in 1812, in the frenzied industrialization of society in the 1930s, in the war against the Nazis and even in the development of the Soviet space programme in the 1950s.

But that is not all, and this leads us to the second factor. It is precisely this community spirit, forming as it does the essence of Russian and Soviet collectivism, 'which helps to make insensitive authoritarianism endurable' (Hickson and Pugh, 1995), and which somehow, and often against all the odds, reconciles harsh leadership and forbearing subordination to achieve a common goal (based on Liferov and Dobrusin, 1969). In the novel *Doctor Zhivago* the hero says: 'A grown man must grit his teeth and share his country's destiny' (in Moynahan, 1994). It is in fact tempting to suggest that Soviet management both emphasizes and embodies an insensitive authoritarianism (hence the characterization that it is directive), while fulfilling a psychological and emotional need for community spirit. The tension between, and the coexistence of authority and collectivism is an enormously strong theme in Russian history. Without an appreciation of the potency of these incongruously positioned forces, Soviet management will to a large extent remain a black box.

Soviet and US management styles analysed

Harvard Business School scholars, Lawrence and Vlachoutsicos (1990), who have compared and contrasted Soviet and US management styles, take due account of these factors. They are particularly reliable guides for characterizing Soviet management. Although their main focus is on differences in decision making, they also emphasize other important distinctions with respect to informal and formal communications, operational planning, attitudes to risk, goals and values, etc. What follows is based mainly on their characterization of the Soviet manager decuced from research conducted in 1987–8. Although, strictly speaking, this characterization applies to Soviet managers during the *perestroika* period (see Chapter 4), it can be taken to reflect the attitudes and behaviours associated with the structures and mechanisms of the command economy.

The Harvard Business School researchers identified 30 differences, with supporting explanations and clarifications, in relation to decision making under the following headings:

1 the use of hierarchy in decision making (11 differences)

2 the use of groups in hierarchical decision making (8 differences)

3 the use of rules in decision making (2 differences)

4 the use of plans in decision making (4 differences)

5 the use of direct lateral contacts for decision making (3 differences)

6 the use of lateral crossfunctional teams in decision making (2 differences).

They also identified 22 differences with respect to a number of managerial practices:

1 the use of time (5 differences)

2 communications (3 differences)

3 attitudes to risk taking and power (5 differences)

4 goals and values (4 differences)

5 personnel (the use of rewards and sanctions) (5 differences).

In total then, if we are to accept the findings of Lawrence and Vlachoutsicos, there are some 50 key differences between US and Soviet managers at the end of the 1980s. There can be little doubt that further probing would highlight even more. For example, factors under 'communications' alone appear to be grossly underrepresented. We do not intend to consider all the key differences between Soviet and US managers identified by Lawrence and Vlachoutsicos, as many will already be apparent to the reader. We will present therefore the main differences in summary form. For this purpose, three categories (based on Hickson and Pugh, 1995) will be used: management of authority, management of relationships and uncertainty avoidance.

Management of authority

The Soviet manager was expected to be an authoritarian, assertive and even inspirational leader with a thorough knowledge of production and human concern for his fellow men. He was also expected to be paternalistic and egalitarian, that is to understand and work with grassroots feeling. In Soviet eyes an enterprise was a democratic institution; in the Russian tradition everyone is entitled to have his or her voice heard, and employees at any level would feel free to speak to the boss. Accordingly, the democratic manager could count on the almost fierce loyalty of his workforce, if he exercised his authority with firmness and frankness, and if he did not avoid straightforward problems or decisions by claiming that 'the centre' (i.e. the cumbersome chain of command from the centre to his enterprise) was somehow failing him. Against that, it is perfectly true, his freedom of action was often severely circumscribed by the demands of the plan, other rules and regulations and the frequent need to report upwards.

The Soviet manager's place was not in his office, but with people, and that meant not only frequent and impromptu meetings with particular groups, but also having to address full-scale meetings of the workforce to explain a problem and his proposed solution. So he had to be a good public speaker. Regarded as a leader, the manager did not merely have to tell his subordinates what to do, but also how to do it. Forceful bosses were likely to get subordinates' hackles up if they did not also reveal the human side of their character (this would be considered not a weakness, but rather a strength among Russians.)

Management of relationships

Concerning management of relationships, the Soviet manager dealt formally and informally with several sets of people inside and outside the enterprise. The 'insiders' included: subordinate managers, who would be competent in their area, but not necessarily be familiar with related areas (they would not be given the information); representatives of the enterprise trade union; the party representative based at the enterprise; the workforce; representatives of social amenities, such as schools or hospitals, which were connected to the enterprise. With all these groups meetings would be frequent. The manager must be there in person; Russians do not like indirect communication as per memo. In a culture that prizes close relationships, encounters must be face to face. Meetings would not, however, take on the character of brainstorming sessions (calling a meeting to review ideas about an issue would be incomprehensible.) They were called to thrash out a problem and agree action. Hence, a valued attribute of the Soviet manager was his capacity to act as a troubleshooter (one translation of this expression in an Anglo-Russian dictionary is 'a specialist authorized to settle conflicts').

If inside his enterprise the Soviet manager could stamp his authority with his subordinates, with people outside (the local party bosses, the regional authorities and his network of pushers) he needed strong skills of persuasion to secure favours and influence, a penchant for petitioning (a long-standing Russian tradition), a knack for grooming apparatchiks and horse-trading with the pushers.

Uncertainty avoidance

As noted earlier, penalties for 'failure' could be both severe and humiliating. Hence, the Soviet manager was ever keen to limit this possibility of failure. He could do it in a number of ways. One decisive way would be to tackle the relevant superior bodies directly to persuade them to moderate the plan targets. A less decisive way would be to 'hide' behind rules and regulations. Another devise would be to refuse to give a commitment to a production deadline unless all the necessary supplies were guaranteed. As a rule, uncertainty avoidance focused on a serious current problem rather than about some issue in the longer term: that would be something that the planners were supposed to anticipate.

Conclusion

The Soviet manager has been hidden from us over many decades through the double fog (as it were) of Soviet propaganda and our own prejudices. What the Lawrence and Vlachoutsicos study shows is that, contrary to assumptions, Soviet managers were, within the restrictions imposed upon them, capable, hard working, and genuinely solicitous of their workforce. They were also democratically minded leaders who led by personal example. As we have seen, they were no mute instrument of an uncaring system. But this same system did force them to be, in the final analysis, hard-nosed implementers. But the single-mindedness they demonstrated in their resourcefulness to secure desperately needed supplies is not much different from the frenzied pursuit of the western marketing management for new customers or new product ideas in a sluggish market.

It is important to see the Soviet manager for what he was in terms of the system in which he operated. Because he did not need to know anything about marketing, cashflow management or business strategy, it is wrong to dismiss him as basically incompetent. The sketch in this chapter has consciously emphasized the positive sides of his behaviour, but it is equally well known that the manager operated in a work culture that was prone to aggravated alcohol abuse (White, 1996), displayed 'shocking disregard for safety' (Cooper, 1991), encouraged 'endemic larceny' (Smith, 1991), 'a blasé attitude to errors', 'social passivity', and 'negative attitudes to work' leading to absenteeism and skiving (Dyker, 1992). Nor does it take much effort to imagine that encounters between enterprise bosses and superiors in the party and government structures were occasionally strained and tense. It is easy to imagine him boiling over with rage at some petty bureaucratic whim or lavish request from the local party boss ('Brezhnev is coming down next week, and your factory has got to look as if it's been working flat out. Don't worry. I've fixed the deliveries of the steel plate. It's definitely coming this time.') But it is true, of course, that when *perestroika* came, the Soviet manager was seriously ill equipped in formal know-how and orientation to operate in conditions which rapidly extended his need for new competences.

So let us leave the Soviet manager in the mid-1980s, at the time when Gorbachev began to preach his gospel of *perestroika*. We can see him activating his party contacts, pressing for a modification to Gosplan output targets, playing off the local politicians, petitioning a minister, using all his native ingenuity to get supplies by hook and by crook, wheedling his network of 'pushers', or browbeating his workers, then sorting their accommodation, and even marital problems. He is an accomplished networker, fostering close personal relationships with those who dispense favours and radiate influence. He has tenacity, low cunning, various skills at playing the system, a record of commitment to the party, and a very strong liver. If nothing else, he continues the centuries-long Russian tradition of being skilled in 'improvisation in adversity' (Hosking, 1997).

Referring to the last years of the Soviet era, a construction manager once told us: 'We had to be ruthless. We were tigers.' In what ways was Gorbachev's great transformational plan really going to change all that? If anything, it might call for more of the same!

THE APPROACH OF THE GREAT

FEARED UNKNOWN

Our entire view of the Western economy has been . . . inculcated in a form that is a caricature of reality.

— *Solzhenitsyn, 1991*

In some sense perestroika *and* glasnost *are the artificial lungs hooked up to the increasingly enfeebled, dying organism of the USSR.*

— *Kapuścińscki, 1994*

Introduction

In Chapter 3 we described the Soviet manager in terms of his working milieu and the pressures and priorities with which he perpetually struggled. In this chapter, we examine the impact of the Gorbachev reforms on the Soviet manager, focusing on the provision of urgently needed skills for managing in an economy

Glasnost

When he introduced his reform process, Mikhail Gorbachev introduced three key concepts: *perestroika, uskoreniye* (acceleration) and *glasnost*. *Perestroika* and *glasnost* survived, but 'acceleration', with its overtones of getting the country moving again, had been dropped by 1988. In literal translation *perestroika* means 'restructuring', but *glasnost* has no nominally exact equivalent in other languages. In Russian English dictionaries the word is translated variously as 'publicity', 'openness' and even as '*glasnost*'! The root of the Russian word is *glas*, which means voice. In old Russian *glas* often referred to the voice of the people (*glas naroda*) as opposed to the voice of a person, and the verb derived from it (*glasit*), meaning to announce, affirm or say (in the sense: the law says) has a rather archaic ring. According to Ozhegov's authoritative Russian dictionary published in 1984 (just before the Gorbachev era), *glasnost* referred to accessibility of information 'for public familiarisation and discussion.'

Once it had been adopted by the 27th Congress of the Communist Party in February 1986, *glasnost* became a by-word for livelier presentation and exploration by the media of deficiencies of corrupt officials. For example, by the March the editor of a newspaper called *Tribuna Energetica* wrote and published her own article about the Chernobyl nuclear reactor. This article exposed serious shortcomings in the supply of construction materials in such a delicate installation 'where every cubic metre of reinforced concrete must be a guarantee of reliability, and thus of safety'. On 26 April the reactor exploded. The fact that the disaster was first reported in the USSR from western sources did little to inspire people in the new *glasnost* policy. Gorbachev was later to admit that Chernobyl meltdown was a turning point in opening up Soviet society: it broke taboos, caused apparently unassailable dogmas to be questioned and the recent past – especially the Stalinist era – to be revealed for what it was. In 1989 even Solzhenitsyn's novel, *The Gulag Archipelago*, was published in the USSR. Only a few years before Gorbachev had been proclaiming *glasnost* as something that would 'reinforce socialism.' In fact, it did precisely the opposite.

moving from central control to market led. We begin with a sketch of the *perestroika* process itself. We then discuss the development of management education in the USSR, making use of a short case study about a private business school in Moscow to exemplify suppositions about the needs of Soviet managers. The chapter also includes a discussion of 'early' Soviet experiences of being exposed to western management educators and their teaching methods.

Perestroika

In 1985 Gorbachev, General Secretary of the Communist Party of the Soviet Union, inherited from his successors a country on the point of economic collapse: hopeless imbalances between plans and their fulfilment, crippling defence expenditure, a scarcely functioning distribution system, shortages of the basic consumer items, a dispirited working population. Gorbachev (1988) described his country as being 'a pre-crisis situation', and the unenviable task of cleansing the Augean stables fell to him (Nove, 1990).

Gorbachev launched his period of rule with 'a blitz' of decrees (Schroeder, 1990), many aimed at alleviating the lot of the hard-pressed Soviet consumer. He also made an abortive attempt to crack down on alcoholism (see Chapter 9.) All too conscious that the USSR was languishing after years of economic stagnation, Gorbachev saw rejuvenation in terms both of relaxing social controls and restructuring the economy under three codewords, *glasnost*, *perestroika* and *uskoreniye* (acceleration). [*Glasnost*; *Perestroika*] Even before he became General Secretary, Gorbachev was already delivering speeches using his three catchwords, but one them, *uskoreniye* with its connotation of 'making the old command economy work better' (Roxburgh, 1991), was to fall into disuse: by 1988 it was clear that acceleration was not only not happening, but was also 'incompatible with the transition from a "command economy" to one in which the market had a large role to play' (Brown, 1996). As for *perestroika*, this was officially launched at the April 1985 Plenum of the Communist Party Central Committee, a matter of weeks after Gorbachev had been elected successor to the decrepit Chernenko.

According to political scientist Archie Brown (1996), the Gorbachev reform process entailed a quadruple transformation,

Perestroika

The principle aim of *perestroika* was, in a nutshell, to transform the Soviet economy, increase industrial and agricultural efficiency and raise living standards. It was also in effect a policy to get the USSR out of the systemic crisis which threatened its position as a superpower. Although the Russian word *perestroika* literally means reconstruction, its rendering by the Oxford political scientist, Archie Brown, as 'constructing anew' captures rather better the idea of fundamental transformation. The very ambiguity of the concept, which meant just a long overdue shakeup of the lethargic and corrupt bureaucracy to some and a revolution to others, ensured that *perestroika* was advocated by almost all proponents of change. It was, however, strongly resisted by those who saw in it the sceptre of anti-socialist reform, but reform was in any case a taboo word.

The leading British historian of Russia, Geoffrey Hosking, has suggested that there were two *perestroika*s. Mark I was a set of measures introduced by Gorbachev shortly after becoming Soviet leader in 1985. These measures included: campaigns to weed out and prosecute corrupt officials, to stamp out 'unofficial' supplementary earnings, to restrict the sale of vodka in a bid to discourage alcoholism. Gorbachev also set up a new inspectorate to control the quality of Soviet goods. By 1988 Mark II was clearly discernible: 'restructured' Soviet society would no longer operate in accordance with administrative notions of economic management; market economy principles of accountability would replace them; there would be 'democratization', underpinned by *glasnost*; and there would be a new alliance between the party leadership, on the one hand, and the scientific and cultural *intelligentsia*, on the other. Under *perestroika* Mark II the Communist Party was to lose its monopoly of political power. In the meantime, the Berlin Wall came down, the odious Ceausescus were assassinated, communist parties were ousted from power, the Baltic republics were getting restive.

There was a joke around at the time: Question: 'What comes after *perestroika*?' Answer: '*Perestrelka*' [the firing squad]. Amazingly, it never came to that.

the like of which no country had ever embarked on before. The elements of this fourfold transformation were:

1 The transformation of the political system, which would eventually lead to a pluralist society.

2 The transformation from a command economy with virtually 100 percent state ownership of the means of production to a market economy with a substantial private sector.

3 The transformation of relationships between the centre and the hundred and more sizeable ethnic groups and nationalities (which anticipated new federal relationships).

4 The transformation of Soviet foreign policy, which was necessitated partly by a desire to improve relationships with the west and partly out of recognition of the fact that the USSR could no longer afford its huge military expenditure.

This book is predominantly concerned with the second issue, not least because the process is still far from completion. But we should note in passing that the fourth issue had – and has – a direct bearing on the second because the Soviet Union consisted in effect of two economies. As Brown (1996) explains:

> One – privileged and pampered and in a number of ways up to world standards – devoted to military production and defence-related industry; and the other – starved of capital, new technology, and esteem – constituting the civilian industrial sector and supposedly providing for the needs of the ill-served Soviet customer. For domestic transformation to be carried through there had to be the kind of change in international relations which would facilitate a reordering of Soviet economic priorities at home. The problem for Soviet leaders was that to tamper with the rationale for their huge military expenditure was to put at risk the only basis they had found thus far for ensuring that the western world treated them with a grudging respect.

In a nutshell, the main objectives of Gorbachev's economic programme were to:

- accelerate growth by stepping up investment outlays
- use these for technological restructuring of industry
- attain better utilization of resources by switching from extensive to intensive methods
- achieve 5 percent annual growth by 1990
- double the 1985 national income by the year 2000 with massive gains for the consumer (Brown, Kaser and Smith).

Within the first three years of his rule Gorbachev pushed through three major items of economic legislation which initiated the process of decentralization of economic management and opened the door on marketization.

The Law on Individual Labour Activity (1986) legalized both family-based and individual enterprise of the kind that was already being undertaken on the black or grey market: car and television repairs, hairdressing, photography, private tuition, and taxi services. The law initially fell short of expectations owing to bureaucratic footdragging over issuing of licences (Brown, 1996; Wilson and Bachkatov, 1992).

The Law on State Enterprises (1987) freed industrial enterprises from administrative tutelage and permitted them to render the remuneration of personnel and capacity to expand, dependent on financial performance (Brown, Kaser and Smith, 1994).

The Law on Cooperatives (1988) permitted cooperatives to be set up independently with three or more members and engage in any activity, including banking and foreign trade. Cooperatives could also sell shares and set up joint ventures with foreign partners (Brown, 1996; Wilson and Bachkatov, 1992).

These reform measures were promulgated for an economic environment that did not yet exist. There were neither the appropriate price relativities nor the financial mechanisms. Beside, legislation could not keep abreast of the changes which were taking place in the system. The entire Soviet economy was marching into no-man's land, and by 1989 it was apparent that *perestroika* was not working. By 1990, in the words of the *Cambridge Encyclopedia of Russia* (Brown, Kaser and Smith, 1994), the Soviet economy had 'plummeted deeply into crisis, reflected in financial instability, depreciation of the rouble and diminution of its role in the economy, growing shortages and disruption of economic ties between regions and sectors'. The economy was awkwardly poised between being a command economy and market economy, and enterprises 'had no idea who was supposed to be running them – the local authorities, the republic, or Moscow' (Roxburgh, 1991). The Soviet Union was in a limbo, in which 'the traditional instruments of economic power were working worse than ever' and in which 'the party and government apparatus were in widespread covert – and often open – revolt against Gorbachev' (Brown, 1996). It was against this ever desperate background that in July 1990 Gorbachev, now compelled to work with the ascendant Boris Yeltsin, commissioned economists from all over the USSR (except Estonia) under academician Stanislav Shatalin to prepare a plan for accelerated transition to the market economy. In September the blueprint was ready. The so-called Shatalin Plan proposed 21 major acts of legislation and countless other measures for introducing the market economy lock, stock and barrel in 500 days flat. 'The USSR had never seen such a reform programme that was as concrete, comprehensive or radical. The word socialism was not even used' (Keep, 1996). This was too much for Gorbachev who produced his own compromise guidelines which 'turned out to be just milk-and-water platitudes' (Keep, 1996).

There was nothing to stop the Soviet economy spiralling downwards. In the first nine months of 1991, GNP fell 12 percent, consumption 17 percent, food output 8 percent, and industrial output 6.4 per cent (Rutland, 1994). Inflation, which for decades had been suppressed, was increasing at a rate of 2–3 percent a week (Keep, 1996). The shops were bare and 'black market prices [rose] 100% in 1991 and [stood] at 3 to 5 times the official prices for the same goods – which had disappeared from the shelves' (Keep, 1996). But it was not all gloom. As a result of 1990 legislation, state enterprises were forming themselves into joint stock companies and were setting up banks and trading networks. Over 100 commodity exchanges had been established in 1991, which provided a valuable service to the emerging market economy: they traded at free prices and so helped to fix prices for commodities and services. But with a 40 percent drop in tax revenue in 1991 and serious problems in servicing its $58bn hard currency debt, the Soviet economy was barely limping.

In August 1991 the world held its breath, when an abortive putsch was made to dislodge Gorbachev. It proved to be a clownish fiasco perpetrated by senior politicians. Although Gorbachev survived, the time-bomb ticked on inexorably. By the end of the year, the Communist Party was stripped of its monopoly of power, the Central Committee had been dissolved, Gorbachev had resigned as President, the Soviet Union had gone. On midnight of 31 December 1991, 'the Red Flag over the Kremlin gave way to the Russian tricolour. There were few on-lookers and no euphoric applause. The Soviet legacy was too heavy, the future too uncertain, for celebration' (Keep, 1996). Meanwhile, in Pushkin Square, there was 'a gleaming apparition of the future' – McDonald's. Strange to reflect, on this night of all nights, that its chief executive was living in a flat once occupied by Beria, Stalin's chief executioner (Remnick, 1994).

Transforming Soviet management

Under *perestroika*, enterprises – some 130,000 of them in the old USSR – were no longer to be guided by the state by means of the old, top-heavy planning systems, but they were expected to run their own affairs on the basis of financial accountability. This is what Gorbachev (1988) meant when he referred to 'the transfer of the centre of gravity from predominantly administrative to predominantly economic methods of management'. But Soviet managers had neither the experience nor the training for effecting the kind of changes of attitude and behaviour which *perestroika* required. Under the Soviet system they did not possess even the most basic commercial skills, as their principal task was to achieve short-term output maximization with only the vaguest idea of costs and no notion of price as a market mechanism (Dyker, 1992).

The *perestroika* project, which as Gorbachev knew full well, depended so much on people's attitudes and their willingness to accept new methods. It required a major retraining programme to inculcate not just 'the very basic commercial skills', but the techniques and concepts of modern (i.e. western) management. As the Russian psychologist Hanin (1991) has pointed out, it is not just a question of training managers 'in the turbulent environment of *perestroika* – decentralization of political power, formation of new political parties, shortages of consumer goods, strikes, and social clashes', it has to be recognized too that 'managers at different levels in different companies all over the country are facing the necessity to learn new ways'.

The principal task of management education, whether it developed with or without the assistance of western experts, was to create a new kind of manager from the old class of administrators, comprising (a) technocrats who ran major industries and utilities and (b) bureaucrats, many under-employed rather than unemployed, who guided the USSR's economic effort at all-union and republican level as planners, administrators and sector specialists. In mid-1990, *Business Week* (28 May 1990a) estimated that 'as many as 14 million Soviet administrators need to be re-educated'.

According to Professor Andrei Manoukovsky of the Moscow International Business School (1990), Soviet managers were completely unprepared for the challenge of *perestroika*:

> The old administrative system not only failed to encourage dynamic and innovative captains of industry, but also discouraged them . . . Most Soviet managers lack basic economic (let alone management) training. They usually consist of experienced engineering staff who rose from the ranks of the Young Communist League, trade union and party functionaries . . . Such people were ill-equipped to take personal creative initiatives.

Specifically, there was (as in China around the same time) a 'shortage of professional managers, especially in market-related disciplines' (Warner, 1992).

This emphasis on industrialists and technocrats excludes, incidentally, two important economic groups in the last years of the Soviet economy, who fulfilled (and still fulfil) management functions of sorts: (a) the entrepreneurs of the burgeoning private sector (translators, restauranteurs, hairdressers, cobblers, private tutors, purveyors of fruit and vegetables etc.), whose activities accounted for anything between 2 percent and 15 percent of the USSR's GNP prior to the collapse (*The Economist*, 1992; Hosking, 1991); and (b) the black marketeers, who as of the mid-1980s had 'suddenly started to crawl out of the woodwork and [be] conspicuously associated with organized crime and racketeering' and whose share of GNP might be as high as 40 percent (Menshikov, 1990).

But neither the entrepreneurs nor the so-called underground businessmen can be said to represent a potential source of manager material. Their needs as managers are not of the same order as the 14 million administrators and industrial bosses who, after 'seventy years of distorted attitudes about economics [are] helpless because no-one has taught them to think' (*Business Week*, 28 May 1990b), and for whom the marketplace was, and is, the 'Great Feared Unknown' (Holden and Cooper, 1994).

Central to the Gorbachev idea was the conviction that a new form of socialist inter-republican relationships could be established on Soviet soil with western management know-how (and resources) having a catalytic role. Gorbachev's prime aim was to rejuvenate the system rather than scrap it and to hold the Union together – this was the task of *perestroika*. If he held back from introducing the much-vaunted market economy, he had at least created conditions for a general dissemination of the hitherto alien principles of western management.

Thus, by the mid- to late 1980s, the English words 'manager' and 'management', russified as *menedzher* and *menedzhment*, began to enjoy a wider currency with the development of Soviet-style business schools (Holden, 1991) and, for the first time, these terms were being applied to socialist conditions and not, pejoratively, to western life. Yet the vocabulary of management was being but superficially assimilated; the operational and organizational implications of the terms were not grasped. Even in the late 1980s, management (i.e. *menedzhment*) was still negatively associated with 'get-rich-quick capitalism' and sorts of efficiency that could only logically lead to unemployment and exploitation. The word that conveyed all the negative things about business was the Russian version *biznes*, which often referred – and still refers to – activities associated with mobsters: protection rackets, prostitution and drugs pushing.

From the first minor exposure to western-style management education in the early 1980s (i.e. before Gorbachev came to power), through the Gorbachev period and into the post-Soviet, management education in the USSR/CIS was hampered by the persistence of a complex 'semantic gap': an inadequacy of language and conceptual terms constraining the smooth transfer of western management know-how into the Soviet and then post-Soviet experience. In the scattered western writing on Soviet management throughout the 1980s, there was repeated reference to this knotty problem. The Danish linguist, Møller (quoted in Holden, 1992), found that the English word management was often translated as *administratsiya*, which had all the wrong connotations. An American journalist, Nancy Trotter (quoted in Holden, 1991) was to discover that Soviet participants on a training course 'had no idea' that leadership and forms of motivation were part and parcel of modern western thinking on management.

This same point was endorsed by Naylor (1988), who emphasized that Soviet managers had been really hampered through lack of experience in key functional areas such as market planning, production management, international finance and organizational development, all superfluous skills under the now defunct socialist regime. There had hitherto been no need for words to describe these activities. Thus, the commentator who noted that 'one of the foremost weaknesses of the Soviet management system' lay in the fact that droves of Soviet workers 'do not know the modern language of business' (Kvint, 1990) was not just stating the obvious: he was addressing one of the core challenges facing management trainers in the USSR. MIT expert on Russian science and technology, Loren Graham (1996) puts it all in context:

> The Soviet textbook on political economy of 1958 contains 231 footnotes, but not a single one to a non-Communist source. Over a third of the references are to Marx, Engels, or Lenin. The rest are to resolutions of the Communist Party, works of Stalin, Khrushchev, and Mao Tse-tung, and Soviet government laws and

resolutions. (In later editions the references to Stalin and Khrushchev are replaced by references to Brezhnev, and the citations of Mao have been deleted.) There is no recognition of the host of economic theories developed in non-socialist countries, no discussion of industrial management, no presentation of business economics. Is it any wonder that after the collapse of Communism at the end of the eighties Soviet engineers and industrial managers had such difficulty adjusting to a market economy? They did not even possess the basic vocabulary for understanding it.

It was not clear then how the inadequacy of Russian to handle the new words and concepts acted as a serious constraint on the transfer and acceptance of western management terminology. It still remains precisely that some ten years on (see Chapter 7). [**Management and marketing: Soviet conceptions**]

Demand for management education

Since 1988 there was a rapid growth of business schools throughout all parts of the former USSR, and in that year the first western-style business school was opened. According to the *Financial Times* (1990; quoted in Warner, 1992), already 100 had come into existence within about a year, not that many of these would pass muster as business schools in the west. They were mere concoctions of departments of economics in institutions of higher education or renamed commercial colleges.

Professor Vikhanskii of Moscow State University pointed to another aspect of the supply side. 'In our country' – and the country was the USSR when he wrote this – 'business schools are almost as easy to set up now as shish-kebab stands at busy intersections' (Vikhanskii, 1991). Incidentally, the back-translation of the Russian for 'business school' is, literally, 'school of managers' (*shkola menedzherov*). If the term business school were to be literally translated into Russian (as 'school of business'), it might conjure up unpleasant associations of coteries of pimps, racketeers and gun-toting mobsters.

Managemement and marketing: Soviet conceptions

In the Soviet period definitions of all economic phenomena conformed to the ideological dictates of socialism. Here are some examples of heavily orthodox Soviet descriptions of management and marketing. The first is translated from a book on management for the construction industry (Koziy,1990). Note that the emphasis is on the management of production, the latter word being almost synonymous with output targets.

> The management of production is a purposeful, complex organized influence, concretized in time and space, affecting individual workers, groups of people, and the entire work force [lit. 'the toiling collective'], and affecting too the processes operating throughout construction and assembly organizations and the functioning and developing of these processes, this influence being the product of a transformation of information about the actual condition and status of specified construction work and the external environment into information necessary for changing these organizations, taking into consideration the potential and the limitations in the immediate period ahead and consciously applying laws, conforming tendencies and principles inherent in the socialist, socio-economic structure.

The following extract is a more or less literal translation of the entry for marketing in the 1970–78 issue of the *Great Soviet Encyclopaedia*:

> One of the management systems of the capitalist enterprise, presupposing careful study of the processes occurring in the marketplace for taking business decisions . . . Some practitioners and apologists of marketing maintain that marketing promotes the social regeneration of capitalist system in the economy, at whose core stands the consumer, his tastes, needs and wants. In reality marketing is an attempt, within the framework of individual capital, to eliminate such contradictions of capitalism, as the contradiction between the

> increasing possibilities for production and the relatively sup-
> pressed consumer, between the growing tendency towards
> the systematic organization of production and selling by sep-
> arate enterprises, firms and monopolistic organizations, on
> the one hand, and the anarchy of production in the social
> context on the other.

A reliable guide to the development of management in the USSR in the last years of the Soviet Union is Professor Andrei Manoukovsky of the Institute of International Relations in Moscow, later to be called Moscow International Business School. Manoukovsky (1990) identified three special factors influencing demand for management education in the USSR and three types of provider.

The first of the special factors was almost certainly directly attributable to the Law on Cooperation and Joint Ventures, promulgated in 1988. This law, which freed enterprises from rigid control from the centre, depended on managers being able to make and carry through 'unorthodox' decisions. Within a matter of months, by July 1988, the USSR's first business school was inaugurated at 'an illustrious and ultra-perestroikian opening ceremony and an orientation directed firmly at profitability' (*Financial Times*, 1988).

Next, a series of decrees deregulating foreign trade created an urgent need for international business managers. Manoukovsky estimated that the former USSR had a need of 200,000 such specialists – four times the number estimated by the Soviet government. Not, incidentally, that Russia was starting entirely from scratch here: the new system was able to draw on the skills of former officials of the old centralized foreign trade system, who possessed some vital professional advantages: 'special perceptiveness, deep general knowledge, linguistic competence, flexibility, contacts and a wide range of interests' (*Delovye Svyazy*, 1990, quoted in Holden, 1992).

The third special factor was part and parcel of the 'wild, rudderless transition to the marketplace (Yarlinski et al., 1991). The upshot of this frenzied activity was the hasty creation of business and management schools and swarms of 'training centres . . . established by existing higher education establishments, cooperatives, youth centres and the like' (Manoukovsky, 1990). The demand came in the main from enterprises who sent their personnel on courses to equip them with market economy skills, however dimly perceived by Soviet industry and the 'new' training institutions.

Manoukovsky (1990) suggested that the best way to classify – and in effect rank – Soviet business schools was according to their possession of any of these assets:

- previous training experience

- teaching experience in free market economics and management

- good teaching materials and facilities.

Some training institutions, primarily those set up by youth organizations and cooperatives, had hardly any of these assets. Their standard was 'very basic'. The only business schools with all three assets were leading former All-Union government organizations and first-rank academic institutions, which had been able to develop links with western governments, universities and business schools, and so attract experienced teachers.

Management training: a glance at the VZ Centre in Moscow

It is impossible to know exactly how many self-styled business schools came into being after 1988. As indicated earlier, they varied enormously in quality and facilities. The following paragraphs describe the approach of the one such institution, the VZ Centre in Moscow, set up in 1988 to provide a general courses in management with an emphasis on international business (Holden, 1993). The company's promotional material, from which this information is extracted, throws useful light on Soviet thinking about management training needs at a time of impending change.

Business, states the VZ brochure, 'is not only the wish "to make money", but first and foremost it is the wish to acquire knowledge about economics, management, foreign trade activity, marketing and advertising, banking and other things, which the contemporary businessman must know about'. At first glance there appears to be nothing exceptional about this statement until we appreciate that in Soviet society the word business (*biznes*) had a decidedly unpleasant ring, as we saw earlier. This is why, according to the VZ Centre, business was not just about making money; it was also about knowledge. This is significant too because, as we shall emphasize again in this book, a general Russian/post-Soviet perception of management is that it is all about techniques.

The VZ Centre aspired to develop 'the contemporary businessman', in other words, the new-style manager. The contemporary businessman was someone who 'has mastered several foreign languages, can get on easily with his foreign business partners, and can conduct business with them without the assistance of interpreters'. Foreign language capability was 'the safe and sure road to success'. VZ's language centre, with its 'highly qualified teachers, using modern tuition methods', existed to help budding Soviet businessmen to 'communicate with confidence with their business partners and friends'.

All participants at the VZ Centre were required to follow a foundation programme in business and management before proceeding to one of the specialized courses. The purpose of this course was 'to give students the necessary knowledge and skills in the fundamentals of business administration and law'. The foundation programme has the following courses: theory of organization and management; sociology of management; economics for managers; macro-economic management; microeconomic management; Soviet civil law; civil and commercial law in foreign countries; introduction to information technology and computing.

VZ runs specialized programmes in the following areas, with the number of individual courses given in brackets: small business management (11); export management (16); marketing management (17); financial management and credit control (13); cultural services management (13); environmental management (12). Each of these programmes contained elements that would be considered normal on any management courses anywhere, but there were some unusual features. We note the inclusion of 'business etiquette and protocol' (protocol being Soviet-speak for note-taking and report writing).

Perhaps the most unusual feature was a course in the marketing management programme on 'the art of rhetoric and polemics'. This literal translation might, at a pinch, be rendered as 'effective communication'. But the telling thing is this. 'The art of rhetoric and polemics', as a topic, came straight out of the now defunct Communist Party manuals on agitation and propaganda (*agitprop*), the activity concerned with 'the political education of the people'.

It should not escape our notice that the VZ Centre philosophy was not just concerned with imparting aspects of functional management know-how. It also appeared to be preoccupied with creating a new-style Russian businessman who was intellectually well rounded, cultivated and skilled in communicating with foreign businessmen. Elsewhere in the burgeoning literature on Russian management we find similar resonances. The article in *Delovye Svyazy* (1990), mentioned earlier, speaks of the Russian international business manager as 'a special person . . . educated, quick-witted [*soobrazitel'nyi*], dynamic . . . and, paradoxical as it sounds, a certain degree of dilettantism!' . It is hard not to escape the conclusion that the VZ Centre was catering to a perceived need for a kind of Russian capitalist who should ideally be 'a business intellectual'.

Constraints on developing management education

A major impetus in the development of Soviet management education was the establishment in December 1990 of the Soviet Association of Business Schools. This was set up to exchange ideas and information on all aspects of management education; identify and meet new needs; develop contacts with business schools abroad. The first Rector of the Association, interviewed in a trade magazine (*British Soviet Business*, 1991), highlighted three enormous challenges facing the Association on the development of management education in the USSR:

- It had to stop 'cowboy courses from exploiting the market'.

- Support had to be given to burgeoning business schools far away from the major centres of Moscow, St Petersburg and Kiev.

- Joint ventures with western partners had to be formed to

upgrade teaching quality.

At the operational level, Manoukovsky (1990) identified four main general weaknesses in the provision of management education:

- lack of adequately qualified teachers

- shortage of teaching materials

- lack of language skills for study of foreign teaching materials

- lack of a healthy competitive spirit as a result of 'excess demand'.

Manoukovsky reported two other problems, which are by no means unfamiliar in western experience: how to persuade enterprises to give young people the time off and how to make the new knowledge meaningful to students over the age of 40. To this Vikhanskii added another constraint, easily overlooked: a lack of understanding of what exactly management education is, and what purpose it serves. In his words: 'The customer is totally ignorant of the commodity he is about to buy. He wants to become a businessman, a manager, but he doesn't know how.' Like the Rector of the Soviet Association of Business Schools, Vikhanskii is critical of the sharkish attitudes of the founders of business schools: 'as long as the money comes in, they will keep doing this activity' (Vikhanskii, 1991).

Concerning that lack of qualified teachers, Professor Abramishvili (1991), also of the Institute of International Relations, described the shortage as 'catastrophic'; and a former economic adviser to Gorbachev estimated that in the entire Soviet Union there were 'no financial experts, businessmen, marketing specialists . . . there are perhaps twenty people with a first-class grasp of these things' (*Der Spiegel*, 1989). We have to bear in mind too that the 'new' teachers of management subjects were all brought up to regard the term 'manager' as synonymous with 'the bigwig seeking to extract profits from anything, disdaining no means in the pursuit of personal gain'. No-one should underestimate the huge intellectual and emotional readjustments required of Soviet teachers.

As for teaching materials, there was severe undersupply both of home-grown material as well as translations of principal western textbooks. In the case of the former, the translations spoke of marketing products that most Russians had hardly seen in their lives or applying financial techniques which might be fine in a fully fledged market economy, but not in the USSR where the term 'bookkeeping' was currently the closest expression for financial management. Regarding home-grown texts we find, even after three years of earnest *perestroika*, Soviet authors, true to their own upbringing, were still generously quoting the grand *troika* of Marx, Lenin and Engels, even though the need for ideological conformism has presumably passed ('guilty' authors, as far as the construction industry goes, include Abramov and Manayenkova, 1990; Afanasyev and Shishkin, 1989; Kaplan, 1990). No wonder then that 'the economic system established by Stalin has proved, despite all its conspicuous deficiencies, to be forbiddingly stable and self-reinforcing' (Hosking, 1991).

Training Soviet managers in foreign countries

As of the mid-1980s, Soviet managers started to attend management courses in western countries. Some had been seconded to business organizations, too. In mid-1990 *Business Week* (1990a) estimated that between 4000 and 5000 young Soviet managers were studying abroad. At the same time the foreign contact was being further extended by western organizations – governments, universities, consultancy firms – working alongside a gamut of Soviet organizations (ministries, city councils, enterprises, training bodies) – to provide management training courses or to supply knowhow in specialist areas such as international finance or agricultural distribution. This foreign involvement was to increase dramatically after December 1991.

Tables 4.1 and 4.2 published in a Soviet business journal show countries in which Soviet managers have received specialist management training in firms for secondments of about three months' duration. The tables are interesting in that they suggest something about Soviet priorities for management training. The numbers relate to managers sponsored by the All-Union Soviet Chamber of Commerce in Moscow and present only a partial picture.

It is interesting that the prestigious All-Union Chamber apparently saw no need for sending Soviet specialists to foreign destinations for training in either production/TQM or human resource development. Further there is no immediate way of evaluating the success of such foreign study. But Professor Vikhanskii of the School of Management of Moscow University does not mince his words. These visits abroad are 'junkets', allowing managers to 'enjoy foreign travel for its own sake, do some personal shopping and generally have a good time'. Seven years later the *Wall Street Journal*, querying the cost effectiveness of bringing over 200 Russian

Table 4.1 Soviet managers in industrial placements of less than three months, to August 1990

	USA	FRG	France	UK	Austria	Finland	Switzerland
Law	4	—	—	5	—	—	—
Management	41	189	19	60	25	15	5
Marketing	—	162	—	—	11	14	—
Finance	—	—	—	—	—	—	—

Source: *Delovye Svazy,* June 90

Table 4.2 Soviet specialists studying in the USA and Germany for more than three months, to August 1990

	USA	FRG
Law	2	—
Management	11	18
Marketing	4	15
Finance	—	12

Source: *Delovye Svazy,* June 90

managers to the USA without a follow-up programme, was to rail against this 'educational tourism' (*Wall Street Journal*, 1996).

Foreign reactions to training Soviet managers

Until the end of the 1980s there was no experience in the west of training Soviet managers. Not only did western trainers know very little indeed about the Soviet economy and its management, they had no clear ideas about Russian managers' training needs: needs not only in terms of knowledge to be supplied, but also in terms of teaching methodologies. Accounts of western experiences of equipping Soviet managers with market economy skills in the late 1980s up to the disintegration of the USSR in 1991 already make it clear that the task was already unexpectedly daunting.

One important source is Noel Hibbert of Coventry University, who has run short courses for up to 150 Russian managers in the UK with follow-up courses taking on up to another 500 managers. In two descriptions of his and his colleagues' experiences, Hibbert (1990, 1991) has highlighted the following factors influencing the Russian learning style. In one article (Hibbert, 1990), the conclusion is that Russian willingness and ability to absorb management knowledge is constrained by their:

- preference for learning techniques based on formal presentations 'with a definite answer approach'

- difficulties with a 'student-centred' approach to learning

- difficulties with role plays involving a director and deputy director of the same enterprise

- conviction that 'we are here to learn, not to discuss our problems'

- unfamiliarity with (a) sharing experience and (b) crossindustry learning

- tendency to assume that there must be 'laws' governing economic development (even if, presumably, Marxist-Leninist laws did not prove equal to the task).

In this same article Hibbert noted the value of case studies which had been translated into Russian. He reported too a Russian tendency to award their UK teachers either a collective vote of confidence or a collective reprimand.

In his second article Hibbert (1991) highlighted three additional points, which stemmed directly from existence and education under the old centralized system. Russian managers:

- had no idea of 'managing resources'

- had no appreciation of 'different outlooks' (i.e. different managers see things in different ways, e.g. according to the industry they are in)

- were accustomed to knowledge being 'vertically transmitted' from the top downwards and being received without demur or discussion.

Sheila Puffer, a leading US specialist on the problems of educating Russian managers for the market economy, rightly emphasized the 'Herculean feat of attitude change' challenging western management educators. In particular she highlighted Russian managers' tendency to be docile; their inability to distinguish between incentives and motivation as management tools; and their lack of appreciation of the role of human factors in management activity. Envisaging that the future would hold substantial opportunities for American institutions to become involved in major training initiatives, Puffer was among the first to challenge a key issue, which is still valid today despite the fact that the Soviet Union is no more (Puffer, 1991): 'In spite of the benefits, sending Soviet managers abroad is expensive, time-consuming, and disruptive, and some critics question whether such an approach provides sufficient linkage with conditions in the former USSR to make application of knowledge possible.'

Another American commentator, writing in 1991, was also well aware of the great task, facing western management educators. Rising to almost oratorical heights he pronounced: 'While dramatic political and economic changes – a managerial revolution – have suddenly opened the doors to Western providers of management education and development, both corporate and collegiate, those who charge into this virtual Klondike of opportunity should be fore-

warned that the successful identification and exploitation of entrepreneurial mother lodes will require a great deal of hard spadework
and artful adaptation of western models' (McKibbin, 1992).

He, like most other writers of the time, seemed to assume that
despite all the difficulties of imparting to Soviet managers (as they
were then) modern management concepts and practices, fundamentally the Soviets would be willing to learn about these things
in order to apply them in their enterprises and offices.

As we shall see, after the collapse of the Soviet Union, this was
going to become an increasingly less tenable position.

Constraints on management development when the USSR collapsed

By the time the USSR collapsed in 1991 it was possible to identify
five key factors which were constraining, indeed almost paralysing, the capacity of western management educators to design and
deliver effective training courses for Soviet managers:

1 Management educators, both Soviet and western, did not know
   for what kind of society they were developing managers.

2 There was an absence of a common language for communicating management concepts: Russian is both producing from its
   own lexical resources and absorbing the new vocabulary from
   other languages (primarily English), but it may take years before
   these become the normal language of business and management
   and by extension part of everyday life.

3 Western assumptions about management did not correspond to
   Russian assumptions.

4 Western management educators themselves lacked know-how
   about the former USSR/Russia and so did not understand the
   psychology of Russians as learners of management.

5 There was an explicit challenge to western management educators: how to communicate management know-how and the
   underlying concepts into Russian/post-Soviet terms of reference.

These factors were to acquire even more significance after the dramatic collapse of the USSR in 1991, because of the scale, complexi-

ty, cost and urgency of the management training challenge. For the moment there was a kind of euphoria about the exchanges. It was understandable then that western management educators should assume that 'new-style' Soviet managers had forgotten all those deeply engrained prejudices about capitalist managers being money-grabbing exploiters. Yet, shortly before the collapse of the USSR, if we care to believe Lawrence and Vlachoutsicos, (1990) 'the prevalent Soviet thinking' about American (western) management was influenced by a conviction that 'American managers operate like economic robots driving aggressively over human values to maximize short-term profits.' On the bright side, Gorbachev's managers also thought that Americans had 'a vast store of specialized and rather miraculous management techniques that Soviets [could] adopt to improve performance'. No-one saw it at the time, but the scene was being set for a reawakening of a strongly Russian posture: oscillation between distaste for foreigners with their superior know-how and the irksome need to rely on them to get hold of it.

THE POST-SOVIET MANAGER: THE

NEW CLASS STRUGGLE

It wasn't their arrogance that hampered them so much as their complete lack of comprehension. When it came to simple economics, they could not connect the dots. The mine director complained that production had fallen at the mine by half, but at the same time he launched into a glorious paean to the central planning system and the web of state orders and subsidies. The fact was that his mine was badly equipped, primitive, and probably defunct. It . . . would never be profitable in a normal economy.

— Remnick, 1994

The Tartars, who once conquered Russia, relieved the peasants of ten percent of the harvest-yield. The present Russian state raises 44 federal, regional and local taxes: it is nabbing 95 to 97 percent!

— Maslov, 1996a

Introduction

In this chapter we chronicle the emergence of the Russian manager from the collapse of the once mighty Soviet Union. We set the scene against a background of Russia's immediate post–Soviet economic woes, noting the subsequent transformation of Russia into its present raw, rudderless capitalism. We examine the evolution of the new Russian manager throughout the transition period, paying particular attention to his ethical concerns, which focus on the seeming impossibility of aligning Russian communitarian motivations with the demands for market efficiency and accountable performance. We also highlight some important Russian studies which suggest that western ideas of the development needs of Russian management must actively take account of the deeply engrained Russian impulse to forge a different path.

Russia's post-communist economic woes: the first years

The dissolution of the Soviet Union at the end of 1991 plunged the former communist superpower into turmoil and most of the rest of mankind into speechless incredulity. By general agreement, the situation in Russia/CIS was vastly more complicated than in the former socialist countries of eastern Europe. One of the root causes, according to *The Economist* (1992) was that 'communism lasted longer in Russia than anywhere else and moulded it more completely. Only Russia went through the transformation to an industrial economy under communist rule. Because many of its current reforms are an attempt to undo communism's legacy, the task is correspondingly greater than elsewhere.'

Russia's economic plight at the end of that epochal year of 1991 was graphically described by Professor Anders Åslund of the Stockholm School of Economics and Professor Richard Layard of the London School of Economics, who are advisers on economic policy to the Russian government. Russia, they wrote:

> faced a horrendous economic crisis. The imminence of Gehenna hung in the air. Shops were more empty than at any time after World War II. The consolidated state budget was at least 20% of gross national product, and public finances were on the verge of collapsing altogether. Production was falling at an annual rate of some 20%, and there were fears of an outright collapse of production. In December 1991, the Soviet Union ran out of foreign reserves and had to cease ful-

filling its foreign debt service. The Soviet Union was no longer a real entity, and its process of dissolution could result in unnamed horrors. Widespread fears prevailed both in Russia and abroad of imminent famine, widespread freezing to death, and mass emigration. It was a truly formidable crisis.

Åslund and Layard (1993)

According to a Polish expert, Dabrowski (in Åslund and Layard, 1993), Russia was 'a non-planned, non-market economy, without sufficient microeconomic motivation or the means to achieve elementary macroeconomic equilibrium'. *The Economist* (1992) even coined a whimsical neologism to describe this ghastly scenario: hyperslumpflation. If this were bad not enough, Jeffry Sachs of Harvard Business School, and another leading western economic adviser to the Russian government, has proclaimed the monetary problems facing Russia to be 'perhaps the most complex in world history' (Sachs, 1994). The economist Dabrowski (1993) cited the main economic reasons for the emerging recession as 'the crisis of the central planning system, the motivational crisis in state-owned industries, the disintegration of trade relations between Eastern European countries after the collapse of the CMEA as well as the gradual weakening of trade links between former USSR republics'.

Observers reel off cause after cause for Russia's terrible crisis. Some causes are the direct result of 70 years of communism, others are deep rooted in Russian history. Sergei Vasiliev (1993), one of Russia's leading economists, lists various traits which impeded the growth of capitalism in the last century: the primacy of communal spirit, contempt for commerce as an occupation, mistrust of the rich, especially of the newly rich, and a grudge against prosperous neighbours – all these things 'have a long history'. These traits were both perpetuated and even intensified in the Soviet period. In a similar vein, *The Economist* (1992) suggests that the widely chronicled Russian aversion to free markets is the product of the commune system in pre-revolutionary Russia and communism: 'in so vast a country communes formed little worlds of their own, protecting villagers from outside'.

These countless, isolated communities never provided Russia with the semblance of free market democracy; there was no notion of ownership of property; there was no notion of Russia being governed by law that was both uniform and internally consistent (*The Economist*, 1992); pre-revolutionary Russia's merchants and businessmen were too small and insignificant (and despised) to bequeath any significant capitalist and entrepreneurial tradition. These factors have perpetuated, through the Soviet period and even to the present day, what Åslund (1993) calls 'an extraordinary contempt for trade and services', which he attributes to 'the old Marxist scorn for, or ignorance of, finance and money'. These factors too help explain why privatization of land and property is 'a nightmare' (Åslund, 1993), and a bane for foreign investors.

The communist legacy left Russia with the wreckage of the 'old hierarchical and gerontological system' (Åslund and Layard, 1993) and associated political and economic machinery unequal to the Herculean task of reform; interminable bickering and consistent non-agreement among politicians, factions and pressure groups about the way forward; a disaffected populace; and industry in a state of exhausted ruin.

For all the formidable complexity of the 'purely' economic situation in Russia, all commentators seem to be agreed that it is up to politicians to create a new political and legal system for the development of regulated free market economic activity. We now consider briefly the political aspects of Russia's crisis. Then, we return, as it were, to economics in order to assess the impact of the collapse of communism on Russian industry.

History provides us for few grounds for optimism about Russia's capability to reform herself. As *The Economist* survey of Russia (1992) noted:

> The three previous attempts at economic liberalization – Lenin's new economic policy (1921–28); the land reforms of Pyotr Stolypin (1906–11); and the freeing of the serfs(1861–64) – all collapsed when the autocrat of the day abruptly withdrew support for fear the reforms might threaten his (unreformed) powers. The failure to implement political reform means economic policies have not had enough political support. This is in turn leading to the possibility of renewed autocracy.

Since the collapse of the USSR, Russian politics have been dominated by tensions between the executive (Yeltsin) and the legislature (parliament), an unhealthy spread of centres of power, and the emergence of interest groups and lobbies. The resulting rivalries make it difficult to formulate, let alone coordinate and implement policy. *The Economist* (1992) argues that these tensions run the risk of making Russia ungovernable, noting that:

> Many of the reversals have been caused not by faults in policy design, but by the difficulty of implementing any policy in a country that lacks some of the essential features of statehood.

But, according to *The Economist*, Russia's main problem is 'not that it has the wrong policies', but that it has a 'political constraint on higher unemployment'.

In the meantime, as Vasiliev (1993) notes: 'A search is under way for the most effective political and economic territorial structure for the market economy and democracy.' As the factors already cited indicate so overwhelmingly, this search is beset with all manner of countervailing influences. But Vasiliev argues that some of the radical shifts that took place in the Soviet period 'are highly important for Russia's readiness to accept a market economy today'. If only to relieve the picture of gloom and foreboding about the future of Russia, it is worthwhile tracing out Vasiliev's argument.

He points to the following key factors. The first relates to social mobility. As a result of the Russian Revolution 'traditional societies were broken down and stratification barriers between estates collapsed'. This was both the cause and result of the intense urbanization of the Soviet Union. These upheavals promoted conditions in which 'huge masses of people' became accustomed to changing 'their habitual way of life in the course of just two or three generations. (Vasiliev says nothing about how harrowing and disorientating this experience was for individuals and families.)

He therefore argues that 'Russia today is in an exceptionally favourable position' for the successful implementation of the market reforms: 'the urbanisation process is practically completed, society has achieved an advantageous homogeneity, and the geographical mobility of the population is high'. Furthermore the old vertical linkages, which are a legacy of the administrative command economy, are giving way to new horizontal structures which 'are taking shape, albeit slowly'.

Paradoxically, Vasiliev suggests that the low expectations that the people at large have of the efficacy of economic and political reform to some extent works in favour of the market economy. The people, buffeted by 'social upheavals, high unemployment, and hyperinflation', appear to have opted for economic stability rather than social confrontation or large-scale civil disorder. But the price the people are paying is, of course, a reduction in living standards – and continued existence under an extended period of political uncertainty (not to say, anarchy).

In addition to identifying various politicians and intellectuals ('the anti-reform lobby') impeding the advance to a market economy, some observers too have accused time-serving industrial managers of deliberating seeking to slow down the pace of reform.

The collapse of the USSR plummeted Russian industry into a severe crisis. This had not merely to do with the general economic and political situation of Russia, but was bound up with (a) the structural overhang from the old centralized system of economic management and (b) the acute dearth of management competence, knowledge and experience for operating in (increasingly) free market conditions.

The 1992 *Economist* survey of Russia sums up the industrial situation thus:

> Russian industry is just too big . . . The resources tied up in industry are not being used efficiently. The Soviet Union consumes 80% more steel, 7% more rubber and two-thirds as much energy as America. But America's economy was many times larger. Per unit of GDP, Russia used 15 times as much steel, nine times as much rubber and six times as much energy as America – a gigantic waste. Comparisons with Germany and Japan are even more depressing. That is why, when a Russian steel factory reduces output, it is an achievement, not a pity.

Noting that these companies own a staggering 46 percent of

Russia's housing (local authorities own only 32 percent of it), the *Economist* survey turns to the question of size:

> Sheer size makes Russian firms inflexible. The average firm employs around 800 workers – twice as many as the average Polish firm and ten times more than the average in the West. Half of industrial output comes from 1,000 super-giants, with 8,500 employees each (and some of these behemoths employ whole cities). The implication is that Russian firms are too cumbersome to change even if they wanted to.

Russian managers: the shock of the new

After 1991 thousands of old-style bosses, virtually all card-carrying members of the Communist Party until the very end and moulded by the Soviet command economy, continued to lord it in their huge enterprises, cruise around in chauffeur-driven Chevvies, learn new games of survival, and activate their network to get invited on a western-sponsored management course which (a) was entirely subsidized and (b) involved travel to a foreign country. Of these managers, Åslund (1993) is scathing. They have, he says, 'all the characteristics one would like to avoid: they have little knowledge of the outside world; their purpose for coming into power is to gain wealth for themselves and their narrow constituency'.

Åslund draws our attention to two specific issues: the impact of industrial managers' blinkered views on contemporary economic development and their conviction that the experience of other countries cannot be applicable to Russia with its 'unique' set of intractable problems. Taking the first of these points, he argues that industrial managers, along with other representatives of vested interests, 'insist that they possess extraordinary competence as business people'. In effect, the managers appear to be confusing their undoubted influence over economic life with business competencies which they assume must be the ones needed for the market economy. But these competencies are nothing more than 'knowledge and connections' to get state subsidies and get rich, while ignoring the welfare of the population and generally operating in ways that do not make for stabilization of political and economic life. The second issue highlighted by Åslund (1993), and italicised by him for emphasis, is that *'Russians have shown little interest in the experiences of other countries that had changed economic system'*.

This sounds like a harsh judgment, but we should not forget that for a race as prickly proud as Russians we must take full account of what Dyker (1992) calls their 'xenophobic populism', which is a kind of romanticizing tendency on their part to underestimate foreigners' ability to understand Russia's problems and exaggerate their appetite for gloating over Russian misfortune. Hence, it can be difficult for them to accept that foreign knowledge and experience are valid for, or even operable in Russia.

Plainly such attitudes betray a powerful self-protection mechanism, but behind that lies an unpalatable truth for Russian management if it is to succeed in the market economy. Throughout the long years of socialism Russian managers have undergone a relentless process of de-skilling; hence, not only do they lack specific competencies for the new conditions, but they also have difficulty grasping why the know-how needed for the market economy is not just a set of techniques, but the foundation of a completely new way of thinking for setting priorities and taking decisions. It is then not unsurprising that a study of 35 Russian managers in 1992 in St Petersburg found that industrial managers had two primary objectives: to preserve previously achieved levels of industrial production and to maintain the existing *kollektiv*, with the latter having tactical priority (Kharkhordin and Gerber, 1994).

The psychologist Yuri Hanin (1991) suggests that all Russian managers to a greater or lesser extent suffer from 'the learned helplessness syndrome as a result of constantly operating within the barriers of the old socioeconomic system which hindered initiative, independence and entrepreneurship'. All this, of course, fits in with the observations of Manoukovsky and the findings of Hibbert, both cited in Chapter 4. Åslund (1993), who was quoted earlier in this chapter, might also support this idea of the learned helplessness syndrome, for it tends to support his view of Russian managers as being 'firmly moulded by the old Soviet command economy'.

Hanin had been involved with management training in the construction sector during the *perestroika* period, and we can profitably turn to this industry for a glimpse of challenges facing managers beginning to operate in the new market conditions. Our informant is Professor Lev Kaplan, one the USSR's foremost experts on construction and, since the grand demise, a passionate supporter of modernization of its management along western lines. In 1992 Kaplan described the particular problems of transforming management attitudes and practices in this industry in these terms:

> One of the most important problems is the fundamental change of management and managers' mentality in the construction industry of Russia which involves learning from western experience. The command-administrative system has created for itself a special convenient type of 'management' and stereotyped mentality of managers and experts working in the construction sector of Russia, which can be characterized as follows:
>
> a) Lack of initiative from managers and experts. It was customary to wait for all instructions from the top, work according to fixed plans, striving for the fulfilment of these plans 'at any cost' – even to the detriment of the production and final results.
>
> b) A deep-rooted practice of deceiving higher authorities, to colour the truth, the actual situation in a company and in production, to use roundabout ways when breaking rigid laws and instructions.
>
> c) No skills to do economic calculations, choose optimal (or even better) solutions to problems which arise; no knowledge of price formation, contract procedures arbitration, court's proceedings and other elements of a market economy.
>
> d) Insufficient knowledge of how to build up rational organisational and production structures of management, management systems and human resources management.
>
> e) Lack of knowledge of how to organise work and work of subordinate employees, poorly equipped managers' work stations; lack of computers, poor knowledge of information management systems.

f) Lack of knowledge of the fundamentals and practice of marketing, advertising, of appropriate presentation of their companies and developing
corporate image.

g) No skills in the area of customer relations or commercial relationships with banks, stock exchanges,
intermediaries and other commercial entities.

i) No cross-cultural skills when working with foreign
partners, no knowledge of their methods of work,
laws of western countries, requirements of foreign
companies.

These are only the main problems which Russian managers are facing now, in the period of the difficult transition to the market economy. These problems will be
exacerbated as Russia approaches the civilised market
and becomes integrated into the world economy.

It is important to point out that organizational structure of the construction industry during the Soviet period 'had been complex in
the extreme' (Dyker, 1992). The industry was also technologically
backward, its style of management was gung-ho, and had not
responded to the challenge of *perestroika*. In this sense, the construction sector exemplified many of the worst aspects of the centralized economy in action. Making due allowance for that, the
above list of constraints on Russian managers' deficiencies concerning know-how and attitudes vital for operating in market
economy conditions is generalizable across most industries with
one possible and significant exception – the defence industry.

In contrast to the construction sector, the traditionally pampered
defence industry enjoyed stable and unquestioned priority access
to supplies of materials and equipment (Cooper, 1991) nor did it
suffer so persistently from that scourge of the construction sector:
'chronic lateness in the delivery of documentation' (Dyker, 1992).
The latter factor affected, but did not unduly hold up the construction of the Chernobyl nuclear plant. Despite its more than
usually centralized administrative arrangements, the defence sector was, 'without doubt, the most successful sector of the Soviet
Union's socialist planned economy' (Cooper, 1991). It possessed
'some of the best technical and managerial talent in the Soviet

economy, precisely those best-equipped in terms of skills, if not always of attitude, to respond to the challenges of a market economy. It is also the only sector of the economy with long experience of external competitive pressure' (Cooper, 1991).

By the very nature of its activities, however, the defence industry is likely to retain a form of management which is essentially administrative owing to the close relationship it has with government departments, not least its security agencies.

Thus, the 'lead' which the defence sector had over less privileged industries in the Soviet period will be inevitably be cut down because newly liberated enterprises can operate in markets with an autonomy which a defence manufacturer, even if nominally in the private sector in any country, cannot enjoy.

Economy, society and industry

In 1992 the Russian government, with the backing and approval of the west, unleashed the first phase of reforms to introduce market economy conditions. This was the so-called 'shock therapy', which in fact administered more shock than therapy and transformed Russia into a bazaar (Maslov, 1996b). The government's economic reform strategy in fact focused on price liberalization and privatization. Other aims, which took account of the recommendations of the IMF and which predicated general western support for the reform programme, included the liberalization of foreign trade, the introduction of tight financial and fiscal policies, measures to reduce the budget deficit, legislation on bankruptcies, the introduction of ownership of land and firm guarantees for foreign capital (Belova, 1994).

In April 1991, in the dying months of Soviet power, price reform was finally introduced. This was a decision that had been repeatedly delayed for fear of mass social unrest as well as out of uncertainties about fixing prices nationwide. There was also concern in Moscow that the increasingly independently minded republics might set up customs barriers to protect their markets. When the reform came, 'the prices of everything from bread to tractors went up by an average of 300 per cent' (Wilson and Bachkatov, 1992). On 2 January 1992, within days of the disintegration of the Soviet

Union, the state liberalized over 90 percent of consumer prices and 80 percent of producer prices, and abolished most wage control (Mikheyev, 1996). The result was traumatic baptism of fire into the free market economics.

The populace, which hitherto had no experience of supply and demand, and could live without needing to know anything about the relationship between cost and price, witnessed the price of food rise by 300 percent, energy by 300–500 percent, medicines by 400 percent, rail fares by 200 percent and airfares by 300 percent (Wilson and Bachkatov, 1992). By August 1993, if we take the December 1991 price level at 100 percent, prices had risen across the board by 8825 percent (Löwenhardt, 1995). Not surprisingly, the post-Soviet economy went into a tailspin. In 1992 industrial production dropped 19 percent, oil extraction by 15 percent, and agricultural output by 8 percent, and by the end of 1992 the net material product had declined by 78 percent over the previous year, the last year of communism (Löwenhardt, 1995). And things were to get worse, much worse, before beginning to get better.

The other main plank of the government reform programme involved privatization – this 'magic word for coaxing aid from the West, where media and politicians mistakenly equate it with West European-style privatization' (Wilson and Bachkatov, 1992). The key aims of Yeltsin and the reformers were to depoliticize firms (i.e. free them from politicians' control) and to concentrate control and cashflow rights in the hands of enterprise managers and out-side investors (Boycko, Schleifer and Vishny, 1995). In total, some 250,000 enterprises were involved; of these approximately 25,000 were the proverbial Soviet-style 'mega-enterprises', hopelessly inefficient for the most part and dominated by Soviet-era management thinking and attitudes.

Brian Moynahan (1994) describes the impact of the first two years of reform in the following words. Note that the country in question is now metaphorically codenamed 'Ru$$ia.'

> Yeltsin's brave new Russia inherited the old problems. All-Union government had collapsed but the center retained an immense payroll – millions of servicemen, bureaucrats, workers in arms plants. Its ability to raise money was circumscribed so it resorted to printing

money on a massive scale. Inflation rocketed out of control. The dollar bought 32 rubles the month after the attempted coup [which took place in August 1991]; by the start of 1992 it had reached 90 and it hit 1,000 in mid-1993. Two societies were spawned. Ruble Russia squatted in the ruins of the Soviet Union, immense, impoverished and angry. Above it was another world, Ru$$ia, small and sleek, peopled by those with access to dollars – tarts, touts, taxi-drivers, traders. Security guards kept the two sides apart. Bulky young men in tight-fitting uniforms defended the Ru$$ian settlements: $350 a night hotels, casinos, nightclubs with $150 Scotch, Mercedes concessionaires, stores packed with perfumes, cashmeres, video cameras.

By 1994, there was warning from the economist Belova (1994), in the prestigious journal *Voprosy Ekonomiki*, that Russia had been reduced by the west to a mere 'appendage', an abject supplier of raw materials to the ever-hungry manufacturing industries of the more powerful economic states. To add insult to injury, the aim of IMF policies seemed to be to remove Russia as an international competitor. For Russia this meant: 'the degrading of national industry, job cut-backs , the problem of chronic unemployment in the future and, consequently, the impossibility of embarking on high levels of consumption'. Not for the first time in Russia's history, foreigners were being blamed for all the problems, being openly accused of subverting the economy. Indeed Belova went further. She declared that 'an economic war is being waged against our country, a war in which we had already suffered huge losses'. Yet Belova is not scaremongering for the sake of it. She is touching a raw nerve: millions of Russian strongly suspect the west's motives.

Behind such outbursts of indignation is a deeply felt Russian conviction that the western-style approach to economic management does create conditions which deliberately foster destitution and other social ills. The communists may not have been in the end such good managers of Russia's vast resources, but they were right about the capitalists. Russians look around themselves and see an ever-soaring death rate, a sharp deterioration in their diet, a rise in contagious and sexually transmitted diseases, an increasing number of abortions, stillbirths and birth defects. Add to this the steady devaluation of pensions, the failure of the government to pay its employees for months on end, the layoffs, the bankruptcies, the organized crime. All these terrible things are more associated in the Russian mind with the consequences of introducing western-style capitalism into Russia than with the legacy of 70 years of communist rule. No wonder that *biznes* is such a dirty word in Russia.

Yet, despite all this, in April 1995 *The Economist* was able to report that:

> The basic institutions of a market economy have appeared with astonishing speed. It is easy to forget that most forms of private business were still illegal until the end of Mr Gorbachev's presidency of the Soviet Union in 1991. Russia now has about 2,500 licensed commercial banks, 600 investment funds and 40m shareholders. The liberalisation of most prices in January 1992 and the privatisation of 15,779 medium-sized and large enterprises in a period of just 18 months have helped to form a private sector which in 1994 produced 62% of officially recorded GDP. Proportionately, Russia's state-owned sector is smaller than Italy's.

Two years later, the *Financial Times* (1997) concluded 'communism is well and truly gone' and that Russia's main challenge is 'to forge a new national identity'. This new identity will be linked to the path that Russia now takes: either towards a western-type market economy system – 'open, fair capitalism' – or towards an inegalitarian, Latin American-type system – corrupt, monopolist capitalism'. The second path is almost the natural one for Russia because it depends less on a middle class and more on authoritarian government. In other words, the first path can only come about if (a) the politicians allow an independent private sector to expand and to flourish (and many on the left and the right of the political spectrum are opposed to this) and (b) Russia – four or five centuries after its west European neighbours – installs a middle class – a bourgeoisie – which will not only fill the vacuum between the increasingly affluent and the increasingly impoverished, but also supply the managerial talent for an efficient private sector.

After nearly six years of reform, the people of Russia find themselves 'on the edge of a precipice' (*Financial Times*, 1997). These have been years of pain and anguish for the many, of undreamt-of riches and opportunities for the few – and continuation of not an uncushy life for tens of thousands of former Soviet apparatchiks with the right contacts in the ministries, growing finance sector and industry. As for managers, have they coped? We have already noted how unequipped they were in 1992. Since then, they have had to learn to run their enterprises as going concerns, forcing to understand and apply rules for a totally new game. Years on, what verdict can we come to?

The emerging Russian manager: Gosplan past and market future

In 1996 the Moscow office of McKinsey & Company, in conjunction with the Russian Privatization Center in Moscow and the United States Agency for International Development, produced a series of seven booklets in English for Russian managers on restructuring Russian companies and developing management expertise for market economy conditions (McKinsey, 1996). The booklets are large format and vary in length from about 80 to 150 pages, each volume containing several pages of exhibits. The booklets, aimed at senior industrial managers, deal with the following topics: understanding financial accounts, restructuring and the role of top management, allying with foreign partners, streamlining through restructuring, performing market research, organizing for marketing, performing market research, and analysing product profitability. The series come with the sub-title: 'managing successfully beyond privatization'. It is, incidentally, a trifle ironic that the Russian translation of 'restructuring' is *restructurovaniye*. Until Gorbachev came along, the translator's first choice of the Russian equivalent would have been *perestroika*.

We will not try to account for the mysterious omission of booklets on business strategy and human resource management (unless these are in preparation), but pay attention first to identical forewords from Maxim Boycko, Director General of the Russian Privatization Center and Anatoly Chubais, who from 1992–1995, pioneered Russian privatization and who in March 1997 was appointed First Deputy Prime Minister with special responsibility for improving tax collection and reforming the pensions system (*The Economist*, 1997).

It is worth quoting these two leaders of business development on their crystallization of challenges facing Russian industrial managers, most of them the direct heirs of the Soviet technocratic manager. Both men are aware that, at the same time as they restructure, Russian enterprises have also got to aspire to become integrated with the world economy through (a) developing foreign markets and (b) attracting foreign investment. It is singularly apt that Boycko and Chubais are writing under the slogan 'From the Gosplan past to the market future', as the quoted passages clearly reveal how the Russian manager is still a victim of the defunct ways of behaviour and thinking. First Chubais in McKinsey (1996):

> Many Russian companies today are taking a decisive step in their economic development and opening their doors to domestic and foreign investors.These investors are very demanding when choosing where to invest their capital, and building a solid reputation becomes essential to a company. The way to achieve this is first of all to conduct business in a professional fashion thus providing high returns on investment.
>
> Russian companies will have to overcome the crisis of working capital, learn how to manage their finances, establish up-to-date marketing services, develop, launch and market new products and services, and discontinue old ones.
>
> Restructuring companies is not a simple matter of a manager's will and a few harsh decisions such as job cuts or closing down some lines of business. A modern manager should be able to analyse different options for developing his company, see its future in the market, and have the will and ability to engage people in implementing decisions.
>
> It is not surprising that many managers of Russian industrial companies who were used to following instructions 'from above', lack the knowledge and experience necessary to implement fundamental changes. On the other hand, Russian industry has

great intellectual potential, well-educated managers, highly skilled workers and rich natural resources. All of these factors fuel ambitious plans to enter world markets and achieve a respectable position. However, in order to realize these plans, companies should understand exactly what restructuring is and what kind of techniques, approaches and tools are available to organize business in this new environment. Making all the decisions alone is never possible.

It is important to remember that the best way to support the country and to improve the overall situation in Russia is to make your own company prosperous, offering high-quality affordable products and creating stable well-paid jobs. Over time this strategy should bring profits – one of the most important performance indicators . . . Achieve good results and you will see that Russian and foreign investors choose to invest their capital in your business, and other companies will be willing to cooperate with you.

Boycko (McKinsey, 1996) both reinforces several of Chubais's points, while highlighting other issues:

Many problems faced by Russian companies today can, to a certain extent, be reduced to a few major issues. These would include the role of top management and its relationship with shareholders, the working capital crisis, the outdated product mix, the lack of information on new and potential markets, the underdeveloped marketing strategy, the company organization ill-suited to the market environment, the mismatch between prices and actual production costs, and the lack of experience in searching for a reliable Western partner and building a partnership. Other important issues are production management, environmental protection, managing social infrastructure and many others.

A number of Russian companies have found approaches to solving these problems through successful restructuring and are growing into important players in domestic and foreign markets. Those who have just started this journey could save time and learn from

other people's mistakes by studying and summariz-
ing their experiences.

Chubais and Boycko are not only leading market reformers, but
also have a very clear grasp of what needs to be done. Hence these
comments deserve careful scrutiny. Between them, in a matter of a
few paragraphs, they indicate precisely where the anti-market
Soviet past is, as it were, invading the marketizing present. Is it
not somewhat remarkable that their statements go under a cap-
tion containing a reference to Gosplan, which was already declin-
ing in significance in the light of the Gorbachev reforms by the
end of the 1980s?

One significant message from Chubais and Boycko is that
Russian managers have not merely to change their attitudes and
behaviour, they must also actively unlearn many habits which
served them well under socialism, and which are a positive hin-
drance in a market economy structure.

This is not easy. Two Russian scholars, Zhukova and Korotov
(1996), have specifically drawn attention to the problem of managing 'the process of clashes between the new and the old'. They
note that many Russian managers are inclined to make quick and
repeated organizational changes believing such a strategy – which
is of course precisely the wrong word – is going to secure profits.
These rapid changes are not only a direct response to the volatile
nature of the business environment, but also create misunder-
standings between managers and the workforce. A problem here
is that the workforce has an 'institutional memory developed over
several generations'. Among other things it holds a view that there
should be a kind of status quo between managers and employees,
whereby the latter enjoy – as they did in Soviet times 'a warranty
of stability' (i.e. job security, as we would express it). Zhukova
and Korotov note that it is often big managers, who have not fully
left the era of 'one-man rule' who are most prone to use rapid
organizational change as a solution. This state of affairs is consistent with a Russian industrial manager's comment noted by the
French researchers, Berelowitch and Wieviorka (1996): 'There is no
strategy at the top. The bosses just fight fires'. (*Les chefs d'entreprise
deviennent des pompiers.*)

There are, however, clear signs that the logic of the market is forcing managers to break with the tradition of operating through networks of the core contacts who could fix anything – the contacts in the party and the apparatchiks – 'the same old faces, the same old shirkers' (Berelowitch and Wieviorka, 1996). Scholars Kharkhordin and Gerber (1994) noted three factors which were forcing enterprise managers to 'disconnect old ties'. The first factor concerned the issue of the quality of supplies. If firms were not getting the quality, they unilaterally changed supplier. Second, the breakup of the USSR meant that enterprises no longer had to depend on suppliers and to supply customers who were geographically remote. Managers were taking control of their business networks in terms of convenience to them. Third, experiences of non-payment were compelling managers to seek new, reliable business partners. No-one should underestimate the extent to which these three factors were forcing Russian managers, many of them from the old school, to readjust their outlook, think competitively, and go with the flow of new market pressures. However, no-one should assume that managers always relished these changes. Kharkhordin and Gerber (1994) note managers' 'negative views' about having to adopt radically different forms of behaviour vis-à-vis the marketplace alone.

While securing the supply base and customer base, they also have to come to terms with other unpalatable issues such as coping with privatization and restructuring their enterprises. These challenges mean agonizing decisions about the workforce. Not just because of socialist notions of 'full employment', but rather because of traditional Russian communitarianism, Russian managers tend to see their workers more as companions, even fellow sufferers, than we do in the west. Hence, the Russian manager sees himself as protector of the *kollektiv*. In the days of socialism he might have goaded his *kollektiv* ruthlessly, but he still looked after it: there was an implicit contract. In this regard it is only too easy to overlook the fact that even today, the factory 'is not just . . . the place where one works: it is also the very centre of existence especially in the small one-industry towns, which are legion' (Berelowitch and Wieviorka, 1996).

It is hardly surprising then that Russian managers not only rank very highly the capability of their workforce (McCarthy and Puffer,

1994), but also disdain the prospect of having to dismiss their comrades. To the workforce the manager, ideally, is *kind hearted* as well as authoritarian. This is what is meant by the designation *le bon directeur*, to quote the two French researchers mentioned above (Berelowitch and Wieviorka, 1996). When Russians petition their bosses for fear of losing their jobs, those bosses often experience guilt and remorse, knowing the misery they will cause, and at a deeper level curse this thing called the market, which seems so ill fitted to the Russian temperament. Forgetting the millions of Soviet lives which were sacrificed and the millions of careers blighted for the sake of communism, the bosses – especially the unreconstructed old guard – now know for certain that Lenin and generations of like-minded followers were right: basically, the market stinks. The point is that many Russians, with their deep communitarian instincts, find the market unpleasantly associated with self-seeking individualism. In the words of Veiga, Yanouzas and Buchholtz (1995): 'Perhaps the biggest enigma facing the Russian manager is the degree to which it is psychologically and socially justifiable to engage in activities that enhance individual versus collective good.'

Of course, not all bosses take a hard line about the market, but there appear to be enough of the old guard around for them to be seen as a potent counterweight to the Russian managers who incline to modernization. French researchers Berelowitch and Wieviorka (1996) neatly capture the dichotomy between the two strains in the interview with industrial managers. First there is Andrei, who 'expects the state to reduce its functions to a minimum, to content itself with looking after [*contrôler*] the country's finances, the stability of borders and the safety of citizens, but definitely not with industry and the economy'.

Against that point of view there is Arkady, who wants Russia to 'remain or reassert itself as a big country, respected throughout the world; which implies state-sponsored initiatives [*programmes d'État*], the establishment of national priorities and support for enterprises whose output is not readily marketable, notably in the sphere of scientific research and space exploration'. Not for the first time in Russian history, the polarization is at the extremes. This is not to say, however, that even the conservative old-style managers necessarily want a return to the old system. They just find it more difficult to adjust to the momentous changes that Russia has experienced. They regard themselves as competent, but they were made for and in another system. According to Berelowitch and Wieviorka (1996), 'the majority of them have been knocked off course [*déroutés*]'. But about one thing we can be fairly certain: both Andrei and Arkady would agree on what constitutes a being a manager – a boss – in Russia, whatever the economic system. The role is to govern the *kollektiv* and, according to Berelowitch and Wieviorka (1996) 'to keep on the same wavelength with it'.

These French scholars amplify the point in a reconstructed conversation between two other informants, also industrial managers:

> Inside the enterprise, being the boss [*directeur*], means first and foremost knowing how to manage people [*diriger des hommes*], having natural authority, a proven reputation, the ability, said Vadim, 'to solve problems'. The boss, explained Yegor, must guarantee the technical viability of the enterprise. 'If he does not understand production, he will not be able to organize it as it should be. There will be no success.' At this point the Andrei mentioned a moment ago adds his point of view. 'The best bosses are engineers, who have got to combine with their technical knowledge a capacity for being a leader of men. The crucial thing is to impress on the *kollektiv* certainty about the future.' Andrei apparently has this vital capacity. He has often asked the impossible [*des buts incroyables*] of his *kollektiv*.

This resonates with the findings of a major survey of management change in east and central Europe conducted by the Harvard Business School (Aguilar, Loveman and Vlachoutsicos (1994). A technical director of a manufacturing plant is quoted as follows:

> In our culture there is a notion that a boss should know everything. To admit that there are no sure and safe solutions for all the problems would be considered a sign of weakness and incompetence.

Russian management: conditions for development

In 1996, the year in which McKinsey brought out its management guides, the National Training Foundation published results on two surveys on management development in Russia. Possibly the most thorough publications of their kind, these reports provide valuable insights into the state of mind of Russian managers concerning (a) their own effectiveness in current conditions (NTF Survey 1), and (b) their perceptions of training needs (NTF Survey 2). In this chapter we summarize the first of these reports.

NTF Survey I, which is available only in Russian, was conducted in cooperation with the Center for Sociological Research of Moscow State University. It aims were to identify the key barriers constraining the development of managers in Russia. The survey, believed to be the most thorough of its kind ever undertaken, solicited the opinions of 232 industrial managers, 127 representatives of educational institutions providing management education, 23 government officials with legislative and executive competencies, and representatives of 10 sponsoring organizations. The 400 and more respondents came from seven major growth regions of Russia: Moscow, St Petersburg, Nizhni Novgorod, Rostov-on-Don, Omsk, Yekaterinburg and Khabarovsk. Of the managers, 72 percent worked in manufacturing industry, 15 percent for various kind of trading firms, 7.4 percent in finance, 2.9 percent in insurance, and 2.5 percent in services.

All informants were asked to rank in importance environmental (i.e. political-economic) obstacles most seriously impeding management. The responses are presented in Table 5.1.

This ranking changes somewhat when we consider solely the responses of the industrial managers, presented in Table 5.2.

From Tables 5.1 and 5.2 it is very apparent that several sharply perceived obstacles impede government's ability to provide conditions for stimulating management development. A comparison of the two tables shows that these factors were more sharply perceived by industrial managers. Political instability, the inadequacies of the tax system and the legal system feature prominently on various rankings and are considered by a wide range of commentators to constrain the advance towards a market economy. It is

Table 5.1 Perceived obstacles to management development in Russia (1)

Factor	Very important obstacle	Important obstacle	Minor obstacle	Not an apparent obstacle
1 Political and economic instability	266 (66.2%)	93 (23.1%)	23 (5.7%)	15 (3.7%)
2 Impossibility of long-term planning	225 (56.0%)	118 (29.3%)	36 (8.9%)	21 (5.2%)
3 Existing tax system	255 (56%)	87 (21.6%)	57 (14.1%)	28 (6.9%)
4 Unsuitable legislative foundation	153 (38.0%)	148 (36.8%)	70 (17.4%)	19 (4.7%)
5 Underestimation of importance of instilling effective management systems	79 (19.7%)	170 (42.3%)	92 (22.8%)	50 (12.4%)
6 Difficulties in locating qualified managers	62 (15.4%)	168 (41.8%)	117 (29.1%)	43 (10.6%)
7 Government officials' lack of interest in management development	108 (26.9%)	126 (31.3%)	90 (22.3%)	68 (16.9%)
8 Absence of tradition of Russian management	85 (21.1%)	107 (26.6%)	126 (31.3%)	72 (17.9%)
9 Absence of literature and information on management development	85 (21.1%)	128 (31.8%)	144 (35.8%)	80 (19.9%)
10 Insufficient number of education centres for management development	39 (9.1%)	134 (33.3%)	126 (31.3%)	93 (23.1%)

[all respondents, n = 403]
Source: National Training Foundation Survey 1, Moscow

Table 5.2 Perceived obstacles to management development in Russia (2)

Factor	Very important obstacle	Important obstacle	Minor obstacle	Not an apparent obstacle
1 Political and economic instability	169 (69.8%)	50 (20.7%)	10 (4.1%)	10 (4.1%)
2 Existing tax system	152 (62.8%)	46 (19.0%)	25 (10.3%)	16 (6.6%)
3 Impossibility of long-term planning	141 (58.3%)	71 (29.3%)	19 (7.9%)	9 (3.7%)
4 Unsuitable legislative foundation	95 (39.3%)	89 (36.8%)	33 (13.6%)	15 (6.2%)
5 Government officials' lack of interest in management development	66 (27.3%)	77 (31.8%)	49 (20.2%)	44 (18.2%)
6 Absence of tradition of Russian management	47 (19.4%)	64 (26.4%)	78 (32.2%)	48 (19.8%)
7 Underestimation of importance of instilling effective management systems	36 (14.9%)	97 (40.1%)	59 (24.4%)	43 (17.8%)
8 Difficulties in locating qualified managers	34 (14.0%)	96 (39.7%)	74 (30.6%)	29 (12.0%)
9 Absence of literature and information on management development	23 (9.5%)	70 (28.9%)	94 (38.8%)	48 (19.8%)
10 Insufficient number of education centres for management development	22 (9.1%)	70 (28.9%)	79 (32.6%)	64 (26.4%)

[industrial managers, n = 235]
Source: National Training Foundation Survey 1, Moscow

perhaps noteworthy that in this survey around 60 percent of respondents in both tables considered that bureaucratic indifference was either an important or a very important constraining factor. Similarly, Russia's lack of tradition in management was not regarded as especially significant by nearly half the respondents.

However, the tabulation suggests that information on management development and the provision of management education are considered serious areas of weakness. Presumably this finding reflects the opinion of those who regard these things as important, and they should not necessarily be seen as constituting a clear majority of the sample. NTF Survey 2, which we discuss in Chapter 6, in fact supports this conclusion: management training, it finds, 'is a luxury that they [Russian managers] can forego and which can be acquired by experience'. That finding, in turn, reinforces the self-perception that the lack of managerial traditions is not in the final analysis disadvantageous.

This self-confidence is in fact reflected in answers in Survey 1 to a question about the possibility of development of Russian management at this stage in the transition process. Table 5.3 summarizes the responses.

Table 5.3 shows an interesting discrepancy between the view of the industrial bosses and the government officials. Whereas a higher proportion of the latter regard conditions in place for management development than the former, they are more cautious about the future. This discrepancy almost certainly reflects the realism of the manager vis-à-vis the remoteness of the officials whose activities are far less directly influenced by the operations of the marketplace.

The managers in the sample were also asked to state (a) those management specialisms for which they lacked expertise and (b) the biggest challenges facing them in the running of their enterprises. Their responses to (a) are presented in Table 5.4 (responses to (b) are in the next table).

The high ranking of marketing reflects a growing awareness of the need to move from a production orientation to one that is customer centred. It might also be associated with a shift in the networking behaviour of Russian managers, which, as we noted earlier, is being forced to break away from dependence on the core contacts in ministries and industry organizations. The seemingly

Table 5.3 Progress towards management development in Russia

	Enterprise Managers	Directors of educational institutions	Representatives of government departments	Representatives of sponsors	Total
Is developing	91 (37.6%)	64 (50.4%)	7 (30.4%)	6 (60%)	168 (43%)
Will take off soon˙	71 (29.3%)	47 (37.0%)	10 (43.5%)	4 (40%)	132 (34%)
Conditions not yet suitable	70 (28.9%)	14 (11%)	6 (26.1%)	0	90 (23%)
Total	232 (100%)	125 (100%)	23 (100%)	10 (100%)	390 (100%)

[˙ The original Russian reads development 'will begin soon', which implies that development has not yet commenced.]

Source: National Training Foundation Survey 1, Moscow, 1996

low demand for accountants is baffling, given the huge pressures on enterprises to cut costs and to institute more sophisticated methods of financial control. Similarly, the need for IT expertise appears low. As for management of quality, we may safely assume that this refers to quality of production and not to TQM, as understood in other countries.

Table 5.4 Russian managers' perception of need for special expertise

Management activity	Percentage of respondents indicating a specific need
Marketing	50%
Legal affairs	29%
Work with banks and financial markets	24%
General management	17.5%
International business	16.5%
Production management	16%
Personnel management	15.5%
Accountants	13.5%
Information technology	9.5%
Quality management	9.0%

[industrial managers, n = 235]
Source: National Training Foundation Survey 1, Moscow, 1996

Table 5.5 shows the managers' assessment of the major challenges in running their enterprises.

A striking inclusion in this list is the revealed necessity to reduce enterprises' administrative staff. Plainly, the new market conditions do not suit the old pushers, whose bureaucratic ways are fast becoming redundant. It is equally striking that no enterprise sees a need to cut down on its production workforce. This may be partly because of the tenacious relationship between bosses and workers, as we saw earlier, and the fear of losing them in case there is an upturn in business. The low priority accorded to personnel management should surprise no-one.

Table 5.5 Russian managers' perception of challenges

Specified problem	Percentage of respondents
Marketing	62%
Search for financial resources	44%
Development of corporate strategy	28%
Supplier relations	20%
Introducing new technology	19%
Reducing administrative staff	12%
Personnel management	8%
Expanding exports	5%

[industrial managers, n = 235]

Source: National Training Foundation Survey 1, Moscow, 1996

The compilers of this report for the National Training Foundation drew the following conclusions regarding constraints on the development of managers in Russia:

1 Overall political and economic uncertainties.

2 A marked tendency to assume that accumulation of experience is tantamount to management development.

3 A marked tendency to get heavily involved in 'operational questions' (i.e. supplier relationships and production) and not to tackle strategic issues.

4 The failure of educational institutions to understand industry's problems and so deliver appropriate courses (against that many enterprises cannot afford – in both senses – to release personnel for upgrading).

5 An assumption that somehow the state will intervene and help resolve some of the financial problems.

6 A reluctance to accept that the biggest constraint on management development is a conviction that management training is not vitally important.

The report finds Russian managers' self-confidence to be misplaced. It pulls no punches. Russian managers 'are inadequately trained and have no fixed ideas on how to make their enterprise one of the most competitive ones in the market'.

The emerging Russian manager: ethical uncertainties

So far in this chapter we have considered various assessments of the 'emerging' Russian manager. In another book the qualifying word 'emerging' might lead the reader to assume that we have in mind the Russian manager who has suddenly come to prominence in the light of the dramatic demise of the Soviet Union. But we should never lose sight of the fact that we are talking about emerging managers who are Russian: Russian in outlook and temperament. Hence, in this book the expression 'emerging manager' has a profounder connotation.

In this book he is the man who has been thrown up by a giant hand out of the mangled wreck of Russia's 20th century; he is a man bearing deep scars; someone in his family has known tribulation, unspeakable terror, inconceivable injustice; someone in his family died for Stalin, mistaking his pitilessness for benevolent wisdom; the emerging manager is a man whose mouth is full of bitter ash, which he can neither swallow nor spit out. Like Doctor Zhivago, he must grit his teeth and share his country's fate. Being Russian, he will accept what history hurls in his face and, while he can, shelter from its most violent knocks with 'an undying passive resistance [which] is at the bottom of the Russian character' (Baring, 1960). He knows that the market too can be pitiless in its way, and he has not learnt to cope with this yet. He feels helpless despite his bravado. But at least the market will not send him and his kith and kin to the Gulag. What he wants to know is this: can this market be compatible with deeply held Russian values and needs about mutual responsibility, egalitarianism and grassroots democracy, all of which foreigners always misunderstand and therefore disesteem?

It is important that we begin to confront these issues. No study of the shaping of the contemporary Russian manager that does not take account of the legacy of the Soviet Union and Russia's age-long burden on its people can claim to unravel his inner logic and make him, his motivations and priorities, comprehensible to foreigners. Bearing this important point in mind, we now turn to western and Russian studies and observations about the transformation of the emerging Russian manager, this considerably troubled man, as Russia lurches towards the market economy.

The characterization of the Russian manager as 'this considerably troubled man' may seem mildly preposterous, but it gives an important clue as to an essential feature of Russian management: its ethical foundation. In the days of the Soviet era the ethical impulses were supplied by the Communist Party and these boiled down to one simple injunction: the end justifies the means. In the new era Russian managers are relying on their native ethics, while beginning to evolve a general system of ethics for the market economy. One of Russia's leading professors of management, Vladimir Maslov (1996a) has argued very cogently that Russia needs SMEs not just to be the motor of the developing market economy, but precisely because in the SME environment the manager 'can take up close personal contacts with the workforce, whereby these relationships are regulated by the cultural norms'. Writing elsewhere Maslov (1996c) adds that such close personal relations should be regulated by these norms, and not by the market.

These factors, which have already attracted a certain amount of attention from commentators, are of exceptional importance because they reveal facets of Russian behaviour which are already contributing to a distinctive management style, one that foreign management consultants and educators as well as investors and business partners in general must try to understand and work with. Not only that, there are now abundant signs (and this point will be developed in greater depth later in this book) that evolving ethical underpinnings of Russian management are already proving awkward to integrate with the values and behaviour codes of foreign collaborators in business and other forms of cross-cultural endeavour.

A major contribution on this issue comes from American scholars, Sheila Puffer and Daniel McCarthy (1995), who likewise acknowledge the difficulty of exploring ethical issues in Russian management against a murky backdrop of 'mafia connections, bribery, extortion, and even murder'. These scholars proceed on the not unreasonable assumption that Russians for the most part value honesty, trust, fairness and just rewards as the basis of a sound ethical system. But they recognize that 'Russia's turbulent history . . . couped with the recent turmoil created by the move toward a market economy, has created ambiguity among business people about what constitutes ethical behavior'. They highlight three powerful historical traditions which have an incalculable influence on the Russian mindset as it has evolved from mediaeval times to communism and beyond.

The first concerns the general state of subjugation of the Russian populace to those in authority – whether Tsar, landowners, church or Communist Party. Striking among these leaders was the Russian Orthodox Church 'which did not value work as a religious virtue'. Hence, 'people who engaged in business were thus often suspected of having selfish motives and, implicitly, unethical motives' (Puffer and McCarthy, 1995). The second influence concerns the period of communist rule, which both 'recognized collective rather than individual achievements' and gave individuals 'little incentive to work hard or take personal responsibility for their actions'. The third influence refers to the absence of civic institutions, including laws, which gave stimulus and protection to individual aspiration deemed for whatever reason to be not 'in the interests of the state'.

Thus, legislation which in the 1980s was meant to liberate enterprises, and post-communist legislation on matters such as ownership and privatization was and is confusing and contradictory. This industrial manager speaks for many. 'What is the point,' he asks, 'of enforcing laws which do not work, which do not or cannot regulate anything properly' (quoted in Berelowitch and Wieviorka, 1996). Little wonder then the Russians view laws as reinforcing the privileges of those in charge and not as offering protection to the individual. Consequently, 'the Russian man . . . sees a law and instantly thinks of ways to maneuver around it. This is just a tradition [which] will take years to overcome'. (Kaplan, F. in Puffer and McCarthy, 1995).

The upshot, not surprisingly, is that Russian managers are struggling to develop an ethical system that is appropriate to their concept of a market economy. In this endeavour they are operating 'in an ethical vacuum' (Puffer and McCarthy, 1995). Their attitudes are further shaped by some powerful influences: an engrained conviction that business is immoral (greed, materialism, differentials, exploitation; the acceptance that, if you need something to be done, you have to use *blat*, influence with one's personal network of fixers). If we add the fact that Russians by temperament wish to pursue their activities on a collective basis, which accepts authoritarianism as the preferred leadership style, while emphasizing mutual responsibility and egalitarian participation, then we are confronted by three major implications:

1 Russian impulses and values are going to be difficult to accommodate in structures which do not suit the Russian temperament.

2 Russians may not be willing to conduct interpersonal relationships which go against their concepts of authority and egalitarianism.

3 Relationships between Russians and foreign educators or consultants seem to be on a collision course.

Business Relationships:

Asymmetries And Anxieties

The foreigner is armed with statistics, plans a month–long market research project and spends long hours analyzing forecasts and projections. The Russian simply wants to do business. He wants to use his connections and navigate the partner through the complicated system so that they can both make a profit. All the paperwork, the Russian will insist, is unnecessary. His attitude is 'We do it my way, just trust me.' The foreign side sees the Russian as irresponsible and pushy.

— Wilson and Donaldson, 1996

Introduction

As we saw in Chapter 5, Russia is slowly but surely beginning to create a new managerial culture, even though as many as 80 percent of Russian managers held down the top industrial jobs in the Soviet era. The logic of the transition to the market economy is forcing even these managers, for whom money, profits and corporate planning were totally alien concepts, to adopt new practices, not the least of which is the exercise of power without reference to a superior organization in the state and political structure. A major element of the new business landscape in which all Russian managers operate is the scale and scope of business contact with foreign organizations. Russians and westerners can almost be said to be partners in creating this business landscape. The key word is 'almost', seeing that the protagonists in this act of joint creation are often at cross-purposes. In this chapter we highlight the findings of a survey focusing on sticking points which habitually beset these cooperative endeavours. Before tackling this fraught issue, we will briefly review the west's business involvement in Russia's post-communist marketplace.

The new business landscape in Russia

In January 1990, after more than 10 years of negotiating and with an initial investment of $62mn, McDonald's opened its first restaurant in Moscow in Pushkin Square. Serving 40,000 Soviet citizens, it was for a time the busiest McDonald's outlet in the world (the Beijing restaurant now holds the record). In 1990 McDonald's golden arches, a stone's throw from the Kremlin and Red Square, were the ultimate western consumer symbol in Russia. It brought more Russians – including the 27,000 applicants for the initial crew of 630 – into direct contact with western big business than anything in Soviet history (personal communication, 1995). Now it is possible for virtually any Russian, at least in Moscow and St Petersburg, to witness the full panoply of western consumer goods in chic boutiques located in emporia that have not quite managed to shake their jaded Soviet look. [*GUM*] Russia is now a market for products and services, which ten years ago would have seemed impossible: London taxis, cellular telephones, advice on setting regional business centres, loans to improve roads, railways and airports, yoghurt parlours, Barbie dolls, Mars bars, Russia–EU city twinning courtesy of Brussels (*sources*: Bulletins of the Russo-British Chamber of Commerce, 1996–97; *The Economist*, 1997).

The world's big names in consultancy and accountancy run vast operations from portentous Moscow offices. They help to sort out the taxation jungle for their big clients, who also have taken up professional residence and are masterminding multibillion dollar ventures in the sectors offering the best looking long-term payoff:

GUM

GUM was the most famous shop in the USSR, the closest thing to a treasure trove of consumer goods that Soviet citizens were ever likely to see. Westerners, of course, found it drab, utilitarian and understocked. The building itself, with three three-storey parallel arcades, occupies almost the entire eastern flank of Red Square. The present-day structure replaced the historic hall of the Upper Trading Rows, which burnt down in 1825 and which had housed some 1200 shops under one roof. It was opened in 1893 and modelled on the great railway termini of London and Paris with their lofty steelframe and glass construction. After the 1917 Revolution the shop was renamed GUM, the initials of State Universal Store in Russian. In the 1920s the building was taken over by bureaucrats and it did not reopen as a store until 1953. It had 130 counters, many selling identical items. On the top floor was the discreetly located 'Section 100', where the top party officials could buy clothing and other articles not available to the rest of the population.

With *perestroika* many leading western firms in toiletries, clothing and up-market food invested in GUM in order to get a foothold in the USSR's vast, untapped consumer market. The bottom floor is almost exclusively occupied by foreign firms, which are paying between $2000 and $4500 per square metre for floor space. This is why GUM is one of the most valuable items of real estate in all Russia (did someone once say that property is theft?). It is far cry from the 1930s when the outside walls of GUM overlooking Red Square were festooned with gigantic photographic portraits of top comrades, so gigantic in fact that they had to be developed in swimming pools.

oil, gas, telecommunications, and automotive engineering. Three South Korean giants – LG, Daewoo and Kia – committed $7.7bn to projects in Russia/CIS in 1996 (*The Economist*, 1997), and the Koreans are not waiting for Japan and Russia to conclude their long-running spat over Russia's post-war annexation of four tiny Japanese islands. In 1996 Coca-Cola and arch-rival Pepsico both made significant investments in Russia, which raises the irresistible question: will it be cola wars in the Kola Peninsula?

Some 200,000 foreigners live and work in Moscow compared with a mere 30,000 when McDonald's first opened its gilded portals. Other foreigners, peripatetic business people, consultants and educators scarcely give Moscow a glance. The Russian capital is a staging post for Irkutsk, Yakutsk, Tyumen or the Kamchatka, cities and regions which hardly saw a non-card carrying foreigner in Soviet times. In the meantime thousands of Russians work for foreign organizations as representatives, managers, consultants, and – important in Russia – go-betweens. Can you imagine it? The saleswoman is a PhD biochemist. She used to work in one of Leningrad's most prestigious research institutes. She has just sold a Mercedes-Benz 220E to a former scientific collaborator, who evasively describes himself as 'an entrepreneur'.

The Russian market, still less than a decade after the implosion of communism, has been described as 'the final frontier of emerging markets, [but] still very much a Wild West for most foreign investors' (*Russia Express*, 1996a). With greater geographical punctiliousness, but with greater emphasis on all the perceived dangers, *Business Week* (1997) dubs Russia 'the wild, wild East'. The Russian government's attempts to create an attractive and stable environment for investment have been beset by a diverse range of constraints. A seminar in London, sponsored by the Russo-British Chamber of Commerce (1996a), cautioned investors that there was 'no fairy-tale ending' for them in Yeltsin's Russia. Four 'serious deterrents' facing foreign investors were highlighted:

- The absence of a constitutional successor to Yeltsin (fears about his state of health have abated for the time being).

- The lack of legal safeguards and the crippling (and complicated) taxation problems remain the biggest practical deterrents to investment. Foreign investors must realize that it may take years to resolve these problems.

- An omnipresent and suffocating bureaucracy, rampant corruption, rising crime and terrorism do little to foster investment confidence.

- The Russian has a preoccupation that foreign companies practise industrial espionage. (In his hour of glory Alexander Lebed, the short-lived national security adviser, stated that foreign companies operating in Russia should be 'prime targets' for the security services. Lebed may have left the scene, but the suspicions still linger.)

To these factors we can add further complications (*Russia Express*, 1996b):

- Comprehensive legislation on ownership of property is not yet in place.

- Violations of intellectual property are serious and on the rise.

- A deteriorated infrastructure adds to the difficulties of doing business – telephones, road and transport are all of poor quality.

- Russian foreign investment regulations regarding permissible activities, prior authorization and notification requirements are confusing and contradictory.

- Foreign participation in what the Russian authorities term 'strategic sectors' are becoming increasingly restricted.

- Russian law offers few incentives to foreign investors.

- In the case of disputes, foreign investors are confronted by conflicting and overlapping laws and resolutions, if obtained, are ad hoc and unpredictable.

The same source continues:

> Despite the problems . . . most foreign companies in Russia believe that if reforms continue, opportunities justify the risks, uncertainties and considerable bureaucratic obstacles. Few established foreign companies are leaving and many continue to show an interest in Russia's rich geological and human resources, sometimes world-class high-technology and large potential market.

The post-communist scramble for Russia by western investors – both private companies and key suppliers of development aid such as the EU, the World Bank, the IMF and EBRD – is a quest for a new Klondike. Indeed, 'Russia-preneur' Richard Poe describes the great suction of western investment into Russia as a Gold Rush. Just as those first to the Klondike got the best nuggets, Poe (1995) warns the laggards not to delay: 'The trend is obvious. The Gold Rush is on. The first wave (i.e. the early pioneers of the "joint venture era") is already past. The second wave is well under-way. Don't wait for the third wave. The competition will be mur-der.' And he was not even anticipating 'an almost complete criminalisation of the gold and diamond industries and foreseeing when mafia gangs would wage open war for control of the energy sector' (*The Economist*, 1996), or the mowing-down of Russian bankers by contract killers, most of whom remain at large.

For all this, the prevailing mood among not only business people but also experts seems to be that Russia will become a sound market for investment as long as the reforms continue in the direction towards a free market system and provided that the mindset of socialism is eradicated. According to *Business Week* (1997), 'investors are swarm-ing to buy Russian equities even in the face of rampant crime, corrup-tion and a 6% economic decline in 1995 . . . big global investors have poured $1.2 billion into Russian utilities since Jan. 1 alone.' Further optimism is supplied by Professor Richard Layard of the London School of Economics, one of the leading advisers to the Russian gov-ernment on economic reform, and John Parker, a former Moscow correspondent of *The Economist*, in their book *The Coming Russian Boom* (*Russia Express*, 1996c). The authors argue that the continued growth of the private sector in a market the size of Russia, in terms of population and sheer territorial extent, will be a sufficient attrac-tion for foreign investors, while Russia enjoys a colossal export mar-ket for its vast metal and mineral resources.

The conviction drew this comment from the authors of *Russia Express* (1996c):

> It is . . . fortunate that Russia has a small population for its size, and a well-educated and ambitious one at that. Russia's superabundance of every resource known to man (it is No. 1 or No. 2 in reserves for a whole range of commodities) fit it to join that select band of countries with huge natural endowments and comparatively small populations, Australia, Canada and Saudi Arabia. With its annual US$45bn energy export earnings and over US$20bn in other commod-ity earnings, it is on track to join them already.
>
> A resource-driven boom should spill over into ancil-lary sectors and engender a boom in construction and

services. Once the economy is picking up, the knock-
on effect becomes positive, not negative as in 1990–5.

Layard and Parker hold the view that 'foreigners will reap good
rewards from investing in the large domestic market and in
Russia's amazing natural resources'. Nevertheless, they concede,
Russia 'will remain a hard place to do business' (quoted in *Russia
Express*, 1996c). No, not a hard place; rather an inexplicably mad-
dening place. Russia is still a topsy-turvey market in which there
is 'an ingrained suspicion of law going back many centuries' (*The
Economist*, 1994); a market which 'brands as pathological and criminal what would be regarded as normal commercial behaviour
elsewhere' (Yergin and Gustafson, 1994); a market where 'capitalism, or pseudocapitalism, in its most primeval, ruthless, aggressive form' (Kapuściński, 1994) will foster all the population's worst
fears about the market system; a market in which energetic outbursts and dilettantish enthusiasm will be 'more important than
the planning, efficiency or details involved in completing a quality
job' (Wilson and Donaldson, 1996).

In a word, the Russian market is almost the polar opposite of
what many Russians aspire for it: to be a civilized place. Except
for those in Russia, who hanker after the good old days of communism, there is a general recognition, but not necessarily a joyous acceptance, that the civilized market will bring release from
totalitarianism, will help Russia to become a liberal society and
raise the standard of living (Yergin and Gustafson, 1994). On this
last point, it is important to grasp the psychological dimension.
Russians want a standard of living comparable to that of people in
western countries, who are regarded in all other respects as
Russia's equals and even in some respects their inferiors.

The envy-tinged frustration, which accompanies this attitude,
explains how emphatically it pains Russians to be compelled to
receive investment from the west in the humiliating form of
aid – and why one of the most despised and alienating things that
a western management expert can ever say in Russia is: 'We're here
to help.' In the meantime, to quote the *Financial Times* (1997),
Russia's 'new wealthy still behave more as plunderers than as
owners' – despite the general perception that it is foreign companies who are exploiting Russia and her people. For the time being,

and certainly for many years to come, Russia will be an uncivilized market, and this will continue to manifest itself in the tensions and uncertainties which beset professional relationships involving Russians and their western counterparts.

In Chapter 1 we quoted writers on experiences of doing business in Russia. It will be recalled that western firms' reports on doing business in Russia were described as a catalogue of 'chilling tales of failure and frustration ' (Dunayeva and Vipperman, 1995); that 'every negotiation is an occasion for Machiavellian intrigues, manoeuvring and posturing' (Richardson, 1995); that foreign investors may become unwitting objects of Russian disdain for allegedly 'buying up Russia cheap' (Kravchenko, 1995.) But it is not just the frictions in professional relationships which create exasperation. There can be quite separate causes as the following examples indicate. First, Wilson and Donaldson (1996) on an entirely plausible scenario:

> When the pre-Revolutionary plumbing system causes water to drip onto the computers, or when the company car has been at the mechanic for two weeks and the employees habitually arrive ten minutes late, smiling, it's tempting to yell something like, 'Doesn't anything in this %$!#$! country work right?'

The second story relates to a foreign participant in a business seminar in a top-price Moscow hotel. When the guest wished to send an urgent fax, no-one in the business centre knew how to operate it and no-one realized that somewhere there would be an instruction book. After 20 minutes huffing and puffing it was clear that nothing could be done. 'That's Russia for you', declared the hotel official using one of the great standard exculpatory utterances for such occasions; to which the foreigner, a Russian speaker, rejoined. 'You can't blame Russia. You should know how to use the equipment.' Scowl and shrug of Russian shoulders.

In Chapter 2, we cited the Moscow representative of the World Bank at a seminar held in December 1996. He claimed that at least 40 percent of management consultancy assignments failed in Russia. If we assume that the failure rate is comparable for similar development programmes sponsored by the IMF, the EBRD,

USAID, the TACIS programme of the EU, it means year in year out a multimillion dollar waste of resources and a staggering squandering of management time. At the operational interface, where western investors, management consultants and educators directly pursue activities with and for Russian counterparts, there is all too often 'a dialogue of the deaf' (Dunayeva and Vipperman, 1995). Where exactly are the sticking points? What are the flashpoints in these relationships?

Developing effective business relationships: a survey

In the following sections we attempt to tackle these issues by presenting the findings of a survey, commissioned by the publishers of this book, on problems of initiating and sustaining effective relationships with Russian business partners. This survey focused on the experiences of fourteen UK organizations across a broad range of involvements with Russia from marketing industrial products to provision of technical consultancy and delivery of management development programmes. We first present the western organizations' reactions and perceptions and then analyse them against what we believe to be Russian managers' psychological needs in relationships. As we shall discover, many of the UK organizations' experiences and perceptions both coincide with and illuminate many of the problem areas we identified in Chapter 2.

The survey had four key aims:

1 To identify factors which significantly influence the development of professional relationships between UK organizations and Russian partners.

2 To gather a cross-section of experiences and perceptions based on a minimum of five years' involvement with Russia.

3 To relate the findings and analysis to the Russian context.

4 To highlight implications for effective relationship management.

The research method made use of a questionnaire, which was followed by a structured interview with the focus of questions on the quality and characteristics of relationships with emphasis on one particular relationship for the survey. The theoretical underpinnings derive from the Interaction Approach, a methodology developed in Europe for the study of interorganizational interactions from episodic involvements to institutionalized relationships (Håkansson, 1982; Ford, 1990). The questions probed informants' experiences of five aspects of their interactions with Russian counterparts:

- *The perceived quality of the relationship*: with reference to factors such as its duration, the role of special expertise, the assessment of professional competencies of Russian counterparts, etc.

- *Coping with business communication and negotiation*: the role of interpreters, perceptions of language problems, professional evaluations of Russians as negotiators, their behaviour at meetings, etc.

- *Highlighting of special problems in relationship formation and management*: relating directly to the business sector or product/service category.

- *Perceptions of risk factors*: to one's business: personal safety.

- *Handling the informal side of business*: with special reference to Russian-style socializing

The following UK and Russian organizations took part in the survey (the year in brackets indicates commencement of the corporate relationship):

ABC [fictitious name at company's request] (consultancy services: gas industry) (1978)
AEA (nuclear safety services) (1961)
Andersen Consulting (consultancy services) (1990)
BP, Moscow (petroleum products/services) (1970)
British Council (1955)
British Embassy, Moscow (1924?)
CLX (chemical fertilizer import) (1990)
GPT (telecommunications equipment) (1989)
Husco (valves) (1992)
Image International (commodity trader) (1990)

Rehab Medical (medical equipment) (1993)
Simon Carves (chemical plant) (1958)
Simon Carves, Moscow (1958)
VP International (consultancy services) (1994)
Wolverhampton University (management training) (1992)
UMIST (1990)
Zeneca (pharmaceuticals) (since 1993 as Zeneca; 1955–1992 as ICI)
Zeneca, Moscow (pharmaceuticals) (1991).

In all, there were seventeen informants representing fourteen organizations (e.g. commercial, academic and governmental). Three provide technical consultancy services, six general management consultancy services (including two UK government departments), seven are suppliers of industrial products and one is a general trader.

The Russian counterpart organizations identified by the UK informants were as follows:

Banks
Belarus (a major tractor manufacturer)
charities
construction companies
an electronics joint venture
Gazprom (the major gas company)
hospitals and doctors
ministries (atomic energy communications health)
regional and local authorities
research institutes
trading houses
universities and higher teaching institutes
wholesalers.

The principal findings were:

- assessment of professional competencies of Russian business partners

- perceptions of risk

- evaluations of Russian business people as business communicators and negotiators

- commentary of business communication and negotiation as a process

- business communication and negotiation in terms of outcomes

- the social side of business.

Assessment of professional competencies of Russian business partners

The respondents were virtually unanimous about three factors. Russian business counterparts as a rule:

1 possessed strong intellectual abilities, especially regarding numeracy and grasp of technical factors

2 lacked good communication skills

3 were more skilled at purchasing than selling.

Concerning the first point, most experienced foreign visitors would agree that Russians are frequently very well educated in their own language, mathematics and in many branches of science. This otherwise positive benefit for the development of Russian management systems tends to disguise the fact that Russians expect to be dealing in business with foreign people as well educated as themselves.

Points 2 and 3 tend to support the conviction that Russians tend to lack flair for, or interest in, business (see Åslund, 1993; Chamberlain, 1995; Holden and Cooper, 1994; Remnick, 1994; Smith, 1991; Wilson and Donaldson, 1996; Yergin and Gustafson, 1994). The poor communication skills are attributable to three factors:

- a Russian cultural tradition which admires modesty in the statement of one's achievements

- the long-standing approach to teaching in Russia, and powerfully reinforced in the Soviet era, which actively discouraged participation and promotion of unorthodox views

- innate Russian bashfulness, which does not make Russians into natural salesmen (see Hingley, 1978; Holden, 1994).

This latter point partly explains the observation that Russians appear to be more adept at purchasing than selling.

This aversion to sales may also be a legacy of the 'old thinking': in the Soviet era industry was dominated by a supply-obsessed culture, and purchasing expertise was in any case more important to the Soviet economy than sales and marketing skills. Wilson and Donaldson (1996) take the view that, as Russia is such a powerful sellers' market, it is not difficult to move products. The hard part, they suggest, is getting those involved in the sales and marketing process to understand the basic concepts *behind the sales*.

Perceptions of risk

The views of our informants on the question of risk – to their investments and to themselves – came as a surprise:

1 normal commercial risk: not significantly high

2 anxieties: taxation, bureaucracy, 'mafias', personal safety and illness

3 crime: 'no worse than anywhere else'.

For several years Russia has been perceived as a very dangerous place (see Handelman, 1994). There is indeed no shortage of horror stories of foreign businessmen being beaten up and even killed by criminal groups; of intimidation to the local staff of foreign companies; of hijacking of foreign trucks; of the operations of middlemen – from shady fixers to well-placed government officials – to arrange deals and favours for foreign firms for an appropriate consideration, and so forth. Yet these facts of life did not seem to deter our informants; which possibly suggests that the picture we have in the west of crime-infested business in Russia is worse than it really is. In general, of course, it is Russians rather than foreigners who are intended victims of attacks.

Interestingly, our informants included 'taxation' and 'bureaucracy' under the questions of risk without any prompting. Foreigners cannot claim that they are uniquely targeted victims of the machinations of the government and its cumbersome, business-averse apparatus. Russian businessmen, as we saw in Chapter 5, share the same frustration.

Evaluations of Russian business people as business communicators and negotiators

Our informants focused on five issues under this topic. The prevailing point of view was that Russian business people in general:

1 want one big outcome

2 want personal relationships

3 'fear' being outsmarted

4 like to harangue

5 like meetings with bluster.

The first point is consistent with foreigners' observations that Russians have difficulty working simultaneously with the major issues and matters of detail, often leaving the latter for subordinates to deal with (Johanson, 1994; Wilson and Donaldson, 1996); that they wish to secure a quick result (Kappel et al., 1992; Wilson and Donaldson, 1996); that they may be blunt in the statement of their own position and make this position known early on without always having fallback positions or ploys at the ready. In other words, the Russian tendency is to pursue an overriding drive for absolute advantage (Kappel et al., 1992; Richardson 1995).

Concerning the other points, it is well known that Russians like to develop close personal relationships (Chamberlain, 1995; Holden, 1995; Kappel et al., 1992; Puffer and McCarthy, 1995; Wilson and Donaldson, 1996; Yergin and Gustafson, 1994). A useful perspective has been noted in a Finnish research programme, and it is worth quoting an extract from a case study on Finnish-Russian business interactions in the high-tech sector. The author discusses first the importance of personal relations in general among Russian business people:

New business emerges on the basis of relations with established friends and previous acquaintances. Good personal relations make interaction easier in any business situation, but their role has been traditionally emphasized in Russia. It is impossible to do business with a Russian if you do not get along with him personally. In addition . . . Russian firms have a short history and they have not had the time to earn a good reputation; therefore, trust is based on the people within the firm rather than on the firm itself.

This observation even concerns Western companies, but for a different reason: due to the limited information exchange and lack of international contacts on the Soviet side in the past, few Western companies are sufficiently well known (yet) on the Russian market for their Russian counterparts to trust them on the basis of reputation alone. Therefore, commitment and business between firms take place only if mutual trust between individuals is created first.

Salmi (1966a)

Another difficulty for foreigners is that Russians, even at the height of negotiation, are easily swung into conversational digressions; or they go off into 'non-listening' mode. The fear of being outsmarted should be seen as directly correlated to the Russian 'ancestral suspicion' of the west. As for points 4 and 5 in our list, these are not completely new to commentators on 'relationship development' with Russian business partners. They tie in with observations of the Russian relish for intrigue and posturing (Poe, 1995; Richardson, 1995) and a noted tendency to be vastly exuberant and enthusiastic about a project and then pull back from a commitment or promise (Hingley, 1978; Wilson and Donaldson, 1996), not to mention a noted inclination to lecture business partners on, say, the evils of capitalism or how they run their business operations (Hingley, 1978; Johanson, 1994; Wilson and Donaldson, 1996). It might be added here that informants found that their meetings were badly organized and that key Russian counterparts were not well prepared. They did not always seem to care or realize how this disadvantaged them.

Commentary of business communication and negotiation as a process

Our informants concurred that:

1 business negotiations are tough, slow and exasperating

2 the Russian side is acutely status conscious

3 the Russian side is obsessed with protocols

4 the boss is the boss

5 younger Russians are easier to deal with.

Our informants' perceptions on business communication and negotiation as a process both support and extend the views expressed here. Several experienced the Russian tendency to bargain hard, but negotiate clumsily. As Wilson and Donaldson (1996) have noted, Russians are inclined 'to see negotiating as a zero-sum game. That is, one side cannot win without the other side losing' and that 'a win-win situation [is] alien to their past experience'.

Three factors stood out as strongly influencing the processes. First, Russians are perceived as highly status conscious, wishing to be treated as equals – shades again of their ancestral suspicions – or want to share their values with business partners (see Dunayeva and Vipperman, 1995; Veiga, Yanouzas, and Buchholtz, 1995). However, as we shall argue later in this book, there is more to this Russian sensitivity than the mere wish to be treated as equals.

Point 3, about so-called protocols, needs clarification. The word *protokol* in Russian is translated in bilingual dictionaries by such expressions as 'minutes', 'record of the proceedings', 'report', 'transactions' of a meeting' (Oxford, 1993; Russkii Yazyk, 1991). Definitions in purely Russian dictionaries cover the same ground, but we find here that a protocol is a document which is described as an *akt* , meaning a document of legal significance, an authoritative deposition (Lyokhin, 1955; Ozhegov, 1984; Russkii Yazyk, 1993). The point is that in their business discussions Russian businessmen like to sign such protocols and even to have them countersigned by their foreign partners.

Under the highly formalized method of trade in the Soviet

Union, it is easy to imagine that a protocol could be regarded as a statement of intent. Our informants never suggested that protocols signed with their organizations had any kind of legal status. They noted that their counterparts seemed to be highly relieved if both sides agreed to sign. Indeed, the 'obsession with protocols' had much more to do with getting them signed than acting upon them subsequently. This is an interesting sideline on a solid Soviet business practice being prolonged into the new era, with the old psychology and the old phobias about having to cover your back when dealing with perfidious foreigners. Our evidence suggests that the bigger an organization, the more likely its thinking will still be Soviet style, and therefore the more likely it is to stick to protocols.

On point 4, we must understand that the role of the Russian boss is to be just that: to make the big decisions and then let various underlings sort out the details. The Finnish research mentioned earlier has suggested that the boss is also likely to want to start discussions about 'mammoth projects, and it is therefore the Western partner's task to suggest limitations and to offer projects of manageable size'. Bosses also 'expect the top management of the Western company to be involved in the negotiations.' The presence of the western boss is a sign of goodwill and commitment . . . although the actual expertise needed is often found at lower hierarchical levels (Salmi, 1996b). He therefore acts as a symbolic counterbalance to his 'all-powerful' Russian opposite number. It is not always easy for senior managers to accept this somewhat irritatingly decorational status with Russian counterparts, to whom delegation of responsibility to get the job done efficiently is not part of tradition.

It is no exaggeration to say that some of our informants often looked upon the presence of Russian bosses more as an elemental force in discussions who hindered rather than helped. Not surprisingly, several informants said they found working with younger Russians more productive: they were well educated, ambitious, quick on the uptake and less handicapped by the Soviet-style thinking which stifled initiative and independence of thought and action.

Business communication and negotiation in terms of outcomes

Curiously, when our informants were asked about outcomes of

discussions, none of them explicitly referred to agreed actions. They spoke either of protocols and contracts. The consensus of opinion seemed to be that:

1 Protocols can be useful – or not.

2 Contracts are not reliable – that is to say, legally binding – agreements as to what both parties agree to undertake.

3 Language differences are minimal.

4 Language differences are acute.

Many informants considered that you often had to trust the Russians to deliver whatever they had promised – and hope for the best. The informant who told us that a contract was 'an agreement in principle subject to change according to circumstances' was being realistic, not cynical. As for the seeming disagreement about language differences, these were specified by speakers of Russian and dismissed by non-speakers. The latter were inclined to find no problems with interpreters; the former were conscious of difficulties, many of which stemmed from the fact that western management and business terms and concepts lacked equivalents in Russian. Many of the tricky issues relating to language and problems of interlingual communication are examined in detail in Chapters 7 and 8.

The social side of business

Our informants were virtually unanimous on the following points:

1 There must be a social dimension to the business relationship.

2 Business entertainment is entertainment (i.e. an occasion for merriment).

3 There will or can be drinking and toasting to one's heart's content.

Russian hospitality is legendary, and so are the boozing and carousing that go with it. The Russians have a mysterious word for it: *otdykh*, which literally translates as 'rest' or 'relaxation', which gives the unwary guest no indication of how punishing a session of

Russian hospitality can be. It is unfortunately no good dismissing the Russian penchant for boozing, toasting and carousing as a quirk or social irritant. Practically any social involvement with Russian counterparts will call for tipple after tipple, toast after toast. All of this is central to the Russian concept of relationship building.

The changes initiated by the collapse of the Soviet Union mean that it is no longer risky for Russians to strike up more relationships with foreigners. They are free to invite them home and even put them up. This new freedom has of course been rapidly extended, as it were, to the domain of business contact. Now it is very common for western business people to spend a convivial evening with their Russian business partners and experience the exuberant and jading rigours of Russian hospitality. Whatever the good-natured motivations behind hospitality, its lasting memory on foreigners is that its main purpose is to ply them with food and drink – notably vodka – and break down their inhibitions as quickly as possible with the latter. All this merely continues at least 300 years of recorded history of Russians' delight in reducing their foreign guests to various degrees of alcoholic paralysis (see Hingley, 1978; Massie, 1992; White, 1996).

For those foreign businessmen to whom the prospect of Russian hospitality in merry abandon is not to be relished, there are glimmers of hope. First, younger Russians may be less inclined to be 'macho' about drink. One of our informants was relieved to find that among the up-and-coming entrepreneurs there was a preference for Guinness. Another informant had been confronted by a company's board members, who were all women. Be that as it may, (and this may appear to be strange advice – until you have been to Russia) foreign managers can benefit in their personal interactions with Russian counterparts through a wider appreciation of vodka as a significant social influence in its own right. Chapter 9 is be devoted to this fraught topic.

Insights for developing effective relationships

Careful scrutiny of our informants' reactions and the way in which these either complement or directly reinforce our current knowledge suggests that four major factors of considerable importance to Russians exert a striking influence on the quality, durability and outcomes of relationship development with foreign business counterparts. These factors are:

- the apparent Russian aversion to handling detail

- their extreme sensitivity about status with western businessmen ('the victorious capitalists')

- their negotiating style which presses for absolute advantage

- their wish for business relationships to have emotional charge.

We discuss each of these factors in turn, relabelling them so that we do not unwisely conflate them with our nominal equivalent notions.

Emotional solidarity and the boring detail

We have noted that Russian business people want warm relationships with their foreign partners, and Russian-style hospitality can swiftly create this effect. What Russians do not want is what they term a dry relationship (Mejevitch, 1993), in other words, a relationship without emotional charge. It may not be too much of an exaggeration to say that, whereas a western businessman wants to get close to his business partner to understand how to service his needs better, the Russian businessmen wants closeness in order to attain emotional solidarity. This particular need overrides the importance of long-term benefits, which may be central to the foreign partner's negotiating stance.

This means that pronouncements about mutual long-term benefits may not have much emotional and psychological appeal to Russians only if and unless there is an adjustment of the social distance between the Russian and his foreign business partner. In other words, whereas closeness in western business parlance implies an interorganizational intimacy to facilitate information exchanges and to respond to one another's business needs, closeness in the Russian context is more allied to concepts of social exchange. The important thing, therefore, is the intermingling of emotions: this often transcends the information need as well as an interest in matters of detail. To understand the Russian psychology on this point, information is often best presented to Russians in the form of innuendo, rumour and on the grapevine, exactly as it was in the Soviet Union (see Steele, 1994).

Wilson and Donaldson (1996) note that Russians get bored with the actual technicalities and intricacies of business, including the accompanying paperwork, which get in the way of doing a deal now. This reluctance to handle detail in preference to the grand design may be connected with traditional Russian gigantomania, which the Soviet system 'exploited' and even magnified with its tendency to proceed with (prestige) projects without adequate information at the working level, and hope for the best – which precisely describes the construction regime of the Chernobyl nuclear plant (see Read, 1993). Johanson (1994) observed a general Russian difficulty in handling 'the big picture' and matters of detail at the same time, and one of our informants commented that Russian managers like to make big decisions – fast. Once the big decision has been made, it will as a rule be left up to subordinates to sort out the boring details – which can place those subordinates in an invidious position (Wilson and Donaldson, 1996). So it is often the case that the boss fronts relationships 'strategically'.

In order to understand the Russian mindset on this rather difficult issue, it is also important to grasp that Russians experience great swings of emotion. All this is part of Russian dilettantism: the much-cherished freedom to be exuberant combined with the compulsion to switch enthusiasms, to embark on a new project – and leave other things half finished (Holden, 1992). In other words, in addition to attributing to Russian businessmen various weaknesses due to lack of experience for whatever reason, we need to take account of the mercurial side of the Russian character: that element in their makeup which inclines them literally and figuratively to change agendas.

The quest for absolute advantage

As in their political and military behaviour, so in their international business activities, Russians seek to secure and keep absolute advantage. Russians, as Wilson and Donaldson (1996) noted earlier, can only conceive of negotiating on a win-or-lose basis. The notion of negotiation as a means of sharing benefits with business partners is far from being a commonly accepted principle. The Russian negotiator is inclined to take up a fairly rigid position *a priori*, so rigid in fact that he only allows himself limited scope for manoeuvrability and hence concessions. Accordingly, it is up to the negotiating partner to make these concessions, a tactic which is seen by Russians as a sign both of the former's flexibility and of his weakness.

Understanding this general Russian posturing is essential knowledge for the foreign business partner. It means of course that the foreign partner must ensure that there is sufficient slack in his negotiating position, including his pricing tactics, to go through the motions of making concessions; which is singularly reminiscent of business negotiations with the USSR's centralized foreign trade corporations (see, for example, Kennedy, 1985). Our informants and the literature in the field give many indications of the Russian tendency to seek absolute advantage; they seek a quick result (Kappel et al., 1992; Wilson and Donaldson, 1996); they tend not to listen and to lecture the other side (Hingley, 1978; Johanson, 1994; Wilson and Donaldson, 1996); they relish intrigue, misconceive or misconstrue foreign partners' motives (*The Economist*, 1995; *Financial Times*, 1996a, 1996b; Kappel et al., 1992; Wilson and Donaldson, 1996); and they do not like handling information, as this is mere detail obscuring the big picture (Dunayeva and Vipperman, 1995; Holden, 1995; Johanson, 1994; Puffer and McCarthy, 1995; Wilson and Donaldson, 1996). In short, the Russian instinct is to seek absolute advantage; anything less means a shift to a weakened negotiating position.

The idea of equivalence

It is perhaps hardly surprising that Russians have a reputation for being hard bargainers, but not for being adroit negotiators. And the foreign businessman who assumes that negotiation with the Russians is a game which is concerned with achieving *da* has failed to understand the Russian mindset. Insight into this mindset requires some awareness of troublesome topics, such as traditional attitudes to money and money making, ambivalence to the west and a need for a business relationship to comprise intellectually and emotionally satisfying elements. Without this awareness the western businessman may not appreciate that the Russian way of seeking accommodations with foreign business partners is based on the conviction that it is the foreign partner who should be the more flexible – indeed demonstrably more flexible – in making adjustments to the relationship.

It is in this aspiration we find what Vlachoutsicos (1995) illuminatingly describes as the Russian desire for equivalence, as distinct from equality in their relationships with western business partners. At the heart of this desire for equivalence is a Russian conviction that Russians are no less intelligent, educated or competent than people elsewhere, but Russia has a lot of problems which make it difficult at the moment to harness all her talents. At the same time, Russia still has undisputed potential as an economic and technological powerhouse. It is, the Russians will point out, the selfsame potential which transformed a largely backward agricultural country into the second most powerful country on earth in a matter of decades; was instrumental in defeating Nazi Germany; launched the world's first artificial satellite; created a scientific establishment which in its heyday (the 1970s) comprehensively rivalled achievement in the western world (Graham, 1993), and presented over many decades a fully fledged alternative model of global economic development.

The fact that the communist leadership sacrificed millions of Russians and non-Russians in the Gulag (see Conquest, 1992), kept the rest behind the country's borders and deprived them of what we consider to be basic necessities of life over several decades – all this does not diminish the argument. The Russian businessman who used the example of Russia's launch of the first Sputnik (in October 1957) to impress a would-be joint venture partner from the UK is using a past – and world-famous – technological achievement to demonstrate contemporary potential. He knows that his enterprise is not technologically equal to the UK firm now, but it has the potential to be. This 'posture' requires of a foreign business partner a recognition of equivalence in the situation. Awareness of a Russian need for equivalence is one thing, but building this need into a viable business arrangement is something else.

Thus the advice that 'western managers should expect to approach their Russian counterparts as equals' sounds sensible enough, but is misplaced. Likewise the assumption guiding a crosscultural management programme in Moscow, which allows 'Russians and Americans to learn from one another . . . preserving the best from both cultures' (Dunayeva and Viperman, 1995) seems to miss an essential component of the Russian mindset. To make the distinction between equality and equivalence absolutely clear: there is only one time-honoured way in Russia of achieving equality with foreigners – at least in the short term – and that is to ply and quite possibly anaesthetize them with vodka (Holden, 1997).

Need, outward expression and coping strategy

Given the results of our survey and exploration of the literature in the field, we now present a framework (Table 6.1) for understanding the mindset of Russian business partners as negotiators and 'relationship developers'. The framework is in the form of a grid, in which four posited psychological needs of Russian businessmen, as reflected in the four thematic factors just discussed, are highlighted in the left-hand column. The central column suggests the outward expression of this need, and the right-hand column posits the basis for a western coping strategy, that is to say a strategy facilitating adaptation, at the organizational and individual level of interaction, to Russia's restless business environment.

This framework is, of course, tentative, but it derives from direct empirical investigation of our informants' experiences of Russians as business negotiators, supplemented by the observations of other commentators. It attempts to suggest partial solutions, in the form of coping strategies, to accommodate what Russians seem to hold dear in their business relationships: the need for absolute advantage, equivalence, emotional congruence and boredom limiting stimulation. Most significantly, the framework gives psychological pointers to foreign negotiators who have somehow got to take control of their interactions with Russian counterparts on those occasions before discussions dissolve into mutual exasperation and brooding miscomprehension.

A comment is also needed on the coping strategy which suggests

Table 6.1 Framework for understanding Russian business partners' mindset

Russian negotiators' need	Outward expression	Coping strategy for western business partners
Need for perceived absolute advantage	Incapability or reluctance to modify the initial negotiating position	Build plenty of slack into offers and the methods of making the offers to give Russians the illusion that they have wrung concessions out of you
Need for equivalence	References to Russia's vast potential as an economic partner and the great technological achievements of the Soviet era	Treat Russians as if Russia is as powerful as it used to be; respect Russia's potential; avoid negative references to Russia
Need for emotional satisfaction/ congruence	Exuberant hospitality; sudden displays of emotion; descent into sentimentality; seemingly inexplicable switchings of position and mood	Understand that Russians expect foreign partners to be more accommodating to them than vice-versa; use language grandiloquently about working together; speak to Russians' hearts and heads simultaneously
Need for antidotes for boredom	Swift verbal commitment to the grand scheme; reluctance to discuss matters of detail; partner expected to take over the problems which the Russian side cannot be bothered with	Move back and forth among key points; alternate between being hard nosed and flexible; use humour to lighten atmosphere

that the western businessman, seeking to accommodate the Russian wish for emotional congruence, needs to address his Russian partners grandiloquently with appeal to their hearts. The western negotiator must develop an understanding for the Russian love of language – of even badly interpreted language – in its poetic and rhetorical modes especially at social gatherings. The Russians prize eloquence, which they (perhaps deceptively) see as a hallmark of a civilized person; they enjoy grandiloquence because it appeals to the romantic and sentimental element of their character. Toasting at meals, when the vodka flows, is when Russian and foreigner alike can indulge this cherished facility with words. For the Russians, hearty feasts, carefree merrymaking and lavish toasting are all very much part and parcel of doing business.

The survey summarized

The survey plainly reveals how western professionals and their Russian counterparts do not bring to their encounters necessarily compatible or even reconcilable assumptions about their role vis-à-vis one another. The atmosphere of interactions can be prickly to the point of hostility. Russian partners, it seems, have a problem with being partners. The impression is that in the Russian perception of relationships one side must dominate and the other be abject and fawning. Little wonder then that the Russian negotiators are inclined to harangue and lecture their western colleagues, to bluster defensively in case they, the westerners, true to form, get up to their tricks of being clever, superior and catching them out. Listening to the other side is not the Russian's strong point.

We saw too how the Russian position in negotiations and relationships is strongly influenced by the boss. He sets the tone, makes the decisions, does not trouble himself with matters of detail: the underlings deal with all that. The boss is much preoccupied with his status. He is definitely *primus inter pares* with his colleagues but is no worse than you, his foreign counterpart. In the more formal sessions he will stress to you the potential of Russia. The potential, he will argue, guarantees the investment. There is, therefore, no problem, hence the detail can be swept aside. The detail gets in the way of the relationship, and the relationship can come alive when the vodka is flowing, when the hearty toasts cement not so much the deal as the moment of boozy bonhomie it has given rise to. All this leaves the inexperienced foreigner bewildered, confused and possibly sizzling with anger, because the impression he has is that his Russian counterpart keeps switching his mood and changing his mind. He may at one moment appear cooperative, charming and friendly, the next hostile and cantankerous. Indeed he may even display both conflicting emotions at the same time (that is what being Russian is). So what gets the business? Answer: sheer persistence, a capacity not to be browbeaten by Russian bluster, and flexibility as a reflex to Russian mutability.

Russians' emotions are on virtual permanent display. Indeed no study of Russians which discounts the fact that an emotional manifestation is an integral part of their normal reaction to events and pressures is likely to ring true. But the problem facing foreigners in their professional contacts is that Russian reactions frequently appear to be contradictory. At this point it is perhaps judicious to leave the reader in the very safe hands of Ronald Hingley (1978), who provides a brilliant explanation of this complicated issue. He comments:

> Since the Russians have already been observed oscillating between the extremes of life-enhancement and life-denial, it will not be surprising if they also exhibit other opposed characteristics. Broad, yet narrow; reckless, yet cautious; tolerant, yet censorious; freedom-loving, yet slavish; independent, docile, tough, malleable, kind, cruel, loving, hating, energetic, lazy, naïve, cynical, polite, rude – they will be found veering in all these directions at some time or other; as what people will not?
> [. . .]
> The Russian speciality is a tendency for a single individual or group to alternate between one extreme position and its opposite; or even, somehow, to occupy two or more mutually exclusive positions simultaneously.

You have been warned!

Conclusion

It is evident that the findings of the survey on relationship management and the findings of the workshop on problems of transfer of western management know-how to Russia tend to be mutually reinforcing. There is all in all no doubt that Russian and western management systems are on a veritable collision course.

The Russians are, in a nutshell, doggedly determined to do

things their way (which is, of course, their prerogative) and are therefore pursuing – not for the first time in their history – yet another alternative path whereby Russia will somehow lead the west 'on to a higher and higher stage of civilisation' (Hosking, 1997). This alternative path is a most distinctively Russian one. It is a quest for an economic system which, as we noted in Chapter 5, can espouse and foster the enduring Russian values of communitarianism, equality, democracy and participation – all concepts which do not dovetail neatly into corresponding western notions and which western management finds awkward to accommodate in its own philosophies and practices.

So far in the book, we have attempted to explain why it is that a complicated and persistent clash of values and assumptions seems to exist between Russian and western managers. We have approached these issues from the perspectives of many disciplines, but even though we may have provided insights into the Russian managerial temper, we have not directly addressed the issue of how to cope with the ever-present potential for mutual miscommunication and recrimination. In the final four chapters of this book we attempt to explore four themes that present themselves as essential intercultural know-how for those who are charged as investors, consultants and educators to agree and harmonize actions with Russian counterparts.

RUSSIANS, LANGUAGE AND

COMMUNICATION

Of all the numerous features of the Russian language one should first and foremost highlight . . . its capacity to express all knowledge accumulated by mankind in every field of endeavour and its semantic universality; from which it flows that its literary language is able to describe human life in its entirety

— *Filin, 1979*

In my experience, the art of conversation is pursued in Moscow at a higher level than anywhere else on earth.

— *Hosking, 1991*

Introduction

Personal relationships are of extreme importance to Russian managers, and we have already highlighted those factors which help to maintain, and those which definitely do *not* help to maintain relationships between western firms and their Russian business partners. 'Relationship management' is very demanding and frustrating for both sets of partners, so great is the scope for mutual misunderstanding and misdirection of intentions. It is therefore not an exaggeration to say management of relationships with Russian counterparts calls for communication skills, not so much of high order as of an unusual kind.

Communicating with Russians means understanding their frame of reference. In this chapter, we continue this process of exploration by investigating aspects of the Russian language. You do not need to know a single word of Russian, but without reading this chapter you will never be able to understand the psychology of your Russian counterparts and know how to communicate with them in formal and informal settings; which means that you will be at a severe disadvantage when it comes to negotiation (Chapter 8).

In this chapter we shall tackle a variety of topics to do with the Russian language, such as modes of address and interpersonal communication 'Russian style'. Russians address and refer to one another in a way that is markedly different from west European and American usages. It is important to understand the principles of the Russian system of address, because the foreign business person can use it to his or her advantage to develop and maintain the appropriate level of social distance: achieving this is crucial for meeting the Russian desire for equivalence in relationships with foreigners. Insight into the Russian style of interacting with others, and the characteristic role of language in these processes, is vital knowledge for the business negotiator: it is a path to their psychology and therefore to the dispositions which they bring to their business interactions with foreigners. But first, with a brief overview of the Russian language.

The Russian language

Russian is a Slavonic language and a close cousin of Ukrainian, Polish, Czech and Bulgarian. Over the centuries, Russians and non-Russians alike have spoken of the vigour, vitality and expressiveness of Russian. German-born Catherine the Great (1729–96) found that Russian 'is richer in hard, concrete words than French or German, and therefore a better instrument for talking about the visible world'. The great Russian writer Turgenev (1818–83) hailed the 'great, mighty, truthful and free Russian tongue' (in de Bray,

1980). The Russian language is spoken by 150 million Russians and by an additional 100 million non-Russian citizens of the former Soviet Union.

Russians and Russian

Arguably, the most important defining feature of Russians and their culture is their language. Every Russian knows, and probably believes in Turgenev's famous description of Russian language as 'great, mighty, truthful and free'. This conviction about the greatness of Russian transcends and has transcended Russia's darkest hours. Russian may not have quite 'the divine status' (Zeldin, 1984) of French in France, but their language is vastly cherished by Russians. The foreigner who walks among them and does not appreciate this fact is a Philistine; he is failing to exploit one of the great cultural clues for 'relationship development' with Russians.

Whereas to the French, their language is a supreme instrument for analytical thought and logical expression, to the Russians their language is a great emotional resonator: a repository of all that is expressible – and pardonable – about the human condition. Their great literature is a perfect testimony to the potency of the Russian language in this regard. The Russians, who love singing and poetry as well as respecting great literature, are easily stirred by language, which makes a direct emotional appeal to them. All Russians seem to know and can quote by heart lines from their great poets, and they like to quote these things in company – not at a business meeting, but quite possibly over a meal with foreign associates and perhaps especially as part of a toast (see Chapter 9). For many Russians advertisements of foreign products are seen as threat to their great literary heritage. According to Wilson and Donaldson (1996), 'sociologists complain that children today can name the foreign candy bars but not recite the poetry of Alexander Pushkin, as they could in the past.'

The vigour and creative verve of Russian have struck native and foreign observers alike. The redoubtable Catherine the Great who learnt Russian as a young woman, liked the language because, in her words, it is 'so rich, so energetic, and you can manipulate it as you wish.' She also declared to a confidante that 'our Russian language, uniting as it does the strength, richness and energy of German with the sweetness of Italian, will one day become the standard language of the world' (in Cronin, 1989).

According to a leading British linguistic scholar, by the 19th century Russian 'had become the instrument to express great, humanistic ideas, which were to become the property and heritage . . . of the whole civilised world' (de Bray, 1980). Another authority has described Russian as a language of 'immense power and beauty, rich in synonyms, capable of expressing the subtlest nuances of meaning' (Leeming, 1994). Part of the sheer richness of Russian is due to the fact that over the centuries it has absorbed thousands of words from European and Asian cultures, giving the language its special flavour.

The point here is not to extol the Russian language, but to bring home an important fact about Russians: they are not only proud of their language, they also respect it and the great literature that has been composed in it. And this has a startling consequence. Russians, when they visit homes in, say, Britain, are shocked not to find the works of Dickens or Galsworthy (pace the *Forsyte Saga*) on bookshelves in people's living rooms. In their living rooms you will find not only the collected works of Pushkin, Tolstoy, Dostoyevsky and Turgenev, but volumes of books in translation by Dickens and Galsworthy. [**Russian literature**] The Russians read these books for pleasure and self-enrichment. They are mystified that foreigners turn their backs on the great literature of their own country.

It may not be an exaggeration to say that Russian visitors find this form of indifference sadly typical of materialistic, money-grabbing societies, unfortunately the very ones that post-communist Russia is supposed to be modelling itself on. Russians, as a rule, prefer to deal with foreigners whom they do not classify as *nekulturniy*, literally 'uncivilized', but implying a moral judgment on someone who lacks proper educational polish. Foreign businessmen may be unaccustomed to being subjected to this kind of moral scrutiny, but in Russia they must take account of it in their dealings. Being *kulturniy* is part of the impression that a foreign businessman should convey to his Russian associates; being *kulturnyi* can also make you look and sound less boring to Russians. If your Russian business partner discovers that you, a foreign business-

Russian literature

In the 19th and 20th centuries Russia has produced writers of international repute. Pushkin (1799–1837) has been described not only as the finest lyric poet of the 19th century, but also 'the Mozart of literature' (Milner-Gulland and Dejevsky, 1990). Tolstoy (1828–1910) 'wrote – to a degree not attained by any other modern writer in any other language – perfect prose, prose that possesses so many capillaries as to elude even the most refined *explication de texte*' (Field, 1971). As for Dostoyevsky (1822–1881), it has been written that he 'possesses a certain quality which is different in kind to any other writer, a power of seeming to get nearer to the unknown, to what lies beyond the flesh' (Baring, 1960). Indeed, many say that it is Dostoyevsky and not Tolstoy who is Russia's greatest novelist. The 19th century produced other great writers: Chekhov, Gogol, Gorky, Turgenev, to mention but a few. Writers active in the 20th century and throughout most of the communist period from 1932 onwards were compelled to obey the ideological requirement for literature to conform to 'Socialist Realism'. This policy was defined as 'truthful, historically concrete presentation of reality in its revolutionary development', which 'must be combined with the task of the ideological remaking and education of toilers in the spirit of socialism'. Many writers did conform, but others such as Pasternak and Solzhenitysn did not, thereby exposing themselves to party-backed hate campaigns and harassment. *Perestroika* was a liberating experience for Russian writers and today there is no censorship. Yet Russia – and perhaps the world – is waiting for an epic of *War and Peace* proportions to describe 'ordinary' life and the impact on it of great and terrible events of the 20th century. There are those who say that the new conditions of literary freedom are not conducive to a sustained creative drive: modern writers lack the necessary restrictions. A very Russian point of view.

man, have read even in translation one of the great 19th-century Russian novels, this will almost be viewed as business competence.

Pre-revolutionary and Soviet Russian

Not for the first time in her history Russia's political upheavals are creating the need for 'a new language'. In the 17th and 18th centuries the great reformers Peter the Great (1672–1725) and Catherine the Great (1729–96), brought new ideas, artefacts and impulses from western Europe. The resulting influx of foreign words to describe these influences, it was disapprovingly noted, engendered 'a thousand new concepts', and 'more than two thirds of the Russian lexicon passed out of use' in the process (Entwistle and Morison, 1949). Words for science and learning came from Germany; the vocabulary of the social graces from France (Hosking, 1997). After the 1917 Revolution the Russian language took on a dramatically different character, stemming from the new socialist-scientific conditions including the growth of literacy, universal education, urbanization, equal rights for women, and the high rate of upward social mobility.

The language sprouted ungainly collections of compound words, discarded unnecessary (i.e. ideologically undesirable) foreign words, and reflected the cult of gigantomania, as evidenced in the effusive glorification of the achievements of the workers (Ward, 1965). Hingley (1978) has described this language of glorification as a 'priestly and hieratic argot', deriving partly from the powerful liturgical traditions of Old Church Slavonic. Although the Revolution was carried out in the name of the working class, the linguistic norms of that class did not prevail, but the old colloquial became stylistically neutral and hitherto non-standard forms became the colloquial standard (Comrie and Stone, 1978).

All in all, the Russian of the Soviet Union became strongly politicized, reflecting new institutions and new ideological positions, generating 'an entire panoply of totalitarian shibboleths' (Fallowell, 1994.) The most conspicuous area of linguistic change in Russian during the Soviet period concerned lexis with the major shifts in the operational (and permitted) vocabularies of politics and public administration; agriculture; industry; the armed forces (Comrie and Stone, 1978). This outward language has been termed *novoyaz*, a newspeak 'formed over dozens of years, great clots of language that had no purpose other than meaninglessness, the putting off of meaning, the softening of meaning . . . [This] Party language had a ruinous effect on Russian, so much so that when people heard a speech by Sakharov, one of the first things they would comment upon – even before the inevitable wisdom of it – was the purity of his Russian'. (Remnick, 1994). Matthews (1967) has drawn attention to 'the demagogic colloquialism' of Soviet Russian, noting that its imaginative literature, which of course tended to idealize socialist life, was 'rich in vulgarisms, provincialisms, and slang, both word and phrase, and in the acronyms, abbreviations and cliches that infest the vocabulary of modern living'. All in all, 20th-century Russian has been characterized by the elevation of its vernacular heritage into literary status for a multicultural empire, that lasted 70 years.

In other respects, Russian became, in effect, the language of social, cultural and political advancement of the Soviet Union (Comrie, 1981; de Bray, 1980; Hajdu, 1975; Isaev, 1977). It further established itself as a major language of science (Buxton and Jackson, 1962); but, despite a sycophantic fraternal claim from the former GDR, Russian never was a language of commerce 'next to English' (Kohls, 1981). Nor did Russian fulfil Stalin's dream that it should be a 'victorious language . . . destined to influence the world language of the remote Communist future' (Hingley, 1978). Perhaps that rightly served Stalin, given his quirky dabbling in linguistics, or rather 'pseudo-linguistics' (Conquest, 1993). Lastly, and significantly, throughout the entire Soviet period (i.e. from 1917 to 1991), the peoples of the USSR had relatively little exposure to foreign (i.e. western) influences. This meant, at risk of oversimplification, that Russian was deprived of lexical resources for the description and apprehension of western phenomena (except, arguably, in fundamental rather than applied science). This ideologically motivated semantic and conceptual vacuum is now proving one of the major influences on Russia's business interactions with western countries.

The Russian language after the collapse of the USSR

With the collapse of the Soviet Union in 1991, the Russian language is again experiencing a new reorientation. One can say with some certainty that three trends are already clearly manifesting themselves. First, the general influence of Russian is shrinking over the territory of the former Soviet Union. Former Soviet republics, which are now independent states (e.g. Ukraine, the Baltic republics, Georgia and Moldova) are promoting their own national languages as a form of new-found national and cultural assertion. One striking feature here is the increasing use of the adjective *rossiiskii*, which refers to the Russian state, in contrast to *russkii*, which conveys ethnic (exclusively) Russian associations (Götz and Halbach, 1994).

Second, entire areas of Russian lexis are becoming redundant: the language of socialism is being eroded. This is most clearly manifest in the extensive transformation of place names, with hundreds of names of cities, institutions and streets being 'depoliticized' or reverting to pre-1917 nomenclature (*The Economist*, 1994a, 1994b.) Third, Russian is absorbing hundreds of foreign terms in either direct and transliterated forms from foreign languages (especially English). One might, incidentally, add a fourth area, which is not discussed further in this contribution: the emergence of underworld slang, based on criminal and camp argots, as a kind of 'in-language' of the new breed of 'gangster–capitalists', who run the former Soviet Union's massive shadow economy (Handelman, 1994). In Chapter 2 we discussed one aspect of language change in Russian: the inadequacies of Russian as a repository of modern management terms and concepts.

A great language, nevertheless

But, whatever its future, the Russian language will for ever be the repository of 'one of the greatest literatures in the history of civilization' (Brown, Kaser and Smith, 1994). It will remain the language of a 'brilliant and vital people' (de Bray, 1980); and, as Turgenev noted, it will give Russians 'succour and support . . . in days of doubt, in days of painful reflection about [Russia's] fate.'

Russian names and modes of address

To the uninformed outsider, the Russian language imposes two immediate barriers to cultural and psychological closeness. The first is the alphabet. [**Cyrillic alphabet**] The second concerns Russian names, or rather the Russian system of naming and the associated conventions of address. From the foreigner's point of view, the con-

Cyrillic alphabet

The Cyrillic alphabet hangs like a portcullis, protecting yet affording glimpses of Russian culture to the untutored eye. Its name derives from St Cyril of Thessalonika (in Russian *Kirill*) who devised the alphabet for the Slavs so that they could read the holy scriptures in the common Slavonic tongue. This was done in, or perhaps shortly before, the year 863, when Cyril and his brother Methodius set about their missionary business. The letters that make up the Cyrillic script come from the Latin, Greek and Hebrew alphabets; in addition Cyril invented some new letters for Slavonic sounds that had no counterpart in those languages. The written language, which the alphabet created, was used exclusively for liturgical purposes and is known today as Old Church Slavonic (also called Old Bulgarian).

The Cyrillic script has been subject to reform over the centuries, and countries where it has been adopted – Russia, Ukraine, Bulgaria and some regions of the former Yugoslavia – each has its own variation. Today the modern Russian alphabet consists of 34 letters.

Anyone who has learnt Russian is acutely aware of the problem of transliterating words written in Cyrillic into phonetically equivalent forms in the Latin alphabet. Any respectable book on Russin produces a commentary on this problem and craves the indulgence of readers with knowledge of the problem. The absence of agreed conventions means that there exist different Latin variations of the same Cyrillic word. For example, the name of the composer Tchaikovsky (which is the conventional spelling) can also be written as Chaikovskii or Chaykovskiy, but no-one would recognize these. Then, too, the transliterations vary from one European language to another. Thus, the composer Shostakovich becomes Chostakovitch in French; Gorbachev is written Gorbatschow in German.

fusion seems to be connected with 'the endless array of names for one person' (Gerhart, 1974). Every Russian, as will be explained more fully later on, has three names, but with full forms, short forms, special usages associated with each name such as nicknames, there are in theory twelve possible ways of addressing every Russian (Comrie and Stone, 1978).

Not only that: first names can have a full form and various short forms that range from the very endearing to the downright contemptuous. With so many permutations of names it is no wonder

that generations of foreigners have been put off reading translations of the great Russian novels – quite apart from having to cope
with formidable-looking surnames like Svidrigailov, Lebezyat-
nikov and Razumikhin (who all feature in Dostoyevsky's *Crime
and Punishment*). It has been observed that handling the Russian
system of address requires discipline (Mattock, 1996). Understanding how it works may not automatically reduce social gaffes,
but the payoff can come when you need to establish a relationship
on a warmer footing. (With Russians, remember, it is better to
think of relationships in terms of degrees of warmth rather than in
terms of closeness).

The Russian 'tripartite' system of naming started to develop in
the 15th century, only becoming formalized at the time of Peter the
Great (Comrie and Stone, 1978). Needless to say, it all evolved
around the families of the upper strata of society; the peas-
antry – the overwhelming majority in the Russian population –
were not provided with surnames before the emancipation of 1861
(Unbegaun, 1972). Everyone who has studied Russian learns the
naming system in order to address Russians properly. Those who
have not studied Russian, but who are professionally involved with
Russians, must understand how the system works, because it forms
a central pillar of all social interaction. From the foreign businessman's point of view ignorance of the system is unlikely to cause a
problem with Russians, but it can perpetuate social distance, and
social distance is something Russians do not like. Social distance
with a foreigner will often be put down, however mistakenly, to his
arrogance and big headedness, Russian pet hates. Now to the
system of address.

Every Russian has three names: a forename, followed by a patronymic and lastly a surname. Until the Russian Revolution of
1917, the forename was literally a Christian name: the Orthodox
Church baptized children with a forename taken from their list of
saints. The best way to explain the system is with an example,
using the plausible name Sergei Ivanovich Pavlov. This name indicates that Sergei Pavlov is the son of Ivan Pavlov, who in turn
might be the son of Konstantin, and so *his* full name would be Ivan
Konstantinovich Pavlov. The suffix –vich therefore means 'son of',
corresponding to Ben in Hebrew and Ibn in Arabic (it is supposed

to be connected with the Latin *filus* 'son' and to the Scots 'Fitz-', referring to illegitimate offspring). There is another form of the male patronymic, which is -in. If Ivan Pavlov had a daughter called Anna, her full name would be Anna Ivanovna Pavlova. Note that Russian female names take a-endings. The female patronymic forms are -ovna and -evna. In fast speech Russians tend to 'swallow' part of the patronymic: Konstantinovich could be pronounced as 'Konstantinich.'

As we have already seen, this system of names permits Russians to address one another in a variety of forms. As a rule, and except in the family circle and with close frends, Russians (i.e. adults) tend to use the combination of first name and patrononymic. Russians on intimate terms would use first names, and often accepted shortened forms of their names. For instance, Vanya is the common short form of Ivan; Seriozha is the corresponding form of Sergei. But there are other variants on their names too, each with specific emotional loading. For example, there are five different forms of Ivan to express degrees of endearment and a specific form (Vanka), which is pejorative. But it is probably the common female name Anna that wins hands down: there are some 20 variations. Actually, Anna only wins if we exclude the word *Papa*, which comes in more than 30 forms of endearment (Gerhart, 1974). **[Papa]**.

For purposes of simplification, we can say that Russians address one another using the forename and patronymic. Use of the forename by itself is largely restricted to the family and among intimates, such as close friends and schoolchildren. In such cases, the shortened rather than full form of the name will be used. It should be noted that these shortened forms are, strictly speaking, not the equivalent of nicknames, which are less common in Russian than in American or British society (with the possible exception of the criminal fraternity).

The neat thing about the Russian mode of address, using forename plus patronymic, is that it allows both intimacy and distance at the same time. Note, however, that the Russian words for Mr or Mrs (the word corresponding to Miss is the same word) are not used as part of the addressing formula. The use of Mr (or Mrs) with just the surname would be, depending on circumstances, facetious, possibly even provocative. When Gorbachev met people throughout

Papa

The Russian word for dad or pop is basically *papa*, but it comes in at least 33 different forms, each with its distinctive level of affection, playfulness, facetiousness and intimacy. Rusians enjoy playing with names, so the list should not be regarded as definitive.

pa	papenka	papunka
pap	papishche	papunya
papanchik	papka	papus
papanechka	papochka	papusechka
papanenka	papulchik	papusenka
papanka	papulechka	papushenka
papanya	papulenka	papushka
papanyushka	papulik	papusik
papasha	papulka	papusya
papashechka	papulya	
papashenka	papun	
papashka	papunenka	

the USSR, he would be greeted by his fellow citizens as Mikhail Sergeyevich: not Mr Gorbachev, not Mr President. By the same token a factory worker would address his boss as (say) Ivan Pavlovich without prior acquaintance. No disrespect would be implied. The thing to remember about the Russian system of address is that the combination of first name plus patronymic is the equivalent of Mr (or Mrs) plus surname. In other words, Mikhail Sergeyevich is the equivalent of Mr Gorbachev in our terms.

In common with other European languages Russian has an intimate form for you, *ty*, corresponding to *tu* in French or *du* in German and a formal form, *vy*, corresponding to *vous* in French and *Sie* in German. As a rule, when you are on first name terms, you might use *ty*; and when using first name plus patronymic, *vy* is appropriate. Although it is possible to envisage situations in which *vy* might be used with first names only, the use of *ty* in conjunction with first name and patronymic is idiosyncratic. With respect to the use of *vy* with first names, Russian men, meeting a woman for the first time, might address her by a diminutive form:

Lenochka for Lena, Verochka for Vera. But, when addressing her as you, they would use the significantly less intimate form *vy*. This 'instant' intimacy is generally not felt by Russian women to be ingratiating.

What are the implications for foreigners dealing with Russians? The first thing is that you need to know all the names of the Russians you deal with. You may know that you are having a discussion with Mr Ivanov, but other Russians will refer to him in your presence by his first name and patronymic. To make things slightly complicated, the English version of Russian names on business cards frequently indicate the patronymic by its first letter, e.g. Ivan S. Ivanov. The full patronymic will always be given on the Russian side of the card. Therefore, if you do not know Russian or cannot read the Cyrillic alphabet well enough, ask for the patronymic.

When it comes to addressing Russians, it is acceptable for foreigners to use Mr or Mrs plus their surname, but often Russians like to be on first-name terms with people they like or hope will like them. In such cases a Russian will say: 'Call me Ivan'. Foreigners who know the Russian language will tend to adopt the Russian usage already described, but it is normal to wait for a Russian to suggest that you address him using *ty* rather than *vy*. Such an invitation can occur in a toasting session or over drinks generally (see Chapter 8). However, as one of our informants noted, there can be a problem the day after: how do you address the Russian on the next occasion. *Ty* may suddenly sound presumptive or overfamiliar; *vy* may be interpreted as a sign of rejection of friendship. If in doubt, stick to *vy*.

Foreign businessmen may occasionally find themselves addressing several Russians (for example, at a banquet). In English the word 'you' does not sound cold, but its equivalent in Russian (*vy*) does. To get round this, you are advised to talk either in terms of 'we' and 'us' (which is good for 'togetherness'); or to address the assembled as 'dear colleagues' or '(dear) friends'. 'Dear' in this instance will normally be translated into Russian as 'respected'. Foreigners are usually advised not to use the word 'comrades' in English or Russian, unless you want to be facetious and provided that you know that the company you are in – which might include the odd unreconstructed communist – will appreciate your waggishness. Those with a good command of Russian and, on the right occasion (such as a toasting session), might use the word *rebyata* (lads) with those he knows well. One of our Russian-speaking colleagues used to amuse Russians (all men) in drinking bouts by addressing them with the word *devushki* (girls).

In conclusion it may be worth adding a few words about Russian names. Many names have direct or very close equivalents in English, e.g. Alexander, Andrey (Andrew), Nikolai (Nicholas), Anna, Mariya (Maria/Mary), Yekaterina (Catherine), Yelena (Helen), etc. Others are slightly more disguised equivalents, e.g. Ivan (John), Pavel (Paul), Yuri (George). In some cases the short form of the first name is not always apparent. Figure 7.1 provides a list of common Russian names with 'non-obvious' short forms.

Male names	
Alexander:	Sasha (*cf* Scots Sandy)
Aleksey:	Alyosha
Anatolii:	Tolya
Dmitri:	Dima, Mitya
Mikhail:	Misha
Nikolai:	Kolya
Viktor:	Vitya
Vladimir:	Volodya
Yevgenii:	Zhenya
Female names	
Anna:	Anya, Nyura
Margarita:	Rita
Yekaterina:	Katya
Yelena:	Lena

Figure 7.1 Some Russian names and their short forms

Lastly, under forenames it is worth noting that Russia in this century has tended to be conservative about adopting non-traditional and foreign forenames. The Russian Revolution of 1917 did not have the effect of dramatically expanding the corpus of names to reflect the new social consciousness, as might have been expected. There have been some notable curiosities such as Vladlen, a first name derived from *Vlad*imir *Len*in (there are still a few Vladlens around); Ninel (Lenin spelt backwards); and Dotnara, an abbreviation based on three Russian words 'daughter [*do* . . .] of the toiling [*t* . . .] people [*nar* . . .]'. There is one attested reference to Embrion ('embryo') – if ever a name was waiting for stardom in a smash-hit sci-fi movie!

Once the Orthodox Church lost its power to give names, the 20th century saw the revival of heroic mediaeval names Russian such as Igor and Vsevolod. Some foreign names have proved popular in the Soviet period such as Eduard, Albert and Artur among men, Nelli, Klara and Emilia among women. The most successful innovation has proved to be hugely popular Svetlana, a 19th-century Russian female forename without saintly claims.

Russian communicative styles

To understand something of how Russians use language among themselves is to gain insights into them as communicators. This is vital knowledge for understanding their psychology and for communicating with them even through interpreters. In this section we examine three striking features of Russian interpersonal communication systems.

Although these are features which can only be experienced by Russian themselves or foreigners with a very competent command of the language, they are highlighted here precisely because they reveal a good deal about normal Russian behaviour which foreign business people may find difficult to apprehend and accommodate (those selfsame foreigners forgetting that it is their behaviour which in Russian eyes is somewhat abnormal). The first feature is to do with a Russian gift for conversation: how a culture converses tells us a good deal about how its business representatives use language in negotiation. The second topic deals with Russians as communicators and undercommunicators. Our third area concerns the Russian love of proverbs.

It is readily conceded that generalization about Russian culture is a particularly notorious pastime. Hingley, a sharp observer of Russians and who is quoted in this section, readily admits this. His advice is 'never to accept in advance that an unknown citizen of Russia or any other country will necessarily exhibit even a single characteristic, however minor, from among any amalgam which may be claimed as typical of the group as a whole'. With that word of caution we proceed to the daunting task before us.

A gift for conversation

One of the most striking features of social interaction among Russians is how easily complete strangers seem to set up a conversational rapport with one another. This ease of interaction is almost certainly connected to the Russian sense of equality, to which we have already referred. Alas, the conversational skills of Russians hardly ever cross the language barrier. A Russian, it seems, can only converse naturally with another Russian or a foreigner who speaks Russian well. Interpreters seldom convey the special features of Russian conversation: wit, pithiness, a penchant for emphatic persistence on one issue (such as the interlocutor's reprehensibleness or intransigence), a tendency to interrupt (i.e. not to listen) and, in the case of those who enjoy some specific form of superiority over the interlocutor, a tendency to bully and badger. Generally we can say that the purpose of conversation among Russian is not to proclaim one's own achievements or to belittle one's interlocutor. Whether it is a purpose of conversational discourse or not, what tends to happen is that each party display its feelings to the other.

An outsider's impression of a Russian conversation is that language moves fast, rather like a flowing stream, now suddenly obscured from view, now revealing a panoramic vista. The course of the stream is thrusting and exuberant, a great flow with no ebb. At any moment this stream is going to burst its banks. When it does, it will often be a moment of uproarious hilarity – before some realizes that we are about to witness a gaffe at best, a cataclysm at worst.

In trying to capture the quality of Russian conversation in these words, the challenge is to convey to the staid westerner that for Russians conversation is an emotional experience, not merely an informational one. The bigger point, of course, is that Russians bring to their interactions with foreign businessmen, in formal and informal encounters, these conversational dispositions. This partly explains why in Chapter 6, in our framework for understanding the mindset of Russian business partners as negotiators and 'relationship developers', we attempted to take account of the central issue of Russian emotion. But it is no good applying the strategies suggested by this model unless you are, at least to some extent, aware of the Russian emotional patterning and its manifestation in communicative behaviour, if only through the refracted utterances of an interpreter.

Compulsive undercommunication

Perhaps the most important contribution on Russians as communicators comes from the world of literary studies. Ronald Hingley, an Oxford don and best known perhaps for his translations of Chekhov, published a book in 1978 called *The Russian Mind*. Hingley brilliantly characterizes Russians as compulsive undercommunicators. What brings him to this most perceptive, yet unusual portrayal? First, this arresting phrase is presented as the opposite of a pronounced Russian tendency to expose themselves 'either excessively or misleadingly'. By this tendency Hingley is referring to preference for using language for:

- conveying emotional nuance: for example, by modifying words, including people's names to convey affection, humour, disdain

- displaying feelings: displaying them, not merely revealing them

- fantasy mongering: the capacity to project a grand scheme – communism being an excellent example – which exists more in the mind than in reality

- evading and deceiving, but not necessarily to trick anyone deliberately, to avoid admitting weakness or fault (think of how many times Russians say 'No problem', the multipurpose codeword for impending cockup).

Undercommunication is the opposite to these tendencies: it refers to the centuries-long tradition of keeping one's lips sealed, of not saying more than one knows, of not saying anything that it might be incriminating or unwittingly advantageous to an interlocutor, of not admitting to knowing anything it might be dangerous to know, of passing information stealthily. Hingley speaks of this tendency in terms of an obsession with secrecy. In this sense Russians reveal themselves as compulsive undercommunicators, obsessed with information based on rumour, innuendo and the grapevine (Steele, 1994), as if information not obtained by non-clandestine means automatically has value.

A penchant for proverbs

Another feature of Russian is significant but easy to overlook. This is to do with the sheer profusion of proverbs (*poslovitsa* (sing.)) and sayings. Discuss with a Russian a situation which he cannot possibly know or conceive of, refer to any kind of human failing or predicament associated with it, and you can guarantee that the vast treasury of the Russian language will have an apposite saying – even if it is literally or metaphorically untranslatable! A *poslovitsa* is a Russian device for sharing experience with friends and strangers alike, a mechanism for creating intimacy and warmth. As we emphasize throughout this book, Russians want warm business relationships: not that manufactured warmth that western businessmen can turn on and off like a tap.

It would, incidentally, be quite mistaken to assume that it is only less well educated people who indulge in proverbs. One of the authors of this book recently met a professor of sociology from the Russian Academy of Sciences, whose language was positively strewn with these ancient sayings. As we note in Chapter 8, proverbs are a frequent component of Russian toasts.

Speakers of western languages do not have this need for dispensing proverbs. Western businessmen, when a proverb is being explained to them, no doubt wag their head, politely acknowledging this Russian foible. But a colleague, convinced that proverbs play an important role as a social cement in Russia, told us that he tried to explain some English proverbs. He described the experience as 'a bit like schoolboys swapping stamps' – somehow a relationship was fostered. On one occasion he used the term 'little acorns' with some Russian managers, going on to explain that it was necessary with a business venture 'to think small' in the beginning. This created gales of laughter. The more or less literal translation of thinking small had sounded like an exhortation to think of smalls (i.e. tipples of vodka).

Conclusion

At the beginning of this chapter it was argued that insights into the Russian language and how it is characteristically used by Russians can be a valuable aid to foreign business people who wish to understand the mentality of their Russian business partners. Although our review of the Russian language was brief and selective, we were able to highlight some notable features of Russian language behaviour which become a set part of Russians' orientation towards foreigners.

Russians believe that all human feeling is expressible in the copious repository of the Russian language. They like to use language as a reflector of their feelings at a specific moment. What they actually say will depend on the state of their emotions at that moment, and the direction in which these emotions are swaying. This is why, to oversimplify, a growling *nyet* can suddenly become a smiling *da* – and then a growling *nyet* and so forth. What is hard for foreigners is first to apprehend and then to cope in a practical way with (for example, in negotiations) the Russian penchant for using language to assert an emotional attitude rather than to make an intellectual point or even tell the truth – again, at a specific moment. So, when a Russian expects you to be flexible, he is challenging you not only to understand his various dilemmas and predicaments (all of these things come under the grand codeword 'problems'), but also to keep up with his emotional changes. Foreigners find all this at best baffling, at worst downright frustrating. To make things worse, effective communication between Russian managers and their western business partners is insidiously undermined by the fact that western management terms and concepts are entering the Russian language and therefore Russian life in a haphazard way.

The New Language Barrier

Wirtschaftliche Öffnung – Sprachliche Neuorientierung

— *Trubel, 1994*

Market (1) Space (still sometimes listed in guidebooks under 'local curiosities') for the sale of produce from collective farms and private plots . . . Market (2) Magic formula for instant riches.

— *Wilson and Bachkatov, 1992*

Introduction

Management consultants and educators who do not know Russian are unlikely to be aware of how acute the language barrier is in the transfer of management knowhow. In this chapter, we highlight the underdevelopment of Russian from the point of view of its lexical and referential resources for handling management terms and concepts. We use the term 'language deficiency' for these ascribed limitations of Russian as a language of management. We introduce the issue with respect to general business and management terms, and then highlight specific instances affecting management development programmes for the Russian construction sector. In passing we comment on the role of interpreters, who are frequently an unwitting source of two-way confusion.

Most of the linguistic and terminological confusions cited in this chapter have been derived from the authors' experiences of management training in Russia with particular reference to the construction industry. But it is of course the case that other management professionals – including consultants and investors – will also find themselves in situations where such confusions influence the progress of interactions.

The language of management

Since the end of the 1980s the peoples of the former socialist world have been experiencing a dramatic, painful change of direction, 'a gigantic political and economic adjustment' (Trubel, 1994), as they struggle to align themselves with western market economy systems. Part of this process of reorientation involves, on the one hand, the immense task of shedding the language of Marxist-Leninist economics, and the associated vocabulary of production and the *glorification* of production and, on the other, the continued absorption of management language from the west. In this chapter, the aim is to note the problems of reorientation of the lexical systems of the Russian language to handle modern management know-how in the context of transition towards the market economy. We therefore examine Russian from a rarely considered point of view: that is, as a language of management.

It is safe to say that the management discipline has never made much use of 'the great human fact of Language' (Entwistle, 1974 [emphasis original]) as an explanatory tool for the description and analysis of management communication, by which is meant the organized use of human and technical communication systems for facilitating goal-oriented corporate endeavour. Yet, as we hope to show, using language in this way can prove rewarding for explaining the nature of human communication and instances of breakdown especially in crosscultural contexts.

In this chapter we explore Russian as a language of management, a term that we must explain. Our starting point is that the language of management is a 'special language'; that is to say, a domain-specific sub-set of 'general language' which facilitates professional communication among specialists. The most distinguishing feature of a special language is its generation and use of a domain-specific lexis (Sager et al., 1980). Regarding management as a domain, we accordingly define the language of management as 'a set of linguistic symbols, manipulable in a given language (such as English, German, Japanese, etc.), and incorporating standardised terms and informal elements (such as oblique reference, humour, pretence, etc.), necessary for the conceptualisation, description and execution of management tasks and sharing of management information' (Holden, 1992).

However imperfect this definition, it makes clear that the language of management is more than merely a set of terms: it both informs and underpins a coherent, shared professional outlook within a specific paradigm. Russian, as we argue here, is underdeveloped as a language of management. It suffers from what we call language deficiency: it suffers from semantic voids pertaining to a wide range of market economy management concepts and functions. This is, of course, the direct consequence of the fact that Russian, which had been a fully serviceable language of socialist endeavour, must now reorient its meaning systems to accommodate the terms and concepts associated with management thinking and behaviour in a market economy. In the Soviet period, either these terms and concepts were not part of the Russian language or they were distorted for ideological effect, that is, to disparage and defame capitalism (i.e. the west) and correspondingly glorify the socialist way of life.

Language deficiency and management learning in Russia

For some years now, Russians have been creating new words using Russian roots, or have been importing fashionable words to describe the new kinds of economic behaviour in which entire millions are willy-nilly becoming involved as entrepreneurial protagonists, discriminating consumers, racketeers or helpless, if not destitute observers. But often these words, while enjoying a vogue, are meaningless to most Russians, who understand neither the concepts behind the words nor the practices they denote. This applies particularly to those activities deemed superfluous under socialism, for example marketing (Abramishvili, 1991; Skurski,

1983), human resource management, financial management and business planning (Hibbert, 1990 and 1991; Puffer, 1992). Entire areas of management vocabulary have got to be invented and institutionalized, replacing the impoverished and discredited lexicon of Marxist-Leninism. But even if the language of socialism is waning in influence, simply because the state is no longer in a position to use this language as an element of social coercion and political direction, Russians in general do not always seem to be interested in assimilating the language of the market economy.

As that trenchant observer of Russians, Hedrick Smith (1991), has noted: 'The language of the market – competition, profits, free prices, and productivity – has come into vogue among urban intellectuals, but so far these concepts inspire fear, not confidence among the masses; they cut against the grain of deep-set attitudes.' There is little doubt that the language of the market is the language not only of the Great Feared Unknown (Holden and Cooper, 1994), but also of the west and all its ways: as Russians sometimes see it, all its anti-Russian ways. Another influence may be the persistence of the 'old Marxist scorn for, and ignorance of, finance' (Åslund, 1993) and the disinclination to save money (Hingley, 1978).

Our experience shows that among Russian managers there is little or no awareness that western-style management, even in the 'mere' application of techniques, requires:

- genuinely radical changes of attitude to the world of work

- the control of new forms of interpersonal relationships

- the steady accumulation of new forms of knowledge and experience (Holden and Cooper, 1994).

This lack of awareness not only perpetuates the mutually distorted view of Russian and western management techniques (Vlachoutsicos and Lawrence, 1990), but it is also symptomatic of a Russian disinclination to convince themselves of the value of management to the kind of society that they wish to create on the ruins of communism (Holden and Cooper, 1994).

We are, therefore, dealing with a major problem of receptivity on the part of Russian managers, and for the moment there are inadequate lexical and referential resources in Russian to make the task of communicating market economy skills easier. In the following sections we shall describe how language deficiency negatively affects the process of transfer of management know-how, with respect first to management terminology in general and then to the construction sector.

Absence of general management terminology

Since Gorbachev unleashed *perestroika* and *glasnost* in the mid-1980s, the Russian language has been absorbing hundreds of words to do with business and management, sexual behaviour, politics and the mass media (Dunn, 1996). All these imported words are the lexis of not merely of the market economy, but the very shibboleths of a new way of life and underlying assumptions and attitudes. The specific significance of the vocabulary to do with business and management is that it is to a large extent being thrust on Russia. This means that western management educators need to be aware that the increasingly documented problems of teaching management subjects to Russians (*The Economist*, 1993; Hibbert, 1990 and 1991; Holden, 1996; Holden and Cooper, 1994; Manoukovsky, 1990; Puffer, 1991; TACIS Magazines Nos 1 and 2, 1993) can legitimately be seen as a form of Russian wariness of, even occasionally resistance to externally imposed language change.

Quite apart from that important attitudinal factor, it is very difficult to convey in Russian everyday management terms and expressions. Indeed some defy direct translation and resort has to be made to paraphrases. Terms such as challenge, product champion, organizational learning, management prerogative, leaner and fitter, performance, track record, corporate identity, total quality management belong in this category. The term environment, which comes with a variety of collocations (business environment, marketing environment, macro-environment, micro-environment, etc.), has proved awkward. Interpreters have said that Russian managers associate the nominally corresponding word *sreda* with the physical, ecological environment. *Sreda* apparently still sounds strange when applied to business and economic behaviour, although presumably one day it will not.

Training is a good example of a key concept for which there is no exact correspondence in Russian, despite the fact that since the mid-1980s many thousands of Russians have taken part in western-sponsored training programmes. Words that are based on Russian roots revolve around ideas of teaching and learning, in which the emphasis is on the communication of knowledge or skills in a fairly formal way, that is to say, in the presence of the teacher; and the teacher in traditional value system is always a mentor, a moral guide (there were vast numbers of these in the Soviet Union inculcating the moral virtues of socialist society). In the Soviet period, there were hundreds of institutes offering specialist courses for 'raising qualifications', but such courses would hardly be classed as training by western standards. The closest word in Russia to training (*obucheniye*) in the management sense does not convey the associations of improving or extending competencies (Ozhegov, 1984), and also has the ring of a 'course of study'. Although Russian has built up words derived from the English word training, these are associated with the preparation of sportsmen (and cosmonauts) and the bringing up of animals (Kotelova, 1984; Lyokhin and Petrov, 1955). The ground is plainly set for a 'new' Russian word *training*.

Problematical too has been the term 'business mission'. The word *missiya* (via the French *mission*) is used, although the word carries stronger religious overtones than in English. Likewise, the English term promotion, which embraces a wide function of unaccustomed activities (advertising, public relations, awareness campaigns, and aspects of personal selling) causes headaches: the occasional resort to *reklama* (lit. advertisement) by interpreters is understandable, but not adequate. If 'promotion' is a problematic concept, so too is the term marketing, which was an ideologically superfluous activity during the communist era (Skurski, 1983). In spite of this, from the mid-1970s we see occasional references to marketing in leading journals such as *Novy Mir*, *Izvestiya* and even the 1970–78 edition of the *Great Soviet Encyclopaedia* (see Holden, 1995a). By 1990, the USSR had appointed its first ever professor of marketing, who described marketing as 'a hazy concept' (Abramishvili, 1991), and so it remains. Russian managers can grasp the nature of functions such as selling and advertising, but they appear to have problems with understanding marketing as a business philosophy, as an organizational disposition.

There is no Russian word for marketing, so it has taken over the English word. As such, the imported word sounds nothing like the Russian word for market. Some western marketing textbooks have been translated into Russian, but when you see terms such as product lifecycle or channel management decisions translated literally into Russian, you wonder what the averagely educated Russian would understand by these new additions to his language. Some Russian books on marketing have also been published, but these tend to parrot the contents of the western books rather than adapt western marketing ideas and practices specifically to Russian business conditions.

We should also not forget that market is itself an awkward term, and there may be some truth in the observation that Russians use the Russian word as a euphemism for capitalism, which may be 'still too tainted to use in polite company' (Morrison, 1991). To a Russian, as the quotation at the beginning of the chapter suggests, it conjures up marketplace in a physical sense as well as a money-making opportunity. But it is hard for a Russian to conceive that a set of electronic impulses spiriting millions of dollars from New York to Tokyo is also a market. It is a characteristic of a market that it facilitates economic exchanges, but these exchanges are not the same as exchanges such as stock exchanges or commodity exchanges, and there are two separate words in Russian. There is a cited instance of a Russian translator using *birzha* (via French *bourse*), which represents a place, to translate exchange in the sense of activities (Holden, 1996).

It is of course especially relevant that the words manager and management have established forms, *menedzher* (pl. *menedzhery*) and *menedzhment*. It has been noticeable to us that in the last two years or so Russian managers, who put the word *direktory* on their business cards, are starting to refer to themselves as *menedzhery*. Referring to on another they are either *menedzhery* or *predprinimateli* (lit. 'entrepreneurs'). It is also noticeable that the steady output of Russian books on management and business, and management glossaries, tend to use the words *predprinimatel* and *predprinimatel-stvo* (entrepreneurship) in their titles rather than the loan-words *menedzher* and *menedzhment*. One glossary (Sinelnikov et al., 1992) illuminatingly translates *predprinimatel* as 'businessman' rather than 'entrepreneur', the latter term implying a degree of risk taking and commercial buccaneering which is absent from the Russian word. This same dictionary, disappointingly, defines manager (*menedzher*) as someone responsible for production. This is objectionable; such a definition would not pass muster in a western management book. This 'deviation' is, it seems, characteristic of the persistence of terminological problems between English and Russian in the field of management.

Incidentally, the term managing director has not proved easy to translate: this may be because the English term, as well as connoting executive power, decision-making capability, and responsibility to shareholders, normally implies membership of a board of directors. Although one encounters *direktor–rasporyaditel* as the translation in various dictionaries, including the European Commission's *Dictionary of Economic and Management Terms* (1994), designed to facilitate the transfer of general western management and business terminology into Russian, it is a term which we have hardly heard, or seen on business cards. Interestingly, the much-travelled chief executive of one St Petersburg firm of our acquaintance styles himself as *prezident*, an American usage which could catch on, especially in those companies conscientiously and actively seeking western business partners.

The central problem is, of course, that the underlying concepts behind these terms, and the realities they connote to westerners, fall outside Russian/Soviet experience. Our investigations of Russian managers (Holden and Cooper, 1994; Holden and Gale, 1993; Holden and Yamin, 1994) have highlighted three aspects of this experiential void that prevents Russian managers, for the moment at least, from understanding the concepts as realities. First, there is a general difficulty of adjustment from a production-oriented and output-oriented frame of mind to one that can conceive of the centrality of customer satisfaction to business success. A second factor is that Russian preconceptions of western management tend to be associated with hard management – making decisions and pushing people to get things done. Russians know all about that kind of management. But as for soft management, which emphasizes motivations, good communications and stresses the importance of individual contributions, this is a source of bafflement to them. It does not fit into any established scheme for handling Russians, who are said only to respond to tough bosses.

Third, we have found that managers seem unable to recognize that the practice of marketing and other unaccustomed management activities is crucially dependent on the systematic and initiative-driven search for specific categories of information – an ideologically superfluous and potentially treasonous activity under the old centralized planning system (Holden, 1995a). We have found that they have particular difficulty understanding management information multidimensionally, as:

- material for creating and updating market pictures

- a resource for outmanoeuvring competitors

- a management tool for motivation and communication

- the lifeblood of the company

- input for strategic planning and decision making

- tactical and manipulable elements in business negotiation

- a commodity of variable time value

- a key component in (competitive) pricing.

In all of these areas of management information processing, the Russian language reveals serious deficiencies, not because the basic vocabulary does not exist, but because this vocabulary is non-standardized and is made up, as we have seen, of foreign words which are not clearly understood.

Construction management terminology

We have worked in the construction industry in Russia and felt that this would provide a good example of the types of language difficulties that arise. With regard to the terminology of construction management (as opposed to the general language of management) we have observed, for example, that problems of misunderstanding result not only from mismatches of experience, but also from perceptions of construction as a process. A major stumbling block is that it is impossible to explain construction management as a process without reference to information flows linking all parties to a contract. In fact, the word contract serves to exemplify the nature of the gulf very well. It has been noticeable that Russian managers only talk about projects (with the emphasis on implementation and completion of a task) and not about contracts, a word which connotes relationships between parties and the acceptance of obligations to cement those relationships.

In a glossary of project management terminology (Shapiro and Sheinberg, 1993), it is pointed out that in the Soviet period the term *proyekt* 'meant a set of design or engineering documentation only'. Recently, however, even the mass media have started to use the term in the wider western sense. It is therefore not surprising that translators and interpreters have come to grief with terms such as procurement, bidding, and tendering, which are, to Russian managers, completely unfamiliar activities involving highly complex forms of interaction between actual or would-be business partners.

With regard to other problematical terms, we have found, for example, that the word developer is virtually untranslatable in Russian (except by paraphrase). Here the problem is to do with the still largely alien notion of ownership of land and the lack of procedures for securing the right to build on it involving a financial investment. We have noted instances of services (i.e. utilities) being translated in Russian by the word *obshluzhivanie*, which rather suggests the idea of servicing. The Russian word for a construction site is *obyekt*, which also seems to serve extremely well as the translation for (building) development (but all Russian translators seem to translate *obyekt* as 'object' until corrected.)

The critical terms contractor and sub-contractor do not cover the equivalent semantic territory in English and Russian. Other problematical words have been: plant hire (being splendidly mistranslated as the 'hire of factories') and speculative building, whereby the adjective ended up in Russian as *spekulativnyi*, a once pejorative (i.e. ideologically charged) term under socialism referring to illegal profiteering, an offence which then could lead to a death sentence (Utechin, 1961). An otherwise competent translator of our management course books misunderstood the term built environment, taking it to mean the environment that a firm builds within itself. Management specialists call that corporate culture, a highly problematical concept to convey. Bill of quantity has been unsatisfactorily rendered by the word *smeta*, which literally means an estimate.

We have encountered another interesting problem connected with back-translation. Many of the construction companies we have been involved with are building portentous residences for Russia's nouveaux riches. These are called, and appear in company brochures as *kotedzhi* ('cottages') The word *kotedzh* listed in a Russian dictionary of foreign words of some 40 years ago (Lyokhin and Petrova, 1955), was defined as 'a small English country home'. In the intervening years, the word seems at first glance to have undergone a major semantic shift. We have cautioned managers and interpreters that the use of the English word 'cottage' with UK business contacts to describe these prestigious homes will convey the wrong impression. It is almost certainly the case that one of the first, if not *the* first 'cottage' in Russia was that built in the Alexandria Park of Peterhof and commissioned by Tsar Nicholas I for his wife around 1830. This 'rambling villa' (Lieven, 1994), known as The Cottage (*kotedzh*), was created 'in the then fashionable pseudo-Gothic style of English country houses with an intricate array of roofs, terraces, balconies and bays' (Baedeker, 1991). It seems safe to assume that this was the prototype of all later *kotedzhi*.

Interpreters

The vast majority of western businessmen operating in Russia do not speak Russian. They are very much dependent on the English-speaking capabilities of their counterparts or must make do with interpreters. Several words of caution are necessary about interpreters. First, even if the interpreters have a general knowledge of commercial terminology, they do not as a rule understand the management thinking behind them. Virtually all the words highlighted earlier present great hardships for interpreters.

We have already noted management terms that prove very difficult to translate into written Russian; they often require a circumlocution. In the case of interpretation, one is dependent on the the spontaneous skills of a linguistic mediator. Anyone who has ever been called upon to act as interpreter, especially in front of an audience, is likely to appreciate the high order of the intellectual demands involved: quite apart from possessing from an extremely good knowledge of the two languages in engagement, the interpreter needs to understand the cultural contexts of the negotiating parties. Beyond that, of course, an interpreter needs to be familiar with the specialist terminology in both languages.

On this last point, we have already established that there is in Russian a general terminological vacuum concerning management concepts. If you want a rule of thumb about interpreters in Russia, assume that they have a very good knowledge of Russian and English (or whatever other foreign language is involved), but sharply discount their competencies in the other areas. Interpreters may well be personal friends of your Russian business partners, who are doing a favour to these friends who need the work and the money!

This state of affairs is not helped by foreign businessmen who do not understand what is easily and not so easily translatable into Russian. We have given some instances of troublesome terms. Figure 8.1 provides three examples of how some Russian interpreters have coped with these terms.

English term	Russian translation
Performance	Achievements
Track record	History of the company
Challenge	Problem

Figure 8.1 Distortion through translation

As on-the-hoof translations, they are very good attempts, yet none strictly speaking is a close semantic equivalent. The term performance is tricky at the best of times, and the translation of 'challenge' by 'problem' is acceptable, as the nominal translation of the word challenge conveys the notion of provocation.

But more serious mistranslations occur when an interpreter is out of his or her depth. Here are some attested examples of mistranslations. On one occasion an interpreter was involved in a discussion about building construction. The British representative was talking about casting concrete. The interpreter did not know that 'cast' in this context means to pour, but he did know that 'cast' can also mean 'to throw'. So he used the Russian word for 'to throw', but this word also means to 'abandon' (i.e. throw away). Another confusion arose with the same interpreter (a friend of the Russian boss, needless to say). The British representative was explaining that the Russian construction firm was liable to damages of $800 to replace a glass door which its workmen had inadvertently smashed. The sum of $800 was reduced in the translation to a mere $8.00. The explanation appears to be that the interpreter 'misheard' $800, as he could not conceive that a glass door could actually cost the equivalent in 1994 of three or four years' average pay.

Another serious mistranslation arose over a reference to the pharmaceutical industry. The interpreter did not know the word pharmaceutical, but she obviously did know the word 'farmer' and so, with weird logic, the pharmaceutical industry became the agricultural industry. It is appropriate to conclude this section with a reference to a truly notorious management-speak term: the word 'change'. This semantic chameleon is on everyone's lips, especially in this context on the lips of management educators. In our experience no translator or interpreter has come up with a satisfactory equivalent in Russian. Oddly enough, the closest Russian word may well be our old friend *perestroika*, which meant, in one helpful explanation, 'construction anew . . . from the foundations up' (Brown, 1996). In any case how can our concept of 'the management of change' be expected to set the Russians on fire? Change, as we mouth the word, is peanuts to Russians who are still reeling from their exit from 'the most grandiose, radical, painful, and disastrous sociopolitical experiment in modern history' (Mikheyev, 1996).

Conclusion

At the end of Chapter 2 we noted a World Bank estimate that perhaps as many as 40 per cent of all consultancy assignments fail in Russia. It is surely undeniable that language deficiency is a major influence on this poor performance: it is a source of semantic confusions and inexactitudes; it perpetuates mutual wariness and reinforces the gap which prevents western managers from understanding their Russian counterparts. All in all, the transfer of western management know-how is seriously impeded by a complicated language barrier conditioned by factors such as receptivity to this knowhow, the depth of the socialist experience, and culture-specific factors influencing language change. At the same time, precisely these same factors are constraining the development of vernacular Russian into a language of management.

Management educators and consultants need to grasp that their real task lies not so much in attempting to transfer techniques as in helping to bring into general service a new language of management which is (a) specifically reoriented to facilitate Russia's economic interaction and exchange with the rest of the world, and (b) explicitly based on the firm as the key socio-economic agent of initiative in a modern market economy. This is no easy challenge to meet. The problem is that management educators and consultants, who do not think about the words they use or are unskilled in adapting their spoken language (for example, slowing down the rate of delivery) to assist interpreters, are unwittingly undermining the implementation of the very processes they are promoting (*The Economist*, 1993; Holden, 1995b).

If these same consultants and educators are not especially knowledgeable about Russia and give the impression that they are also perceived by Russians as not being genuine specialists, then one begins to see in what insidious ways consultancy assignments and the training programmes can easily sink into quicksands of mutual misperception and antipathy.

Afterthought

Catherine the Great, who learnt Russian as a foreign language, declared to a confidante that 'our Russian language, uniting as it does the strength, richness and energy of German with the sweetness of Italian, will one day become the standard language of the world' (in Cronin, 1989). It conceivably had this chance in the days of communism. The chance may come again, but only if Russian becomes a fully equipped language of management *and* dislodges English from its pre-eminent international role. The first may happen; the second . . . never.

Coping With The Green Snake:

The Social Side Of Business

Alcohol . . . the main entertainment, the main currency, and the main scourge.

— Quinn-Judge, 1990

That's me all over! Why, do you know, my good sir, that I've even sold her stockings to pay for drink? Not her shoes, though, which would be more in the order of things; not her shoes, but her stockings – sold them for drink, I did.

— Dostoyevsky

Introduction

In this chapter we explore business entertainment Russian style. The dominant theme is vodka, which can claim without much exaggeration to be the driving force behind Russian notions of attaining bonhomie and equivalence with anyone including their western business partners. Foreign businessmen, for whom the consumption of vodka is an inescapable experience, are offered this extended narrative on Russia's fearsome national drink to show once more the aptness of military aphorisms to the battlefields of commerce: in this case 'Know thy enemy'. This is a way of saying that the significance of vodka in Russian life is certainly misunderstood and probably underestimated in western countries and that foreign managers can benefit in their personal interactions with Russian counterparts through a wider appreciation of vodka as a significant social influence in its own right. As is generally known, the downing of vodka is often initiated with a toast. Therefore we take a look at toasting; there is more to this practice than meets the eye (or ear), especially if you do not know Russian and do not understand what has been shielded from you. The chapter concludes with some comments on vodka and business socializing in Russia, and some hints on how to drink that slightly notorious tipple.

Russians and business socializing

Russians value close human relationships with their business partners. The Russian way of understanding human relationships in business involvements is not the Japanese way, which always requires a tactful observance of social distance. For Russians, even in their business dealings, social distance must be obliterated, and business entertainment, smoothed with vodka, can help achieve precisely that, and quickly. It is only in this way that Russians can get on an equal footing with western business partners, who have a stereotype of being on occasion disagreeably tutorial and patronizing. Russians seek human warmth in their relationships with business partners (which is something that the Japanese emphatically do not seek in their dealings with non-Japanese businessmen). Some years ago, a Russian construction manager, who had experience of working with both Finnish and German contractors, bemoaned the fact that his involvements were 'dry' (Holden 1995). He did not mean merely that the business meetings were formal and tedious; he was complaining that they did not give much opportunity for displays of feelings. From all this we may deduce that the social side of business is extremely important to Russian managers.

Until the collapse of the centralized trading system in 1991, western businessmen had relatively little occasion to experience the social side of business with their Soviet business partners. This was in the main a function of the old system which actively discouraged unnecessarily close contact. The signing of a major contract in Moscow might be a significant enough occasion for foreign trade representatives to accept an invitation to join the victorious western company for a restaurant dinner. But those involved in such festivities found them low key. The Soviet side appeared under orders not to enjoy themselves; the atmosphere was generally stiff; the Soviet businessmen might propose one toast, would make a collective getaway after an hour or two. It was not always like that and the few foreign business representatives who lived in Moscow or technical personnel who were, say, supervising the construction of an industrial plant out in the sticks had different experiences of socializing with Russian counterparts.

The changes initiated by the collapse of the Soviet Union mean that it is no longer risky for Russians at large to strike up relationships with foreigners. They are free to invite them home and even put them up. This new freedom has of course been rapidly extended to the domain of business contact. Now it is common for western businessmen to spend a convivial evening with their Russian business partners and experience the exuberant and jading rigours of Russian hospitality. Whatever the good-natured motivations behind hospitality, its lasting memory on foreigners is that the main purpose is to ply them with food and drink and break down their inhibitions as quickly as possible with the latter. This is no flippant observation: there is a recorded history of 300 years of Russians' delight in reducing their foreign guests to various degrees of alcoholic paralysis. And it is not so long ago that the KGB was actively continuing the tradition as an instrument of surveillance (and who is to say that its successor organization has abandoned it?). Ronald Hingley, writing in 1978, had this to say on Russian hospitality, noting a tendency to ply guests with drink 'by all means short of intravenous injection':

> Can it be that to cause a guest to vomit, or to suffer distressing after-effects, qualifies a Russian host for bonus points on some award scheme? There are those among them who seem to confuse hospitality with hospitalisation. To such overzealous dispensers of good cheer, nothing short of the guests's collective expiry through surfeit of alcohol, caviare and suckling

pig could, it seems, be accepted as an adequate response. Here, not for the first time, excess of zeal must be recorded as a feature of Russian *mœurs*.

For the most part the entertainment takes place in restaurants, but other venues such as a sauna or bathing station on a river or lake are possible. The vodka will flow and toasts will be proposed: the entire event is likely to stay in the memory – according to one's knowledge of Russian – as an occasion of merry gregariousness, spiced with sharp Russian humour, and concluding with splodgy kisses, fumbling bearhugs and vice-like handshakes. Russian businessmen, and they are no different from their western counterparts in this, look upon a meal and drinks with their actual or potential business partners as an important means of cementing a personal relationship. One of our Russian contributors, who has experience working for a major UK industrial corporation, told us that he finds western business entertainment somewhat stiff and formal, 'as if it were a duty'. For Russians, he added, duty does not come into it. They issue their invitations in anticipation of mutual enjoyment.

There is no neat expression in Russian for 'business entertainment' or 'business socializing'. One is invited to a 'dinner', which normally implies an evening as opposed to lunchtime function, or to a 'banquet', which generally means the same food, more people, as much to drink and considerably more toasting. In Russia one's scale of enjoyment is often directly proportional to the number of people indulging themselves at the same time. Russians may simply refer to such events as 'rest' or 'relaxation'. But these are wholly inadequate, even dangerously misleading literal translations of the Russian word *otdykh*. In fact, to anyone familiar with the Russian language, this particular word is one of the most loaded in the entire language: it can encompass anything from a teabreak to tramping in the forests for mushrooms, from a cosy chat (one of Russia's more charming experiences) to a whole gamut of extended liver-punishing experiences. It therefore implies some kind of joyous release from daily labours and the trials of life. 'Relaxing' with one's Russian business counterparts can usually be expected to be a bracing test of stamina. For example, if your Russian hosts meet you at midday on a Saturday or Sunday, it is best to assume that the hospitality will last late in the evening.

Western managers working with their Russian counterparts will normally find that socializing entails the consuming of vodka. The place of entertainment might be a restaurant or hotel; it may be a Russian bath (*banya*) or you may be a guest in your Russian host's home. It is safe to say that, when you are the guest of your Russian business partners, business is unlikely to be one of their conversational priorities. The purpose of the entertainment is to get to know one another better and determine each other's integrity. It is an occasion when you can freely drop your guard, display your emotions and generally add cheerfulness to the gathering. Nothing acts faster (or more fatally) than vodka in delivering these effects.

Vodka

If there is one word that conjures Russia more rapidly than any other it must be *vodka*; and if the word itself conjures up thoughts of the Russian penchant for hard drinking and carousing, that is only half the story. The point is that vodka plays a part in Russian life that is similar to the role of wine in France. Although the behaviour associating with drinking habits differs dramatically in the two countries, the fact is that a vodkaless Russia is about as imaginable as a France from which wine – its production and consumption – has been eradicated. Books on wine like to say that wine has a property that is 'life-enhancing'. There the comparison might end: in Russia vodka is, after all, life-threatening. But it does, even so, have its life-enhancing side in that vodka can be symbollically associated with any aspect of the human condition. In the words of one commentator, vodka does wonderful things for simple people. It 'warms them in the cold, cools them in the summer heat, protects them from the damp, consoles them in grief, and cheers them up when times are good' (Christian, 1990, in White, 1996). In short, there is always a good reason to partake.

But a Russian, whether one who likes the occasional tipple or one who likes to pour 200 grams – the equivalent of nearly four doubles – down his throat in one draught for breakfast, would say that vodka is life-enhancing and that it has long been so. It makes one forget 'the drabness of life of the average citizen and the inadequacies of alternative relaxation and entertainment facilities' (Brown, Kaser and Smith, 1994). According to Lev Kopelev (1994),

Zakuski

Why should I trust you? We haven't eaten cabbage soup from the same bowl.

Solzhenitsyn

Although Russia is famed for its hospitality, it is less well known for its food and style of cooking. Perhaps the most distinctive feature of Russian meal is the *zakuski*, which are described, slightly misleading, as starters, 'nibbles', appetizers or *hors d'œuvres*. It may not be an exaggeration to say that the partaking of *zakuski* is the most important ritual of the Russian table. *Zakuski* are items presented on the table, which are freely taken according to taste or hospitable insistence of one's hosts. They can be salted items, such as cucumbers, gherkins, mushrooms, and fish such as herring, salmon, trout, halibut or sprats; marinades of tomatoes, peppers and radish; various kinds of salads, often garnished with dill, fennel or parsley; stuffed eggs and tasty pies, or rather pielets (*pirozhki*), filled with vegetables or meat; and, of course, caviar (*ikra*). The word *zakuski* comes from a verb which suggests taking something to eat in small mouthfuls, flittingly (*naskoro*).

The eating of *zakuski* is accompanied by vodka, though other drinks, such as wine and mineral water, will probably be available too. If you are lucky, your hostess may have made a delicious juice from berries. Traditionally the host makes the first toast – only with vodka. Other guests – but seldom the ladies – deliver their toasts too, and thus is achieved the carefree – and often boisterous – bonhomie, which is the supreme aim of Russian hospitality. Traditionally, all the guests and the host himself fall on the *zakuski*, while the mistress of the house makes the final preparation for the main course. Foreigners have a habit of confusing the *zakuski* with the main course; in other words, having partaken amply of them, they find that they do not much room left for the next course.

drabness and deprivation are not the only factors, Russians drink 'from grief and from joy, because they're tired and to get tired, out of habit and by chance'. A contributor to this book knew of an industrial boss with a legendary reputation for hard drinking who once consumed two bottles of vodka at a friend's funeral. We know this man: his toasts to his deceased comrade would have been long, eloquent and vibrant in emotion; he would have reduced everyone to tears and the starchiest mourner would have been swept along with it. It has, after all, been well said that the Russian drinks for effect (Bridges, 1994).

Kopelev adds that vodka, taken in company, promotes 'liberty, unprecedented equality and good-hearted fraternity' (Brown, Kaser and Smith, 1994). In other words, for Russians, vodka not only provides escapism, but is an essential ingredient for collective exuberance and merriment. Thus vodka in part belongs to 'a cultural tradition which made drinking a necessary part of socializing and various festivities' (Brown, Kaser and Smith, 1994). Vodka has also been a traditional source of tax revenue for Russian governments since the 15th century, and has been used by Russia's leaders as a form of social control, as a prop to martial fortitude, and a device for compromising foreigners, Russia's guests. Rightly then, vodka has been described by one Russian historian as 'a most sensitive area of our national identity' (Pokhlebkin, 1992).

Vodka is so associated in foreigners' mind with excessive drinking and alcoholism that it is easy to overlook the traditional gastronomic aspects. Pokhlebkin (1992) makes the point that 'the correct role for vodka as a table drink is to accompany and to highlight exclusively Russian national dishes'. Notably, vodka accompanies *zakuski*, Russian hors d'œuvres. [**Zakuski**] According to Pokhlebkin, in the 18th and 19th century vodka was consumed in a cultivated way by the well-to-do. The rot set in, as it were, when 'the popular consciousness' began to dissociate the two, a process abetted by industrialization and an apparent decline in the richness and variety of *zakuski*. While it was largely the uncouth plebs in society who vulgarized the drinking of vodka, Pokhlebkin accuses two groups in pre-revolutionary Russia of compounding the damage. The offenders are 'those standard-bearers of Russian boorishness, officers and merchants', who more than anyone else had the 'opportunity to represent Russian society before foreigners.' He presumably means misrepresent. Note, incidentally, how Pokhlebkin, an intellectual, likes to stick his knife into vulgar businessmen.

Before proceeding, it is as well to be clear about what exactly vodka is and to distinguish among some well-known types.

What is vodka?

Vodka is distilled liquor, whose raw material is mash from a natural product such as cereal grains, notably rye in the form of both malt and grain (in the past potatoes were also used). The distillate is normally refined by a further process of filtration and then reduced in strength by the addition of so-called 'living' water, (i.e. soft water from rivers), which these days is purified. The resulting liquor is bright and clear without any specific aroma or taste. The most important quality of vodka is purity, which refers to the absence of dissolved substances in the basic distillate. Pokhlebkin considers only *Moskovskaya Osobaya* (Moscow Special) to be outstanding in all respects. The better known *Stolichnaya* does not compare: tiny quantities of sugar are used in its preparation. Commercially produced vodkas have an alcoholic content ranging between 40 and 55 percent. In Russia the strength is usually 40 percent by volume (80 US proof), and in Poland, where vodka is also the national drink, the normal strength is 45 percent (*Encyclopaedia Britannica*, 1993)

Some vodkas are produced with deliberate retention of the taste of the raw material; others are infused with a particular flavour. Examples include the somewhat aromatic *Zubrovka*, which is based on buffalo grass; *Pshenichnaya*, which is based on wheat; *Pertsova*, which is a pepper vodka; and *Limonnaya*, which is flavoured with lemon – 'ladies' vodka'. According to Pokhlebkin (1992), only *Moskovskaya Osobaya* (Moscow Special) outstandingly complements Russian *zakuski*. *Stolichnaya*, he claims, is particularly well suited to cocktails. *Russkaya* (Russian) he regards as 'an unsuccessful modern brand first produced in the 1970s, and the addition of cinnamon is evidently dictated by the need to mask the potato spirit included in the formula.' Three well-known vodkas have strengths exceeding 40 percent: *Sibirskaya* (Siberian) (45 percent), *Yubileynaya* (Jubilee) (45 percent) and *Krepkaya* (Strong) (56 percent).

The word vodka

The word vodka is derived from the Russian word for water (*voda*). Thus, a more a less literal translation of the word *vodka* would be something like 'drop of water'. At precisely what point vodka lost its watery associations to its alcoholic ones is a matter of considerable uncertainty. It is to be found somewhere in the history of vodka production. But, as William Pokhlebkin notes in his *History of Vodka* (1992) 'vodka really became vodka when it became a product cherished and protected by the state'. According to this author, the distilling of vodka as a distinct alcoholic beverage commenced in Russia in the mid-14th century, but the word had been in use for at least 100 years to denote grain spirit. Before then the word *vino* (wine) had been used to refer to the beverage, and was used in this colloquial sense until the 20th century. By 1474 vodka production in Russia was placed under state control, and that is the way things have largely remained ever since.

When they fancy a drink, Russians will often use the diminutive *vodichka*, rather as a Scotsman might talk about having 'a wee dram' rather than a Scotch. Vodka has been called 'Russian sunshine.' But relentless indulgers in marathon vodka sessions will find themselves passing rapidly from light to shade and into a state of total inebriation called 'the green snake'. This vivid, demonological expression refers to alcoholically induced hallucinatory experiences, which may also be accompanied by what Russians call 'the white fever', in other words, the DTs (Ozhegov, 1984). The word green, incidentally, occurs in another drinking expression. A green conference means a booze-up in a park or forest – environmentalists, beware on your next trip to Russia.

A brief social history of vodka

Drink – that is to say, intoxification from drink – has been common in Russia since time immemorial, and drunkenness has long been regarded by Russians and non-Russians alike as a national failing (Utechin, 1961). In the 10th century the Grand Prince Vladimir of Kiev had described drink as 'the joy of the Russes' (Massie, 1981). Of this same Vladimir it is said that he rejected any idea of nascent Russia becoming a Muslim country on the grounds that this religion forbade the drinking of alcohol (Hingley, 1978): whereby hangs one of the great imponderables of history. What if Russia had been an alcohol-free society? To which incidentally an unkind response might be: where could the Finns have gone for their cheap, protracted alcoholic binges?

Countless travellers to Russia confirmed this excessive indulgence. From the first influxes of foreigners to Russia from the 16th century onwards – merchants, engineers, doctors, artists, ambassadors – it has been regularly noted that Russians of any station were much taken with drink, often to forget the miseries of life. Giles Fletcher, an English ambassador sent from the Court of Elizabeth I, noted that at a Russian meal all those present would 'drink themselves speechless' (Hingley, 1978).

By the time of Peter the Great (1672–1725), no mean drinker himself, it was well known among travellers that 'to be drunk was an essential feature of Russian hospitality. Proposing toasts that no one dare refuse, hosts and guests gulped down cup after cup, turning their beakers upside down on their heads to prove that they were empty. Unless the guests were sent home dead drunk, the evening was considered a failure' (Massie, 1992).

Shades of plus ça change

Then, as now, the Russians appear to show remarkable tolerance to what Hingley (1978) aptly terms 'alcoholic befuddlement' as opposed to aggressive drunken loutishness. He suggests that the tipsy person is often treated with 'high regard . . . even tenderness' by the average sober bystander, adding that the capacity to hold one's drink and be a source of relatively harmless mirth is a kind of meritorious feat, the outcome of long years' apprenticeship. But that is only half the story. The Russians, it seems, enjoy the matey boisterousness that drink engenders, and any festivity – or even an excuse for festivity – supplies the occasion for carefree, exuberant merriment.

It has been observed that drinking is a festive, collective pastime in Russia and therefore that alcoholism is seldom a condition springing from isolated self-indulgence. Peter the Great and his fellow boozers formed themselves into their so-called 'Jolly Company' (Massie, 1992). The phrase is apt. Every Russian drinks for precisely that: jolly company. But merriment aside: if before the Russian Revolution of 1917 drinking and the abuse of alcohol were not considered serious social problems (i.e. did not merit alleviative action by the Tsars and their governments), the position under the Soviet regime was at first less tolerant and later ambiguous. Besides, 'at the end of the 19th century income from alcohol sales was the largest item in the Imperial budget' (Steele, 1994).

In 1917 the new regime banned the production of vodka until order was restored in the country in 1923. In 1924 a delegation of British trade unionists visited Russia and nowhere did they find signs of that well-known phenomenon, 'universal Russian drunkenness'. This was heralded by the British visitors as a triumph of Bolshevism: no longer was the working class oppressed and demeaned by the pervasive and corrupting influence of drink. The trade unionists' report noted that:

> On the street one may at times encounter people who are somewhat merry, but to those who remember pre-Revolutionary Russia it is quite clear that there are virtually no drunkards on the street or in public places.

> Pokhlebkin (1992)

There were severe restrictions on vodka production until 1936, and until 1941, the outbreak of war with Germany, 'drunkenness was condemned and punished as a social evil irreconcilable with proletarian ideology' (Pokhlebkin, 1992). Then in 1943, after the epochal Battle of Stalingrad, the Red Army was issued with a daily dose of 100 grams. [**Battle of Stalingrad**] According to Pokhlebkin, this measure had the effect of completely undermining the gains made in the first 20 years of the Revolution, when 'disapproval of drunkenness, and indeed of the consumption of alcohol in general, had been essential to being regarded as a true Communist'. By 1945 virtually every Russian (Soviet) male capable of holding a weapon was in the Red Army. Tens of millions of them had, as it were, rediscovered the pleasures of vodka as a palliative to the hell of war. This acquired taste was taken back into civilian life and, according to Pokhlebkin, it was workers in heavy industry, mining and construction who 'displayed a special need' for vodka.

The official party line was still one of strong disapproval against drunkenness, but by the early 1950s it was again recognized that sales of vodka (and alcoholic drink in general) made 'a singularly

Battle of Stalingrad

In 1942 Hitler commanded his armies in the Soviet Union to plunge south by seizing the Donetsk industrial belt, the city of Stalingrad on the Volga and the strategically important oilfields in the Caucasus. Achievement of these objectives would deal an irreparable blow to the Soviet economy. By the end of August the German armies had reached the Volga, entering Stalingrad on 12 September 1942. Before the month was out they occupied two-thirds of the city that bore the name of the Soviet leader. Possibly for that reason alone, Hitler was as determined to capture the city as Stalin was to save it from his clutches. The following seven weeks showed the Red Army under the great commanders, Zhukov and Vasilevsky, at its very best, engaging in 'ferocious street fighting . . . with small, courageous groups of infantry . . . while the German Panzer armies were hopelessly constricted, operating on greatly overstretched communications, and quite unable to display their true qualities' (Hosking, 1992). In the words of one observer, day and night were on fire. Another eyewitness reported that howling dogs would plunge into the Volga to escape the searing heat of battle. The fatal mistake made by the overconfident Germans had been to detach part of their armies for the next phase of operations before the attack on Stalingrad. On Christmas Day 1942, in temperatures of minus 40 degrees, the German 6th Army, knowing it was doomed, began to pull back. On the last day of the year the Germans surrendered. Thousands of shattered German soldiers, including 24 generals and, 2500 other officers, went east into captivity. They had started the assault on Stalingrad with nearly 250,000 troops and had lost 200,000 of them, not counting 30,000 wounded who were lucky enough to be evacuated by air.

In November 1943, at the Teheran Conference, Churchill, by command of King George VI, presented a sword of honour 'to the steel-hearted citizens of Stalingrad . . . in token of the homage of the British people'. By common consent the Battle of Stalingrad in 1942 was the turning point of the Great Patriotic War between the USSR and Nazi Germany. After Stalingrad the military scales tilted away from Germany: from then on Hitler would never fight on any front on his own terms. The Red Army began its inexorable march westward. It had been the biggest single battle in world history, and certainly one of the most terrible. After the war the city was rebuilt and, following the discrediting of Stalin by Khrushchev, it was renamed Volgograd.

important contribution . . . to state finances' (Brown, Kaser and Smith, 1994). To be precise, 'since the 1950s turnover taxes (sales taxes) on alcoholic beverages have contributed between 10 and 14 per cent of total state budget revenues, accounting for some 40 per cent of all direct and indirect taxes'. By the same token, the increased consumption of alcohol, notably vodka, abetted absenteeism in the workplace, reduced labour productivity, contributed to industrial and traffic accidents and caused suicide, violence and alcoholism. The total cost of alcohol abuse in terms of confinement, treatment and law enforcement has been put at between 5 and 8 percent of the Soviet state budget; and by the end of the Gorbachev era there may have been 15 million registered alcoholics and millions more non-registered ones in the USSR out of population of some 250 million (Brown, Kaser and Smith, 1994). If we are to believe two American experts on Russia (Feshbach and Friendly, 1992), the number of registered and non-registered alcohol abusers combined in 1989 could be between 20 and 30 million.

As already noted, Stalin placed heavy restrictions on alcohol, making drunkenness incompatible with party discipline and conduct during the 1920s and 1930s. Subsequent Soviet leaders also tried to curb excessive drinking using the full power of the state. Khrushchev made a bid in the 1960s; Brezhnev made two efforts to cut consumption in 1972 and 1979; Andropov introduced restrictive measures, cushioned by the introduction of a new, cheaper brand of vodka, which became humorously dubbed 'Androvka' (Feshbach and Friendly, 1992; Roxburgh, 1991). But it was Gorbachev, shortly after he became General Secretary of the Communist Party in 1985, who unleashed the biggest anti-alcohol campaign in the USSR since Stalin.[1] Gorbachev believed that, in addition to reducing a whole range of social ills associated with alcohol abuse, he could save some 300,000 Soviet lives a year, of which the majority would be 'Slavic', i.e. Russian, Ukrainian and Byelorussian.

In May 1985 the Politburo announced its sweeping anti-alcohol measures, which included the banning of drink from all places of work, at holiday resorts and at official banquets and receptions; liquor stores could not open before 2 pm and drink could not be sold publicly in the vicinity of industrial enterprises, building sites, educational establishments, hospitals, railway stations, airports and so forth; drunkenness on the street would be outlawed; there would be an 'All-Union Voluntary Society for Sobriety' with its own newspaper to promote the virtues of restraint (Roxburgh, 1991). At one point this society had enrolled no fewer than 11 million members who had been drinking 'on the job' (Wilson and Bachkatov, 1992).

In 1989 the entire campaign was called off as a failure. The state had lost 37 billion roubles in sales tax since 1985; wine and beer producers – not the original targets of the campaign – were forced to close down; high-quality vineyards were ripped up in the Caucasus and Moldavia; and, most seriously, the nation's hardened drinkers either resorted to making their own firewaters (*samogon*) or turned to substitutes such as perfume (which had to be rationed), anti-freeze, toothpaste, insecticides, cleaning fluids, shoe polish, varnish and glue (Roxburgh, 1991; Wilson and Bachkatov, 1992). These abuses led to 44,000 cases of poisoning in 1987, of which a quarter proved fatal (Roxburgh, 1991). Indeed, between 1985 and 1987 nearly as many Russians died from poisoning from substitutes (11,000) as had perished in the war with Afghanistan, which had started in 1979 and in 1987 was still going on (White, 1996).

The illicit moonshine – literally millions of hectolitres of it – became a major commodity on the black market: 'huge amounts of money accumulated in private hands, and powerful criminal bands arose that were mixed up with the mafias in the distribution system' (Medvedev and Chiesa, 1989). If you wanted legal stuff, you had to queue for it in the ever-dwindling number of outlets. On New Years' Eve 1987 3000 people lined up outside a solitary Moscow liquor store in sub-zero temperatures. Neither did the campaign have a serious impact on 'drinking on the job', which still crippled productivity (Smith, 1991).

This is not to say that the anti-drink campaign had been a complete failure. Sales from state-controlled sources had been cut from 10.9 to 3.9 litres per head per annum (*The Times*, 1995b). Despite the surge in homebrews, the campaign led to a reduction in overall drinking, in drink-related crime and industrial accidents. The Moscow correspondent for the *Guardian* summed up the failure of Gorbachev's campaign thus:

It was the first of his mistakes, and did much damage to his image among ordinary Russians. Instead of trying to handle alcoholism as a social problem with a variety of causes, he fell back on old-style disciplinarian methods. Intellectuals and government officials tended to laugh off the ban on alcohol sales as a mild inconvenience but male manual workers saw it as a new blow in their already difficult lives. It undermined Gorbachev's effort to portray himself as a man in touch with the popular mood.

Steele (1994)

In the reform period, all the signs are that alcohol abuse is as strong as it ever was. In July 1994 *Izvestiya* reported that 'the typical Russian male now consumes more than 80 litres of vodka annually' and that 'life expectancy for men has dropped from 65 years – in 1987, at the peak of Gorbachev's crusade – to 59' (*Financial Times*, 1995). Alcohol abuse is being blamed for up to 14 percent of deaths in the Moscow region and cited as a factor in two-thirds of all murders (*The Times*, 1995a). According to the Russian health ministry, alcoholic poisoning was claiming 37 deaths per 100,000 people in the mid-1990s, a fivefold increase over 1986–89 (*Financial Times*, 1994e). Vodka is also widely used to bribe the police. To test how serious this matter was, the interior minister sent a lorry full of vodka on a 700-kilometre journey through southern Russia. It was stopped by the police 24 times; they asked for bribes on 22 occasions (*The Economist*, 26 August 1995).

At the same time weakened state control over production means that vodka is no longer as pure as it used to be. The indigenous vodka industry is in a permanent crisis through 'growing foreign competition, increased duties and domestic underground distilleries turning forgeries' (*Financial Times*, 1994a). Not only that, some highly dubious spirituous concoctions are being sold in vodka bottles with standard labels. Which prompts this advice: only drink vodka with Russians you know and trust.[2] With respect to the foreign competition, the major international drinks firms have now secured 30 percent of the Russian vodka market (*Financial Times*, 1994). This situation provoked this outburst from Vladimir Iamnikov, director of the seriously ailing Kristall factory which produces *Stolichnaya* and 70 other hard liquors, in an interview with the *Financial Times* (1994c). The company had just been declared bankrupt by the Russian government. This was 'incomprehensible' to Iamnikov, who raged: 'We are Russia's flagship vodka factory, and vodka is the heart of everything which is Russian.' Such is the cruelty of the new winds sweeping the market economy.

Toasts and toasting

It may truly be said that toasting is a kind of spontaneous social art form among the Russians. Many westerners who have experienced Russian toasting, tend to find it an innocuous, quirky distraction from the main meal. But, to Russians, it is a central feature of the entertainment. It should also been seen as a form of business communication in its own right. Westerners without a good knowledge of Russian – an absolute majority of them – are frequently deprived of appreciating a good toast. Interpreters, alas, have an unhappy knack of not communicating the humour and emotional content of many toasts, making due allowance for the fact that these may include various forms of semi-untranslatable double entendres and other forms of linguistic playfulness.

Toasting often gives way to recitals of poetry, recountings of experiences, jokes, and anecdotes.[3] These contributions can be long or short depending on circumstances, and the person making his toast must always be on his feet. On one occasion, one hard-drinking manager (he who consumed two bottles of vodka at a friend's funeral), took ten minutes to recite a poem he had written especially for a banquet in our honour. This can only be described as a super-charged paean to the good old days of communism with its camaraderie and sense of purpose. It was an epic performance, and he was cheered to the ceiling. He reduced himself and half of our company (all market reformers to a man) to tears. This was not, strictly speaking a toast, but it had achieved the supreme effect: it had tugged at the heart strings of everyone, and most people showed it.

It is customary for the main host at a banquet to give the first toast. This is by definition the most sober toast of the evening and therefore the most serious. It often contains references to friendship and good relations and sounds *un peu soviétique*. The third toast is traditionally the Hussar's toast: it takes the form of a compliments to ladies, both present and absent, who are invariably beautiful, charming, and a wonderful source of strength to gallivanting menfolk. The host for the evening may sometimes invite persons in the company to say a toast. If the designated person jibs or hesitates, this may bring a friendly (or indeed not so friendly) rebuke.

One host, an octogenarian communist of aristocrat bearing and background, gave one such vacillator a public dressing down. 'Young man, I have just requested you, most politely, to pronounce a toast to our distinguished guests, and you are choosing to treat my request most casually. Most casually, I say. I tell you, young man, that this behaviour is by no means becoming, and I ask you again to raise your glass to our honourable guests with an appropriate toast. What is that young man's name, by the way?' Upon which, the shamed offender gets himself to his feet and dutifully complies with the command. 'Thank you, young man. Well done, but don't forget that I had to speak to you so severely' is the host's parting shot. Russian actually has a word for such a toast-master-cum-master of ceremonies. The word is *tamada*, but in fact this comes from the Georgian language. As any Russian will tell you with knowing envy, it is in Georgia that toasting reaches is most exalted form. 'If you think this is hospitality, you should go to Georgia.'

It should be mentioned that some Russians, even under the influence of vodka, do not always make good toasts. Some retain a kind of befuddled bashfulness and some do not know quite what to say in front of foreign guests. There is, however, a way out in such circumstances. It is always possible to drop in an apt saying or proverb. The Russian language is awash with these wiseacre apophthegms, which are seemingly adaptable to all human circumstances, including the transition to the market economies. Unfortunately, most of these these crusty bits of folk wisdom tend to get mangled in the translation. Many contain obscure, dialectal or archaic forms, and it is beyond the capabilities of most interpreters to convey the flavour of the sayings, let alone the meaning.

If you know Russian well, it is easy to be impressed, even moved by the resonant eloquence of some toasts. One Russian-speaking manager we interviewed admits that he has shouted 'bravo' after a toast of uncommon spontaneous elegance. Could their business counterparts from other countries, armed with their glittering MBAs, stand up in front of an audience of partial strangers and deliver something so deeply expressed from the heart? How is it that these Russians, admittedly fired by drink, can make such naturally sounding and captivatingly expressed speeches? Part of the answer may be that Russians are highly emotional as a race and need the toast as a kind of channel for their deeper feelings. Another part of the answer is that the Russians are easily drawn to poetry, to rhetorical language and declamation. Yet another part is that the Russians love their language and cherish those who as natives or foreigners speak it well, that is to say, know how to use Russian with elevated potency of expression. We have often been listening to Russian managers delivering a heart-felt toast, thinking 'Why can't our managers be as eloquent as that?'

When it is the foreign guest's turn to deliver a toast, his attempt may be fumbling and stilted. The 'safest' route is to deliver a short toast in English, which can be translated unambiguously by the interpreter. It is almost de rigueur that the toast flatters one's hosts and says kind words about individuals present (Russians are very susceptible to flattery. This is perhaps to be expected in a society in which sycophantism has been so noticeable feature of life.) A toast that directly or indirectly praises the greatness of Russia and her people will be much appreciated. If you are prepared to speak to Russian hearts in your toast, then beware. Our experience, as already observed, is that interpreters drain the emotional content from toasts. They simply deliver verbal cardboard.

Those with a command of Russian will quickly absorb and use some of the set phrases: 'Respected guests, friends, colleagues permit me to express on behalf of those present my profound thanks to Ivan Ivanovich for his invitation to this evening's splendid banquet . . . Respected guests, I raise my glass to Ivan Ivanovich for his great generosity.' The foreign guest can use such an occasion to demonstrate not only his command of Russian in a technical way, but also his ability to speak to Russian hearts. If he can do this by the judicious use of a Russian saying or convert a piece of earthy folk wisdom from his own culture or (and this is where brownie points are scored) he can quote one of the great Russian writers, this is warmly received by Russians.

If you are invited to the *banya*, the Russian bath, you find that taking a sauna and bathing is either followed by, or interspersed with, drinking sessions. You will be crammed into a pine cabin, sitting around a pine table which your hosts will festoon with bottles of vodka, beer, mineral water, a sickly sweet fruit juice and maybe Coke or Pepsi. They will also bring black bread, gherkins, some cold meats and dried or smoked fish. The *banya* is the place of male relaxation par excellence in Russia, not to mention a place of boozy refuge for skiving workers. Provided that there is some kind of common language that can keep the lines of communication open to everyone, the *banya* can prove to be an invigorating and agreeable experience.

Once the ice has been broken with the first two toasts (and some friendly thrashings with birch twigs), Russians will often reveal a curiosity about the life and background of a foreigner or two in their midst. But you, the foreigner, should not expect to be the sole topic of conversation. Russians have a habit of reminiscing and, as a foreigner, it is hard to keep pace with the speed of change of topics. Someone talks about his boyhood in Chelyabinsk. Chelyabinsk? Where's that? Someone else talks about his time in the army. Did you say you served in Afghanistan? No, it was in Germany. Germany? Yes, the Germany that used to belong to us. Have you really been to the Kamchatka? What's it like? I don't remember. I was only born there. Do you really speak Karelian? Yes, listen. There is an outburst of song in Karelian, which intrigues and amuses the rest of the company, non-Karelians to a man. It might as well have been in Yakut or Evenki (but Yiddish might be a bit risky in untested company). In between the reminiscences there are jokes and witticisms, which tend to exclude you as the foreigner.

A lot of these increasingly boozy reminiscences are about life in the army, from which you conclude all armies are equally stupid. Is there no army on the planet that does not give its new recruits completely illogical, mindless tasks to do? Your hosts will soon remember that you are no longer in the conversation and will close the gap by sharing common knowledge about Manchester United or the horrible fogs in London (but not the death cloud from Chernobyl). They seem hurt when you say London's peasoupers are a thing of the past. Better change the topic by drinking something and chewing on some smoked fish. Then, you resume the questions. Choose the best one, which is always: What is the coldest temperature you have ever experienced? Every Russian knows exactly when and where. Someone says Leningrad 1942. [**Siege of Leningrad**] This brings twitches of horror to the Russian faces, at

Siege of Leningrad

No city in modern times has endured such a sustained enemy attack, which led to the death of a million or more non-combattants. On 22 June 1941 the Germans launched their attack on the USSR. Buoyed up by his early military successes against the Red Army and convinced that the Soviet Union's defeat was both inevitable and imminent, Hitler ordered a major assault on Leningrad, the birthplace of bolshevism. The city was to be obliterated, its population starved into oblivion. The blockade of Leningrad began at the end of August and, until the siege was lifted in January 1944, the city was cut off from overland communication with the rest of the country. The city was completely unprepared for a siege. The 1941–2 winter was the coldest for many decades. The daily military food ration was 9 ounces of bread, often 'supplemented' with sawdust, cottonseed oil and cellulose; for the rest of the population it was 4.5 ounces. Soup was made from boiled leather, glue scraped off wallpaper and even book bindings. Domestic animals, not to mention rodents and birds, were eaten by the starving population. There were also acts of cannibalism. There was no transport and no electricity for 'non-essential' purposes. The only supply line was the 'Road of Life' across the frozen Lake Ladoga, which lorries used to bring food into the city. In all 200,000 people died of cold and starvation in that terrible winter. The German lines were first broken in January 1943 and the blockade was lifted a year later after 880 days. In the memorial to those who died in the siege of Leningrad, an inscription carved in stone speaks volumes for the indomitability of Russian courage under the fiercest conditions imaginable: 'Death is more afraid of us than we are afraid of death.' It is said that Soviet newsreels of Leningrad under siege are so horrific and harrowing that to this day they have never been shown publicly.

the thought of the ghastly experience of the Nazi siege. A respectful pause, then someone else pipes up: minus 55 near Lake Baikal (Celsius, for the uninitiated). **[Baikal]** No-one can match that. Grunts of admiration.

From all this, if you deduce that business and pleasure are not to be mixed at sauna parties, you are absolutely right.

Reactions to business socialization

Our contributors all held slightly different views regarding drink as an element of informal relationship building. This is no doubt due to different experiences. What seems to be the case is that the

---

Baikal

Lake Baikal is a huge freshwater expanse, located in the mountains of southern Siberia. It stands 1513 ft above sea level and covers an area of 12,500 square miles. Described as the eighth wonder of the world, it is 'a natural wonder 25 to 30 million years old, an ecosystem as distinctive as the Amazon rain forest, a scenic marvel on the order of the Grand Canyon, but seven times as deep [5669 ft], and a laboratory for what may be the oldest freshwater organisms on the planet' (Feshbach and Friendly, 1992). More than 2000 unique animal and plant species are supported by the lake, including the *nerpa*, the world's only freshwater seal. Laurens van der Post visited the lake nearly 40 years ago and he described a type of fish which was 'found at levels from a hundred metres below the surface, which had no bones and was so transparent that one could read one's newspaper through it' (1964). The lake, which has the dubious honour of sparking off the first environmental protest in Soviet history in 1963, is today chronically polluted. The cause of the outrage then was a factory built on the shores of the lake to make aircraft tyres from cellulose, and this is still the main source of pollution. That campaign failed like many others, even though the plight of Lake Baikal was championed by many leading scientific and literary personages, who repeatedly warned the Soviet authorities about irreversible ecological disaster. 'Conserve this glorious sea, our blessed Baikal', the writer Mikhail Sholokhov pleaded in vain. Today, it faces an additional threat to its existence: tourism.

Russians will not invite you to a *banya* unless they genuinely like you. They want to be sure that you are someone who is going to enjoy the festive occasion, which to the Russians is a form of collective innocuous revelry. One of our contributors had been to sauna parties with his Russian colleagues. The 'naked equality', as he graphically phrased his experiences, made for socially levelling interactions and, as it were, naturally precluded any necessity to mix business with pleasure. Hence the *banya* experience is one where your character – not your undoubted business competencies – is the essential sine qua non of a memorable occasion, as far as Russian hosts are concerned.

As for business drinking, there were various views which, as it happened, revealed a kind of progression about the degree to which one may find oneself a captive of Russian hospitality. Here are some quotations from our contributors. Note the perverse progression from level one, which indicates extreme likelihood, to level five, which indicates inevitability:

1 You must be prepared to drink vodka.

2 You can sip it, but you must not say 'no'.

3 Once there is vodka in your glass, you have to finish it.

4 There is pressure to drink.

5 They force you to drink.

Whatever your attitude to drinking, the inescapable fact is that it is the most direct way for western firms to find and develop the all-important social dimension to formal business relationships with Russian partners. This may be slightly unpalatable to some firms or to individual executives, but this is essentially a fact of life. Russians tend to use drinking together and all the associated toasting as a way of seeing how much they like you. Or, to quote a leading management consultant: 'If the Russians don't like you, they won't do business with you.' This may strike western managers as naive. It is, of course. But, as we emphasized in the chapter on negotiation and business communication, foreigners must make allowance for the fact that Russians are more easily swayed by emotion than by purely rational appeals.

Only two contributors made direct references to toasting. One, who does not speak Russian, found toasting 'boring and formal' – the almost diametric opposite of how the Russian regard it. The other informant, a Russian speaker, noted how important it is to communicate a positive attitude to Russia and Russians in toasts. This contributor also added that an invitation to any form of business entertainment should be 'graciously accepted'. Unless you have a genuine excuse, such as a previous engagement, a Russian will be deeply offended if he thinks that you have turned down his invitation for dubious reasons. The fact that you have been out with Russians for the last five evenings and simply want a break from 'the intense hospitality is no excuse, no matter how diplomatically phrased, and will not be appreciated by a would-be host. His attitude might be summed up thus: 'It is my turn now. I want to show you my hospitality, and you will enjoy yourself just as much as on the previous evenings.'

Drinking vodka

The standard measure of vodka is 100 grams, about the equivalent of a double. Vodka is normally served chilled and is traditionally drunk in one gulp. Russians often press their guests to drink, as they say, 'to the bottom' (*do dna*). Experience suggests that two glasses of vodka taken in fairly rapid succession without the fortification of food or some mouthfuls of soft drink can bring about – shall we say – an agreeable tipsy mellowness. After that one's resistance to the further onslaughts is dramatically reduced. In this state, the golden rule is: Don't drink any other form of alcohol that may be around such as beer or *shampanskoye* (Russian sparkling wine). Unless you actually poison yourself (which can happen), vodka does not provoke much of a hangover (although you may be doing long-term damage to your liver). Despite the assumption that the glass must always be drained in one go, it is possible to take sips. But expect the nearest Russian to keep replenishing your glass.

The way Russians drink vodka is like this. They drink it in one gulp with an inhalation of breath, although before this they may have sniffed some rye bread. They promptly follow this up with a soft drink or mineral water to dilute the vodka in the system, and then take a bite of pickled fish, cucumber or bread. On the pleasures of vodka drinking, here is John Lloyd, the *Financial Times* Moscow correspondent:

> Without question, the cold simplicity of vodka is an invitation to toss a glassful down the throat and wait, eyes watering, for the lovely blast in the stomach as the liquor explodes. It lacks the subtlety of whisky and the bourgeois splendour of brandy but, in its craggy purity, it stands on a peak of its own.

Financial Times (1993)

But let us leave the final word on this topic to William Pokhlebkin (1992), who, as the following passage clearly shows, feels that the art of drinking vodka has become vulgarized, and by the Russians themselves:

> Ideally, vodka should be poured into clear, colourless glass or crystal *stopki*, either cylindrical or in the shape of a truncated cone, with a capacity of 100 millilitres. These vessels should be filled only two-thirds full. To fill the glasses to the brim, so that it is difficult to drink, is the mark of a Philistine. It is a sign of Russian taste, to be sure, but of the lowest provincial and uneducated kind.
>
> That is everything a foreigner needs to know about the correct, and at the same time enjoyable, way of drinking vodka. Anything that does not conform to these rules should be mercilessly rejected as vulgar, uncultivated and historically unauthentic, that is as the mark of a boor and not of a Russian gentleman.

There would seem to be few Russian gentlemen left.

Notes

[1] In his autobiography Gorbachev (1995) recalls a incident, when his father's friends plied him with local hooch at harvest time. He was 15 at the time, and the youngest member of his work brigade. In his words:

> Then the brigade leader started to give me a hard time. 'What on earth are you hanging around for? The harvest is in. Let's have a drink. It is high time you were a real man.' I glanced at my father. He remained silent and smiled with sweat on his brow. A tumbler was produced. I thought it was vodka, but it turned out that it was pure spirit. There was a special technique for drinking spirit. The thing was to drink after exhaling and then without hesitation follow it down with cold water without inhaling. I did not know that and drained the contents of the tumbler.
>
> What was happening to me?! The other workers rolled about laughing and my father was laughing most of all. That was to teach me a really good lesson: from then on neither vodka nor spirit had any particular appeal for me.

This partly explains a strongly personal motives for Gorbachev's anti-alcohol campaign

[2] A chilling cautionary tale was reported in *The Times* (1995 c and d). Their journalist, honouring the long-standing tradition that 'in Russia you never refuse a glass of vodka', was plied with an almost lethal concoction and nimbly relieved of his wallet. He was lucky to survive, later diagnosed as having been poisoned with clonidine, a treatment for high blood pressure, which criminals have latched onto for its narcotic properties.

[3] Russian interpreters and other English-speaking Russians frequently use the word 'anecdote' for 'joke', although there is separate word in Russian for 'joke'.

TOWARDS EFFECTIVE

RELATIONSHIP MANAGEMENT

Most of the early professors [in the first decade of the 19th century] were foreign, and lectured in German or Latin, to the dismay of their less educated listeners . . . Conflicts often broke out between Russian and foreign teachers, with the Russians complaining that the foreigners were indifferent towards the students, and the foreigners dismissing the Russians as boorish and unscholarly.

— Hosking, 1997

Who are we and where are our roots? Where should we seek our heritage and what should we take from the past so that our present and our future do not turn out to be a tragic dénouement of the past?

— Zaitseva, 1994

Introduction

After the turmoil of the Russian Revolution and the horrors of the Civil War, Russia was plunged headlong into the experiment of communism. Even Lenin admitted that he and his cronies had been wrong to assume that 'an immediate transition would take place

229

from the old Russian economy to state production and distribution on Communist principles.' He even conceded that 'we made the mistake of deciding to change over directly' (Conquest, 1993). The founder of the Soviet state, who was not exactly known for admitting error, is conceding that the uncompromising drive to set up the economy on communist lines had proved counterproductive: the inference is that the people were unable to adjust to a radically new set of circumstances unless that particular transition – from autocracy to communism – were taken more cautiously.

Today, over 80 years later, the Russian (former Soviet) population again finds itself in a period of transition – towards another dubious utopia called 'the market economy'. This strange occurrence of history repeating itself helps to bear out the conviction that there are powerfully striking parallels between the decline and fall of Imperial Russia and the Soviet regime (Lieven, 1994). This may be illuminating, but not necessarily a consolation. And, pragmatically, we do know this from history: when Russia and its people are 'on the edge of a precipice' (*Financial Times*, 1997), other countries must hold their breath.

In the Russia of the last years of the 20th century, the speed of change is creating new imbalances, social tensions and anxiety; there is even a yearning for old-style stability, a yearning that overlooks the abominable nightmare of Stalinism. Not that there are many Russians left who genuinely look upon the Stalinist era as a cherished golden age. But at least, after the austerity of Stalinism, society was under control: the Soviet population was being looked after, and there was, until the 1980s, a general conviction that all the sacrifices of creating and maintaining 'socialism in one country' had resulted in the USSR achieving superpower status – Soviet citizens could be proud of their country. It was not until the Gorbachev period (1985–91) and after the demise of the communist party that the people of the former Soviet Union became aware of the ghastly dimensions of these 'heroic' sacrifices.

Whatever mistakes had been made, the Soviet Union – now Russia – always had potential. The attitude to this potential was well expressed by a Russian businessmen in an interview with the *Financial Times* (1997). 'I was born in a country called the Soviet Union. Subconciously I always understood that I lived in the greatest country on earth. That sense of greatness made it possible to feel not only a sense of enormous spaces, but also of enormous possibilities.' The political system may have changed, life may have become topsy-turvy, yet there is always a burning conviction that Russia has 'enormous possibilities'. The problem is how to channel them in order to convert Russia into an industrial democracy suited for the information age (democracy here means a non-totalitarian system of government.)

Those concerned with management education in Russia, whether as implementers or sponsors, must accept these tricky realities. They must first understand that Russia, exactly like the Soviet Union before it, is often unfathomable to westerners. To paraphrase Robert Conquest (1994), a leading western chronicler of Stalinism, Russia is a country with extraordinary idiosyncrasies and special characteristics, 'some of them hardly credible to foreign minds'. Second, western investors, management educators and consultants must realize that Russians are disinclined to become pawns and victims in yet another disastrous social scheme, dreamed up by political zealots and enforced by ruthless dictatorship. But the adoption of western political and economic models is not overwhelmingly seen as a way out for Russia. Who is to say that the much-vaunted market economy may not be yet another form of crippling exploitation? Who can deny that certain aspects of western management practices and business practices, as we have suggested earlier, go against the grain of deeply held Russian values?

For such reasons, the west is sometimes seen by nationalistically minded Russians (often in bizarre alliances of the political extremities) as stoking up 'the fires of change' to the extent that Russia will be an exhausted, corrupted and humiliated wreck. The west for its part is disinclined to see itself in this light. More to the point, after the collapse of the USSR in 1991, the west made a grave miscalculation. It assumed that the Russians would immediately embrace western forms of economic management and political development as enthusiatically as they had bought western jeans and Beatles tapes on the black market. But it was not to be. As we have already noted, the ideologically motivated xenophobic wariness of the Cold War has unexpectedly reasserted itself in a different garb.

It is on this somewhat sombre tone that we introduce the final chapter of this book. Our main task is to draw implications for western managers and decision makers, focusing on specific challenges facing three identified groups of protagonists:

- management educators

- management consultants and business representatives

- policy makers, including sponsors of management education initiatives.

Review of general implications

In 1991 a Russian manager was quoted as saying: 'If you want to make headway in our country, you must understand our mentality and get wise to us. Psychology is the decisive thing, not factual argument' (*Manager Magasin*, 1991). His conviction is no less valid today. In whatever capacity a western manager is working directly with Russia, he or she needs a sharp appreciation of the following Russian concerns, attitudes and elements of their psychological makeup, which have been emphasized at various points in this book:

- entrenched attitudes ('pre-Marxist scorn') towards money, wealth and business

- legitimate fears about being drawn into yet another ghastly social experiment

- deep-felt anxieties about western ulterior motives in 'helping' Russia (intoxicating fuel in a country where conspiracy theories run riot)

- an assumption that key facets of western life and practices have little or no relevance to Russian conditions.

In Chapter 2, we highlighted the nature of areas of frictions and sticking points in relationships between western consultants and educators with Russian counterparts as recipients of advice, instruction and know-how. The directors of the seminar where these issues were debated submitted a report to the National Training Foundation in February 1997. It is worthwhile quoting from a summary of key insights into factors that severely strain relationship development between western managers and Russian counterparts:

1 A central insight to emerge from the workshop is that 'the West' has generally not been successful in managing effective relationships with Russian counterparts because Westerners *have failed to understand Russian expectations and align them with their own*. Management educators do this repeatedly by not building Russian expectations into their training needs analysis and therefore not into the actual programs. Western firms seldom meet Russian expectations to be taught about Western management methods and business principles.

2 Russian staff feel very strongly that they are both undervalued and underutilised; as such they are deprived of making a significant intellectual contribution to the Western firm that employs them. Consultants do this by hiring otherwise talented Russians, but using them mainly as *mere facilitators* to progress the company business.

3 The atmosphere of working relationships is antagonised by points made under 1 and 2 and is negatively reinforced by (a) perceptions that consultants and trainers do not have much interest in understanding the 'Russian mentality' and (b) the severe disparities in remuneration.

4 Relationship management between Russians and their Western counterparts must be based on *equivalence*. By equivalence is meant the mutual realisation that, while inputs from each side in terms of knowledge, experience and resources are *different*, they are *of equal relative importance* to achieve effective communication and productive cooperation.

5 The relative severity of the gap is determined by Russian and Western partners' respective understanding of each other's frame of reference as well

as by more elusive factors such as personal affinity and professional competence as intercultural communicators.

6 Not only is there a gap between Western and Russian managers, but also a gap between managers who operated in the Soviet system and younger managers who have a greater stake in their country's transition to the market economy. (Vlachoutsicos, Bogatova, Holden, 1997)

The report continues:

Investors and managers who aspire to successful operations in Russia, depending on the specific managerial requirements of each investment, will position themselves (a) to work closely with their Russian colleagues, applying the optimum amalgam of Western and Russian management methods; and (b) to seek *alignment* both on objectives, expectations of each side, and on implementation plans as well as on the process through which decisions will be taken. Otherwise, they are likely to encounter significant problems in implementing decisions and monitoring results effectively. In the meantime, however, until some measure of political and economic stability can be established in Russia, old attitudes and habits are apt to persist . . . A knowledge of Russian (however limited), a demonstrated familiarity with Russian and Soviet history and (this goes a long way) with the great Russian literary figures – all these factors positively influence Russians, who expect their teachers to be well read (i.e. outside their nominal field of specialisation).

There is nothing in these insights which is at variance with the findings of the survey which was the centrepiece of Chapter 6. The question now is what can be done to reduce the scope for crosscultural clashes. We address these issues by focusing challenges in relation to:

- management educators
- management consultants and business representatives

- policy makers, including sponsors of management education initiatives.

Implications for management educators

In the light of these factors management educators are strongly advised to:

- shift their emphasis from mere delivery of courses to tackling the underrated (and underresearched) question of how Russian managers learn

- tackle as a central issue on any course claiming to impart market economy skills Russian misconceptions of management and ignorance of the nature and significance of business information

- grasp the importance of the emotional dimension to interactions with Russians

- treat the language barrier not as a 'mere' irritant, but as a central obstruction in the management know-how transfer process.

Educators who develop a conviction that they are learning more on their management courses than the Russian participants may well be on the way to gaining insights into the Russian frame of reference.

The report to the National Training Foundation emphasized the following points:

- Management educators are expected to be fully expert in their field, but able to communicate this expertise in ways which have practical relevance for Russian conditions.

Problematically, there is still a conviction in Russia that western business and management can be mastered through familiarization with sets of techniques. A further complication concerns the fact that western management concepts have only been partially absorbed into Russian, which has not yet developed adequate lexical resources, based both on native roots and foreign terms, to facilitate the onset of market economy thinking, structures and institutions.

- A key policy issue for management educators is the realization that their fundamental aim must be to help to bring into being a new language for social and economic development in Russia.

From this it follows that standard western teaching materials, *'translated into a nominal form of Russian,* actually undermine the effective transfer of management know-how. *The attractions to Western management consultants and educators of obtaining substantial management education contracts from official sponsor organisations have largely outweighed a willingness to apply their intellect to this daunting challenge'* [new emphasis].

The report adds:

> *Effective* communication of management know-how into the Russian frame of reference is immensely challenging. Part of the solution appears to be able to satisfy an entirely justifiable Russian expectation that normal Western teaching materials – and even the teaching approach – must be adapted to suit Russian conditions and priorities. This is not easy, but it can be done.

Implications for sponsors of management education initiatives

Sponsors of management education in Russia, including governments, tend to have no detailed knowledge of Russia as a management training environment. Their otherwise generous donations may end up only partially achieving stated aims without anyone knowing exactly why. It is now time to take stock of the financial effectiveness of western management training aid to Russia. All sponsors have a vested interest in this. This means providing funds to investigate, on a systematic basis, at least two crucially important questions:

- the competence of management educators they are sponsoring to deliver training programmes which meet the learning needs of Russians

- the use and dissemination of western management know-how

in Russian companies, whose managers have attended sponsored programmes.

Competence of management educators

The availability of generous funding for training projects is prompting some educational institutions to 'go for the money': this motive, although fully understandable, may not in all cases be associated with a capacity to devise and implement programmes that are based on a clear appreciation of:

• the historical and wider background to the collapse of the USSR

• Russians as educational participants.

Sponsors, many of whom are publically accountable and concerned not to waste the resources allocated to management education in Russia, may need to establish tighter criteria for evaluating the professionalism of institutions delivering the know-how.

The problem here is that it is the case that western teachers of management are often sorely inexperienced when it comes to educating or training Russians. Given that the vast majority of trainers do not speak Russian, have probably not mastered the Cyrillic alphabet or have any informed appreciation of the nature of socialist economic management, and would never had looked east in other circumstances, it is almost inevitable that in course after course, programme after programme, the trainers are simply reinventing the wheel. Not only that, this state of affairs is reinforcing Russian objections that the educators and trainers are only in it for the money and have no special commitment to Russia. This situation is placing a heavy burden on resources, and donor agencies may not be entirely aware of it.

There would therefore appear to be overwhelming arguments for setting up or designating centres in western countries for equipping consultants with know-how about teaching management to Russians and, by extension, other nations of eastern and central Europe. It is one thing to lay on a course for Russian managers; understanding them as learners and receivers of management education is quite another. About that crucial issue there is enormous ignorance in the west.

Use and dissemination of western management know-how in Russian companies

This is the great unknown of management training in Russia. Sponsors will have to pay more attention to this issue in future. Requiring trainers to follow through by systematically assessing knowledge implementation will bring two important benefits. First, it will make the trainers committed to the results of programmes and not just delivering them. Second, Russian companies, whose managers have attended a course, will in effect be required to indicate in what ways they have implemented the new knowledge and, by implication, justify the training investment they have received.

Implications for management consultants and business representatives

We can usefully draw on the report to the National Training Foundation for elucidation of the key issues:

- Russians who work for or with western firms feel undervalued, underutilized and even intimidated.

- Russia's ancestral suspicion of the west is just below the surface and can be easily provoked.

- Consultants and business representatives must anticipate these possible reactions, and one way of neutralizing them is to build into company policy procedures and systems which take into account the complexity of Russian expectations.

- A western firm may need to develop an educational function for its Russian employees and counterparts, not to mention introducing innovative forms of remuneration for expatriate staff and Russian employees which reduce the perceived disparities.

As noted in Chapter 6, relationship management between

Russians and their western counterparts can be developed on the basis of equivalence and not on psycholgically misplaced notions of equality. Russians, historically speaking, have no tradition of equality in the western sense. Rather, they have been subjected to social and cultural processes of equalization under a dominant authority. Equivalence 'requires the mutual alignment of expectations and an appreciation of the '"Russian mentality"'. (Vlachoutsicos, Bogatova and Holden, 1997). It is important to emphasize the critical importance of meeting Russian expectations. They expect management educators to be experts; they expect vastly over-paid consultants to give advice that automatically shows insights into Russian problems; they expect their business partners to cement relationships with copious tipples of vodka as 'a sort of seal on ceremonials' (Smith and Christian, 1984).

The report to the National Training Foundation expresses the underlying challenge in these terms:

> The specific challenge concerns ways in which Russians can feel valued for their potential contributions to a Western company as an employer or business partner. One potentially effective approach is to institutionalise joint problem-solving teams; another is for Western representatives to see themselves as coaches or mentors, but without pedantry and arrogance which Russians much resent.
>
> Vlachoutsicos, Bogatova and Holden (1997)

Implications for policy makers

Policy makers in the form of national governments and supranational bodies such as the European Union and the United Nations Industrial Development Organization have allocated millions of pounds in assistance to Russia to facilitate the introduction of the market economy (see Chapter 2). These contributions have been criticized by some commentators as being too small: too small to trigger real change in Russia with its tendency 'to wait for history to do something'. Yet, as we have noted, there may be a 40 percent inefficiency factor associated with these 'small' donations. Are substantially bigger donations really going to be more cost effective?

At all events policy makers will be sorely tested over Russia, and the position of management education is likely to be an important factor in their equations because every kind of aid to Russia – whether in the form of foodstuffs, advice on narcotics control or assistance in rendering nuclear installations safer – will perforce entail an upgrading of Russian management competencies.

In the final analysis, everything will depend on the Russians' ability to identify their own best interests, determine what kind of society they wish to create and to help one another to achieve it. Western policy should presumably see that as its long-term goal, but this in itself does not resolve the issue of how much assistance to grant to Russia and how to construct aid packages that do not give the Russians the appearance that the real beneficiaries, financial and otherwise, are western trainers and consultants.

Conclusion

In this book we have attempted to take account of a whole range of factors which appear to confound and even wreck working relationships between western managers and Russian counterparts whether these are clients, customers or even employees. We have made every effort to present the Russian perspective, as representatives of foreign organizations may not be aware of Russia's quest for renewal which seeks a specifically Russian way; of the aspiration to rediscover and restore traditional Russian values; and of the complex nature of anti-western resentments. It is therefore not easy for western governments, companies and organizations including even 'open-minded' organizations such as universities, to find the right formula to allay Russia's fears and, at the same time, to communicate confidence in the Russian way of doing things.

The authors of the report to the National Training Foundation in Moscow addressed this issue. They too had no quick solution, but expressed a firm belief in the importance of commitment to Russia. This commitment, they explained, 'has to be demonstrably personified, must be both intellectual and emotional'. In other words, westerners must be able and willing to develop a special sense of identification with Russians and their problems and be prepared to go beyond the normal confines of 'rational economic thought' (Vlachoutsicos, Bogatova and Holden, 1997). The point is that western businessmen, consultants and educators are not merely involved in opening up Russia's vast internal market, restructuring the wrecked economy or transforming managers to understand the workings of the market economy. Whether they fully appreciate this or not, they are also protagonists bringing about conditions to enable Russia to cope with what the *Financial Times* (1997) has described as 'its final, and perhaps most daunting, challenge: the need to forge a new national identity'. That is why all the market economics in the world and all the best management theory and know-how continually fall short of Russia's needs and why Russian expectations of the west time and time again remain at best half-met.

Russia is coming to terms with its ever-changing identity, very much like when Alice finds herself in Wonderland and everything starts to change so rapidly that she no longer knows where or who she is any more (Gardner, 1960):

> Let me think: *was* I the same when I got up this morning? I almost think I can remember feeling a little different. But if I'm not the same, the next question is, 'Who in the world am I?' Ah, *that's* the great puzzle!

The 'great puzzle' is beginning to be resolved, and that should make it easier for the west to understand the Russia of today as revealed through the contexts of the Russias of yesterday – it is important for us in the west to appreciate Russia in her multilayered historical dimensions.

Whatever Russia was, is or will be, it seems that Mother Russia will ever elude our complete understanding. In a famous verse the fine 19th-century lyric poet Tyutchev wrote that Russia is not to be apprehended by mind alone nor measured in everyday units of distance. 'One can only believe in Russia', he declared.

He might have added 'and hope'.

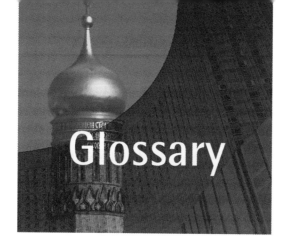

Glossary

This is a select compilation of notable historical and contemporary terms, acronyms and personalities.

Words in *italics*, except personal names, are transliterated from Russian. An asterisk by an entry refers the reader to the information panels (see pages 261–269).

→ by an entry refers the reader to that entry in the glossary.

Academician (*akademik*). The foremost rank of scholarship in the USSR/Russia, corresponding in prestige to a Fellowship of the Royal Society in the UK. Perhaps the best-known Soviet academician in the west was Andrei Sakharov.

Aeroflot. The Soviet state airline, established in 1923, was notorious for its 'service with a scowl' and disconcerting air safety record. In its heyday it employed 600,000 people, including 20,000 pilots, ran 3000 aircraft and served 3600 destinations from major airports to ice stations. Aeroflot also operated air ambulance services, fought forest fires and sprayed agricultural pesticides. Following the collapse of the USSR, Aeroflot has broken up into 300 or so airlines, which run the incountry services, and is now re-equipping itself with Boeings in addition to its ten Airbuses for its international routes. Watch out for big battles ahead between Aeroflot, with its pro-west purchasing policies, and Russia's peeved manufacturers of airframes, avionics and engines.

Andropov, Yuri (1916–1984). Head of the KGB from 1967–1982 and General Secretary of the Communist Party from 1982–84. He was influential in promoting the career of Mikhail Gorbachev.

→ Communist party

→ Gorbachev*

→ KGB*

Apparatchik. A colloquial term for Soviet officials in the party, government and state machine. The term is especially associated with those officials working in the Central Committee of the Communist Party.

→ Central Committee

→ Communist party

Arshin. An old Russian measure of length, approximately 0.7m, the word *arshin* occurs in the famous poem by Fyodor Tyutchev, quoted in one of the concluding paragraphs of Chapter 10.

Autocracy. The supreme power of the Russian emperors. The title of autocrat, which derives from the Byzantine emperors, was used by the Grand Princes of Muscovy when they threw off the Tartar yoke in the 14th century. From the time of Peter the Great, autocracy acquired the meaning of absolute ruler.

Baikal*

BAM. The Russian initials standing for the rail line north of the original Trans-Siberian Railway. BAM attracted thousands of young volunteers in the 1970s who helped build the railway to open up Siberia for economic development and to protect the militarily vulnerable southern rail route.

Banya. The Russian bathroom, as opposed to bathtub: originally a small, one-room log hut, these days the *banya* may be a kind of outhouse or communal bathroom with a changing area, sauna, showers, bathing pool or equivalent (i.e. lake or river). The *banya* is one of the Russian's favourite forms of relaxation. See Chapter 9.

***Borodino*, Battle of** (1812). One of Napoleon's costliest victories and the one he considered the most terrible. His Grande Armée of 113,000 soldiers (with 28 million bottles of wine) was lured into a trap by the Russian general Kutuzov commanding 120,000 troops. Russian losses were 44,000 and French losses 33,000. His weakened army went on to occupy a deserted and burning Moscow. Unable to subdue Russia, Napoleon made his retreat during the bitter Russian winter. Only 25,000 of his men returned from Russia. The great Russian triumph was commemorated in Tchaikovsky's *1812 Ouverture*, which was never heard in public during the Soviet regime, as the music contained fragments of the Imperial Russian anthem which was banned.

Boyar. A male member of the higher aristocracy in mediaeval Russia.

Bear → Russian Bear

Beria, Lavrentii (1899–1953). A Georgian like Stalin, Beria was virtually in charge of internal security in the USSR from 1938, when he liquidated his predecessor, the odious Yezhov, until 1953, when he was shot as 'an imperialist agent' in the power struggle after Stalin's death.

→Stalin*

***Beriozka*.** The luxury hard currency stores of the Soviet era. In 1991 *beriozki* virtually disappeared, as their monopoly of hard currency retail transactions was no longer tenable.

***Bolshevik*.** The word is derived from the Russian word for 'majority'. In 1903 Lenin obtained a majority at the 1903 Congress of the Russian Social Democratic Labour Party – after several delegates had left. After 1918 the Bolsheviks became known as communists.

→ Communist party
→ Lenin
→ Mensheviks

Brezhnev, Leonid*

Catherine the Great (1729–96). Daughter of a Prussian field marshall, Catherine married the future Tsar Peter III, whose murder in 1762 was, as they say, highly convenient. As Empress of Russia she was the apotheosis of the 18th-century absolute monarch, but was a remarkable ruler noted variously for being 'a politician, diplomat, commander-in-chief, educator, builder, picture-collector, lover, mother, playwright, writer of fairy stories, autobiographer and indefatigable correspondent' (Cronin, 1989). Under her reign Russia considerably extended its power and dominions.

Caviar (*ikra*). Caviar comes in two varieties: red, which is the roe of salmon inhabiting the rivers of the Russian Far East; and the more valued and therefore expensive black version, which is the roe of the sturgeon family which lives in the Caspian Sea.

Central Committee. Officially the highest organ of the communist party, whose members were elected by party congresses, but more a machine for rubber stamping the decisions and policies of the inner body of communist leaders forming the Politburo, the executive core.

→ Communist party

→ Politburo

Cheka. An abbreviation for 'Extraordinary Commission', in full The All-Union Extraordinary Commission for Fighting Counter-Revolution and Sabotage. The *Cheka* was the Soviet Union's first political police force from 1917 to 1922, from which all other Soviet organs of state security take their provenance. To this day the word *chekist* is still used to refer to a security official. The founder of the *Cheka* was Felix Dzerzhinsky (1877–1926). In August 1991 a crowd of 50,000 daubed KGB headquarters in Lubyanka Square with slogans and swastikas and dismounted the six-metre, fifteen-ton bronze statue of 'Iron Felix' by a crane, the head in a wire noose.

→ *KGB**

Chernenko, Konstantin (1911–1985). General Secretary of the Communist Party and stop-gap Soviet leader for 13 months between 1984 and 1985. An unreformed Brezhnevite, he left no mark on Soviet history except that he was the immediate predecessor of Mikhail Gorbachev.

→ Brezhnev*

→ Communist party

→ Gorbachev*

Chernomyrdin, Viktor (b. 1939). Appointed Minister of the Soviet gas industry in 1985 and in 1989 Chairman of the new state company, Gazprom. He became Prime Minister in 1992 and has had to grapple with Russia's economic and political troubles while coping with his mercurial boss, Boris Yeltsin.

→ Yeltsin

Chubais, Anatoly (b. 1956). A radical reformer, Chubais was appointed Deputy Prime Minister in 1992 to head the State Property Commission, responsible for privatization. In March 1997 he became First Deputy Prime Minister and Finance Minister, charged with dealing with the Russian government's number 1 problem, poor tax collection.

Civil War (1917–1922). This was fought between the Reds – the Bolsheviks – the Whites, who comprised anti-communist parties, such as the Mensheviks and Social Revolutionaries, Cossacks, Tsarist loyalists, and foreign interventionists from western Europe and Japan. The Reds, under the charismatic revolutionary Trotsky, crushed the fragmented opposition.

→ Bolshevik

→ Cossacks

→ Mensheviks

→ Trotsky

Comecon, alias the Council for Mutual Economic Aid (CMEA). Set up in 1949 Comecon's role was to further trade and technological cooperation among socialist countries. The biggest beneficiary was the leading socialist state, the USSR. The organization was dissolved in Budapest in February 1991. There were no tears.

Communist party. The sole agency and executor of political power and expression in the Soviet Union, and the only political party in world history ever to have ruled an empire. The communist party achieved its dominant position through 'the seizure of political power [in 1917], the suppression of all other political parties and non-communist organizations, the nationalization of industry and trade, the collectivization of agriculture, the elimination of foreign influences and the imposition by decree of specific views, doctrines and tastes' (Utechin, 1961). The gradual disintegration of the Soviet Union led to the demise of the party in 1991.

→ Politburo

Cossacks. The folklorish, legendary South Russian frontiersmen, outlaws, cowboys and Gurkhas all rolled into one. Once subdued by the Russians in the 19th century, the Cossacks became an elite sabre-rattling cavalry, very adept at sweeping through grounds of demonstrators in pre-revolutionary Russia and dispersing them. The ethnic and historical origins are a matter of fierce controversy and so is their present status in Russia and Ukraine. In 1990 they restored a 500-year old custom by electing a new *ataman*, 'father of horsemen', to promote and protect their rights.

CMEA → Comecon

CPSU. Communist Party of the Soviet Union. The Russian initials are КПСС.

Dacha. Descriptions such as 'country cottage' are misleading, as *dacha*s can range from hovel-like dwellings to modest, even elegant residences. *Dacha*s are best seen as the place of retreat from the more soul-destroying aspects of urban life. They 'offer peace and quiet, country air and unhurried living'. Many *dacha* dwellers grow their own fruit and vegetables and distil various alcoholic concoctions on the side.

Duma. Literally 'deliberation', *duma*s existed in pre-1917 Russia as representative assemblies. The most notable was the State Duma, which existed from 1906 to 1917. In post-Soviet Russia the *Duma* has been revived as the Russian parliament.

Dzerzhinsky, Felix → Cheka

Fabergé. The most illustrious court jeweller in history and Russia's most famous brandname even after 70 years of communism.

February Revolution. This was the event in 1917 which led to the downfall of the monarchy and allowed the Bolsheviks, through their soviets, to exercise political power with the increasingly ineffectual provisional government.

→ Soviet

Five Year Plans*

Gagarin, Yuri (1934–1968). The first Soviet cosmonaut, he completed an orbit of the earth in a Vostok spacecraft in 108 minutes on 12 April 1961 – the epic event which created the space race with the USA. Back on earth, Gagarin was swept to Moscow and received a symbolic welcome on Lenin's mausoleum. He died in a plane crash seven years later. He achieved genuine hero status in the Soviet Union and after his death still remains an icon of Soviet technological achievement.

Golden Horde. The mediaeval Mongol–Tatar state founded in 1236 by Batu, grandson of Genghis Khan, it occupied most of European Russia and Siberia (not then part of Russia). Russian princes were its vassals until it broke up in the mid-15th century. The successors of the Golden Horde formed khanates in Southern Russia, which posed a threat to Russia until they were subdued in the 17th century.

Glasnost*

Gorbachev, Mikhail*

Gosplan. The ministry-level State Planning Commission of the USSR, founded in 1921 and responsible for developing the Five Year Plans; discontinued in 1991. Its effectiveness and prestige were badly undermined by the Gorbachev reforms, which gave enterprises more control over their own affairs.

→ Five Year Plans

Great Patriotic War*

Great Terror*

Gromyko, Andrei (1909–1989). Influential Soviet Foreign Minister from 1957–1985 and known abroad as 'Mr Nyet', a nickname already associated with his predecessor, Molotov. 'He played his cards so close to his chest that he once paused carefully before answering a western diplomat who asked him if he had had a good breakfast with a non-committal "perhaps"'. Crucially Gromyko supported Gorbachev for the post of General Secretary after the death of Chernenko. Within months of Gorbachev taking office, Gromyko was replaced by Eduard Shevardnadze, who reflected the 'new thinking', but was given the ceremonial position of head of state until he retired in 1988.

*Intelligentsia**

Internal passport ➔ *Propiska*

Intourist. Soviet state travel agency, responsible for policing foreign tourists in the USSR rather than ensuring that they had a good time (let alone value for money). *Intourist*'s monopoly was broken in 1990.

Izvestiya. Daily newspaper, founded in 1917, and later published by the Presidium of the Supreme Soviet of the USSR. In 1990 the newspaper had a readership of 9 million. Its circulation is now about 0.6 million.

Kalashnikov. The name of the inventor of the AK-47 assault rifle, by which the weapon is also widely known. The gun can fire 30 bullets in three seconds and fatally wound a person at 300 yards. The model for AK-47 is believed by some to be the MP44, an assault rifle issued to German soldiers towards the end of the World War II. It was estimated in 1994 that at least 50 million AK-47s had been manufactured and distributed to armies and fighters worldwide. 'What Coca–Cola is to the export of American capitalism, the Kalashnikov was to Soviet Communism', wrote the *Sunday Telegraph* in 1994.

*KGB**

Khrushchev, Nikita (1894–1971). Foxy politician, fervent Leninist, but erratic 'destalinizer' who was leader of the Communist Party and Soviet government from 1958 to 1964, when he was ousted from office in the time-honoured way: by conspiracy when he was out of the country. He once delivered a memorable tirade at the UN, taking off his shoe and striking the podium with it to emphasize his point – handbagging Soviet style.

Kolkhoz. A collective farm in the Soviet period, nominally a collective enterprise of peasants in a locality, but in fact an ideologically driven confection of the 5 million peasant households that existed in pre-revolutionary Russia.

Kollektiv. A wide-ranging word referring to a group of people whose work together is linked by common interests. Thus a *kollektiv* can be people in the same office, the same scientific laboratory, the same factory or department of a ministry. In line with Russian group values the *kollektiv* protects the interests of its members, and the individual – in theory – never stands above the group. In the Soviet period the *kollektiv* was a principal channel for imposing control from above.

Komsomol. The Young Communist League, the Soviet boy scouts and girl guides all in one, with the aim of produce right-thinking young people for life and work in a socialist society.

Kosygin, Aleksei (1904-1980). Had a meteoric career as an apparatchik, becoming Chairman of the Leningrad City Soviet in 1938. He became prime minister in 1965, introducing some cautious economic reforms, but he was eventually overshadowed by Brezhnev.

→ Brezhnev*

Kremlin*

Kulak, the Russian word for 'fist', but referring, even before the 1917 Revolution, to comparatively prosperous merchants and peasants who allegedly exploited the less well off. After the Revolution the word became a term of abuse for peasants who resisted the collectivization of agriculture. Stalin ensured, true to propaganda, that the *kulak*s were liquidated as a social-economic class.

→ Stalin*

Lenin, Vladimir (1870–1924). Founder and leader of the Communist Party, creator of the Soviet state and first head of Soviet government; one of the most influential political revolutionaries of the industrial era. Shortly before his death from brain disease, he attempted to persuade his successors to drop the uncouth Stalin.

→ Communist party

→ Stalin*

→ USSR

Leningrad, Siege of *

Lubyanka. The headquarters of generations of Soviet security police and its post-communist successor, the FSK (Federal Counter-intelligence Service). Formerly the head office of an insurance company, the Lubyanka, named after the Moscow square where it is located, was taken over by the newly established security police, the *Cheka*, in March 1918. Across the square from the Lubyanka is Moscow's biggest children's store (*Detskiy Mir*). This was built in 1957 as a tribute to Dzerzhinsky, founder of the *Cheka*, who, other duties permitting, chaired a commission on children's welfare. Very touching.

→ *Cheka*

Mensheviks. Originally non-Leninist faction of the Russian Social Democratic Labour Party from 1903 onwards. In 1917 the Mensheviks united various social democratic groups, but were suppressed in 1922. In the show trials of the 1930s Stalin's victims were often branded as having menshevik tendencies.

Molotov, Vyacheslav (1890–1986). Faithful Stalinist, serving twice as Commissar (Minister) for Foreign Affairs and, from the mid-1930s, ranked number two after Stalin in the pecking order. His hallmark as a diplomat was his extreme stubbornness. His career waned after his master's death in 1953. His leading protégé was the USSR's longest serving foreign minister, Andrei Gromyko.

→ Gromyko

→ Stalin*

Muscovy. The Russian state from the 14th to 18th centuries, centred on Moscow. From Ivan III (1462–1505) to Peter the Great (1672–1725), Muscovy extended its control over the other Russian principalities (Novgorod, Vyatka, Pskov, Tver and Ryazan) and well beyond the traditional Russian lands. The first to declare himself Tsar of all the Russias was Ivan the Terrible in 1547. The last Tsar of Muscovy was Peter the

Great, who became the first Russian Emperor in 1721.

Nemtsov, Boris (b. 1960). In March 1997, after five years as governor of Nizhny Novgorod, Nemtsov was appointed First Deputy Prime Minister responsible for welfare, pensions and break-up of monopolies. He has described it as a kamikaze appointment.

Nicholas II (1868–1918). First cousin of George V and last Emperor of Russia. He was forced to abdicate in February 1917. After the Bolshevik seizure of power in 1917 he and his family were exiled in Yekaterinburg, where they were gruesomely murdered on Lenin's orders in July 1918.

*Nomenklatura**

Oblast. A major territorial administrative division within a Soviet republic, for which the word 'province' may be a rough translation. The fifteen republics of the USSR were divided into 150 *oblasts*. A second meaning of the word *oblast* is 'field' or 'sphere.' Other words for territorial divisions, in descending order of magnitude, are *okrug*, *krai* and *raion*.

October Revolution (25 October 1917 in the old Russian calendar; 7 November by today's reckoning). A damp squib of a revolution, but enough of a coup for the Bolsheviks to overthrow the Provisional Government and initiate Soviet rule under Lenin's communists.

→ Provisional Government

OMON. The acronym stands for 'special purpose militia detachment'. Set up by Gorbachev in 1988 under the Ministry of the Interior for use against separatists and other law breakers, its troops, known as the Black Berets, saw action – notoriously in January 1991 – in Latvia, where they killed four civilians.

Pasternak, Boris (1890–1960). Possibly Russia's greatest literary figure of the 20th century and for many intellectuals, disillusioned with the empty promises of communism, the spiritual leader of dissent. Best known for his novel *Doctor Zhivago*, Pasternak was awarded the Nobel Prize for Literature in 1958, but forced to reject it. He endured officially inspired harassment and vilification with great equanimity.

*Perestroika**

Peter the Great (1672–1725). One of the towering figures of Russia history. Boundless in energy and ruthlessness, he introduced the west, especially in the form of science, military technology and commercial practice, into Russia. Like all the reformers of Russia, he encountered massive attitudinal resistance. One of his contemporary admirers wrote: 'The great monarch works hard and accomplishes nothing. The Tsar pulls uphill alone with the strength of ten, but millions pull downhill.'

Politburo. The chief policy-making organ of the communist party and therefore arguably the most powerful Soviet institution. It virtually ran the USSR until 1990, when many of its powers were transferred to burgeoning parliamentary bodies.

Pravda. Communist party daily, founded in 1912, but not by Lenin as is sometimes asserted. Throughout the Soviet period it was a propaganda sheet highlighting production achievements (page 1), party matters, foreign news (courtesy of TASS), as well as correspondence and sport. *Pravda* always set the editorial tone for other newspapers. Its readership, peaking at 11 million readers in 1980, declined throughout the Gorbachev years. In 1992 it had only 1.4 million readers. In the same year it failed to appear for several weeks only to be saved by a Greek millionaire.

Propiska. Introduced in 1932, this was the name of an internal passport which also served as a residence permit. With this document residents anywhere in the USSR had to register with the local police and could not move to a new location without permission.

Purges → Great Terror*

Provisional Government. This was the government which ruled Russia after the abdication of the Tsar in February 1917. It was overthrown in the October Revolution.

→ October Revolution

→ Tsar

Red Army. The Workers' and Peasants' Red Army was formed in 1918 largely as a volunteer force to fight anti-Bolshevik troops. It was the revolutionary leader, Leon Trotsky, who transformed it into a professional fighting machine. But it was not until the 1930s that the Red Army became a modern professional army, although strongly politicized. It became the official Soviet Army in 1946.

Refusenik (or refuznik). A twisted version of the Russian word *otkaznik* (*otkaz* = refuse), refuseniks referred to Jews who had been denied exit visas for emigration to Israel and who also suffered a certain amount of persecution such as loss of employment or expulsion from university. Later the term applied to any Jew waiting for an exit visa. The last act of official persecution took place in 1987.

RSFSR. Russian Soviet Federative Socialist Republic. The largest and economically and politically most important constituent republic of the Soviet Union. Comprising three-quarters of Soviet territory, it was overwhelmingly 'Russian': at least 80 percent of the population were Great Russians. With the collapse of the Soviet Union in 1991, the RSFSR became the Russian Federation.

Russian Bear. The brown bear, known as *ursus arctos*, is the animal most identified with Russia. In Russian culture the bear, 'the lord of the forest,' is considered an intelligent animal and not feared as is the wolf. Its habitat is the *taiga* in European Russia, Siberia and the Far East. 'Bear' was also a NATO codename for a Soviet strategic bomber carrying cruise missiles.

→ *Taiga*

Russian Orthodox Church. After 70 years of atheist communism, the Russian Orthodox Church has restored its place as a powerful focal point for the mystical sense of Russianness. Despite a rapid increase in numbers of spiritually hungry adherents in recent years, the church as an organization is expected to continue its centuries-long role of being a mere appendage of the state.

Samizdat. Literally 'self-publishing' and a pun on *Gosizdat*, the state publishing organization, *samizdat* refers to the clandestine circulation of dissident literature from the mid-1970s until the advent of *glasnost*.

Samovar. Invented in the 18th century and still going strong, this mini-boiler (the Russian word literally translates as 'self-cooker') provides hot water all the time for making tea. The *samovar* does not however make the tea: it boils the water to be poured into a glass containing tea leaves. In Tula in the 19th century there were no fewer than 50 factories producing these 'pot-bellied kettles', which were a traditional wedding present.

Siberia*

Solzhenitsyn, Alexander*

Soviet. The Russian word for council. As of 1905 *soviet*s were increasingly run as strike committees (but not necessarily communist ones). After the Bolshevik Revolution in 1917 *soviet*s became integrated into the formal hierarchical structures of government. The highest levels of representation were the Congresses of Soviets and from 1917 to 1936 these institutions were ostensibly the supreme organs of state power, but in reality rubber stamped the decisions of the party leadership. Under the 1936 constitution the Congresses of Soviets were replaced by the Supreme Soviet.

→ Supreme Soviet

Sovkhoz. State farm of the Soviet period as opposed to the collective farm, *kolkhoz*. The main difference between the two was that the state farm was run more like a factory with hired labour who were paid regular wages.

→ *Kolkhoz*

Sputnik*

Stalin*

Stalingrad, Battle of*

Stolypin, Pyotr (1862-1911). Statesman of outstanding calibre and a notable reformer with particular reference to agriculture. He was nevertheless a ruthless suppressor of insurrection: thousands of agitators and malcontents were executed at gallows known as 'Stolypin's necktie'.

Supreme Soviet. The highest legislative organ of the Soviet Union, consisting of two chambers, the Soviet of the Union and the Soviet of Nationalities.

→ *Soviet*

Taiga. The boreal forest covering almost all the sub-Arctic north of Russia. It is the largest forest in the world, of considerable economic and ecological importance, and contains around half the world's reserves of softwood.

TASS. Abbreviation for Telegraph Agency of the Soviet Union. The official news agency of the USSR, attached to the Council of Ministers and responsible to the Propaganda Department of the Central Committee of the Communist Party.

→ Central Committee

Tsar. The title of the rulers of Muscovy from the 15th century, derived from the Latin Caesar, until Peter the Great assumed the title of Emperor [Imperator] of all Russia. The appellation of *Tsar* was used by all subsequent autocrats until the demise of the Romanov dynasty in 1917. The wife of the *Tsar* was the *Tsarina*; the heir to the throne was the *Tsarevich*.

→ Autocracy

Trotsky, Leon (né Bronshtein) (1879–1940). Revolutionary politician, Siberian exile, menshevik, bolshevik, creator of the Red Army, brilliant orator, a thorn in the side of Lenin and later Stalin, who exiled him. He was assassinated in Mexico in 1940 – the famous NKVD icepick job.

→ Red Army

→ KGB* (for NKVD)

Tundra. The treeless cold desert covering the extreme north of European Russia and Siberia. Winters are long with up to nine months of sub-zero temperatures. The sub-soil is permanently frozen (permafrost).

USSR. Union of Soviet Socialist Republics. In Russian the initials are СССП.

Verst. A traditional Russian measurement of length, equivalent to 1.06 kilometres.

Vodka. 'Commodity Number One . . . Calamity Number One.' See

Chapter 9.

War communism. The name of the bolshevik's social and economic policy during the Civil War. See Chapter 3.

Whites. The collective enemies of the Bolsheviks – the Reds – during the Civil War, 1917–1922.

→ Civil War

Yeltsin, Boris (b. 1931). The first Russian leader to be democratically elected. During the Gorbachev era period he was a politician of some prominence, notably as First Secretary of the Moscow Communist Party. As President of Russia, since 1990, he has strongly supported measures for introducing a market economy system. However, his style of leadership has been far from democratic. He has many of his predecessors' tendencies to 'go it alone', take policy from all-suited cronies (such as his former bodyguard), govern by edict, and dismiss and appoint senior colleagues seemingly on a whim, and allow newly appointed deputy prime ministers to override the Prime Minister, Chernomyrdin.

→ Chernomyrdin

*Zakuski**

Zek (pl. *zeki*). General slang expression for a labour camp inmate, first used by the convict workforce building the Moscow–Volga Canal in the 1930s, an acronym based on the Russian version of 'prisoners of the canal building directorate'.

Zemstvo. Pre-1917 institutions of local government which were abolished and replaced by soviets after the Bolshevik seizure of power.

→ Bolshevik
→ *Soviet*

Zhukov, Georgiy (1896–1974). The most brilliant Soviet military commander of World War II – with the exception of Generalissimo Stalin, of course.

→ Great Patriotic War*
→ Siege of Leningrad*

→ Stalingrad*

→ Cheka

ZIL. The name of the bulky, black limousines for transporting officials of the highest rank, notably presidents and ministers; most famously observed sweeping in and out the Kremlin when all other traffic is forced to a standstill. *ZIL* is actually the name of the car plant in Moscow, which is named after Ivan Likhachov, a Stalinist industrial boss and former Chekist, who was manager of the plant 1926-1950. The next level down of official conveyance is the *Chaika* followed by the *Volga*, which was standard issue for Red Army generals.

Glossary references

Brown, A. (1996) *The Gorbachev Factor*, Oxford: Oxford University Press.

Brown, A., Kaser, M. and Smith, G. (eds) (1994) *Cambridge Encyclopedia of Russia and the former Soviet Union*, Cambridge: Cambridge University Press.

Brun P. and Le Prat, A. (1990) *Russian Cooking*, London: Hamlyn.

Chambers Bibliographical Dictionary (1990), Edinburgh: Chambers.

Colton, T. J. (1995) *Moscow: Governing the Socialist Metropolis*, Cambridge, MS: Belknap Press of Harvard University Press.

Cronin, V. (1989) *Catherine, Empress of all the Russias*, London: Collins Harvill.

Cronin, V. (1994) *Napoleon*, London: HarperCollins.

Davies, N. (1996) *Europe: A History*, Oxford: Oxford University Press.

The Economist (1996a) 'On a wing and a prayer: aviation in Russia', 5 October.

The Economist (1996b) 'Nowhere to go but up: Aeroflot takes off', 14 December.

The Economist (1996c) 'A super-ethos in Russia's ribs', 21 December.

The Economist (1997a) 'Now another go at self-reform', 22 March.

The Economist (1997b) 'Orthodox yes-men', 5 April.

Gerhart, G. (1974) *The Russian's World: Life and Language*, New York: Harcourt Bruce Jovanovich.

Hill, G., Smorodinova, G. and Ulyanova, B. (1989) *Fabergé and the Russian Master Goldsmiths*, New York: Park Lane.

Hosking, G. (1992) *A History of the Soviet Union*, London: Fontana Press.

Keep, J. (1996) *Last of the Empires: A History of the Soviet Union 1945-1991*, Oxford: Oxford University Press.

Massie, R. K. (1992) *Peter the Great: His Life and Work*, London: Abacus

Milner-Gulland, R. and Dejevsky, N. (1990) *Cultural Atlas of Russia and the Soviet Union*, Oxford: Equinox (Oxford) Ltd.

Remnick, D. (1994) *Lenin's Tomb*, London: Penguin.

Richardson, D. (1995) *Moscow: The Rough Guide*, London: The Rough Guides.

Sunday Times Magazine (1992) 'Landing in the soup', 2 February.

Telegraph Magazine (1994) 'Sgt Kalashnikov regrets' and 'Any fool can fire one', 5 February.

Utechin, S. V. (1961) *Everyman's Concise Encyclopaedia of Russia*, London: J. M. Dent & Sons Ltd.

White, S. (1996) *Russia Goes Dry: Alcohol, State and Society*, Cambridge: Cambridge University Press.

Guide to information panels

The following list ranks the information panels in alphabetical order.

The key bibliographical sources for each topic are provided here; they do not occur in the references section of the book.

Baikal, (p. 223)

Brown, A., Kaser, M. and Smith, G. (eds) (1994) *Cambridge Encyclopedia of Russia and the Former Soviet Union*, Cambridge: Cambridge University Press.

Feshbach, M. and Friendly, A. (1992) *Ecocide in the USSR: Health and Nature under Siege*, London: Aurum Press.

Utechin, S. V. (1961) *Everyman's Concise Encyclopaedia of Russia*, London: J. M. Dent.

Van der Post, L. (1964) *Journey into Russia*, London: The Reprint Society.

Wilson, A. and Bachkatov, N. (1992) *Russia Revised: An Alphabetical Key to the Collapse of the Soviet Union*, London: André Deutsch.

Battle of Stalingrad (p. 214)

Bullock, A. (1991), Hitler and Stalin: Parallel Lives, London: HarperCollins.

Dear, I. C. B. and Foot, M. R. D. (eds) (1995) *Oxford Companion to the Second World War*, Oxford: Oxford University Press.

Hosking, G. (1992) *A History of the Soviet Union 1917–1991*, London: Fontana Press.

Moynahan, B. (1997) *The Russian Century: A History of the Last Hundred Years*, London: Pimlico.

Brezhnev (p. 61)

Brown, A., Kaser, M. and Smith, G. (eds) (1994) *Cambridge Encyclopedia of Russia and the Former Soviet Union*, Cambridge: Cambridge University Press.

Golubev, A. (1991) *Istoriya SSSR v Anekdotakh*, Smolensk: Izdatelstvo Smyadyn.

Hosking, G. (1992) *A History of the Soviet Union 1917-1991*, London: Fontana Press.

Nagel's Encyclopedia-Guide (1973) *Moscow and its Environs*, Geneva: Nagel.

Wilson, A and Bachkatov, N. (1992) *Russia Revised: An Alphabetical Key to the Collapse of the Soviet Union*, London: André Deutsch.

Climate and geography (p. 11)

Brown, A., Kaser, M. and Smith, G. (eds) (1994) *Cambridge Encyclopedia of Russia and the Former Soviet Union*, Cambridge: Cambridge University Press.

Kapuściński, R. (1994) *Imperium*, London: Granta Books.

Cyrillic alphabet (p. 177)

Matthews, W. K. (1975) *Russian Historical Grammar*, London: Athlone Press.

Unbegaun, B. O. (1967) *Russian Grammar*, Oxford: Clarendon Press.

Five Year Plans (p. 3)

Brown, A., Kaser, M. and Smith, G. (eds) (1994) *Cambridge Encyclopedia of Russia and the Former Soviet Union*, Cambridge: Cambridge University Press.

Dyker, D. (1992) *Restructuring the Soviet Economy*, London: Routledge.

Hosking, G. (1992) *A History of the Soviet Union 1917-1991*, London: Fontana Press.

Nove, A. (1990) *An Economic History of the USSR*, London: Penguin Books.

Glasnost (p. 86)

Brown, A. (1996) *The Gorbachev Factor*, Oxford: Oxford University Press.

Brown, A., Kaser, M. and Smith, G. (eds) (1994) *Cambridge Encyclopedia of Russia and the Former Soviet Union*, Cambridge: Cambridge University Press.

Hosking, G. (1992) *A History of the Soviet Union 1917-1991*, London: Fontana Press.

Ozhegov, S. I. (1984) *Slovar' Russkogo Yazyka*, Moscow: Russkii Yazyk.

Read, P. P. (1993) *Ablaze: The Story of Chernobyl*, London: Mandarin.

Gorbachev (p. 29)

Gorbachev, M. S. (1996) *Memoirs*, London: Doubleday.
Oxford Dictionary of Quotations (1985), London: Guild Publishing.

Great Patriotic War (p. 14)

Dear, I. C. B. and Foot, M. R. D. (eds) (1995) *Oxford Companion to the Second World War*, Oxford: Oxford University Press.

Moynahan, B. (1997) *The Russian Century: A History of the Last Hundred Years*, London: Pimlico.

Whymant, R. (1996) *Stalin's Spy: Richard Sorge and the Tokyo Espionage Ring*, London: I. B Tauris Publishers.

The Great Terror (p. 70)

Conquest, R. (1993) *Stalin: Breaker of Nations*, London: Weidenfeld and Nicolson.

Moynahan, B. (1997) *The Russian Century: A History of the Last Hundred Years*, London: Pimlico.

Utechin, S. V. (1961) *Everyman's Concise Encyclopaedia of Russia*, London: J. M. Dent.

Volkogonov, D. (1991) *Stalin: Triumph and Tragedy*, London: Weidenfeld and Nicolson.

Gulag (p. 62)

Brown, A., Kaser, M. and Smith, G. (eds) (1994) *Cambridge Encyclopedia of Russia and the Former Soviet Union*, Cambridge: Cambridge University Press.

Conquest, R. (1990) *The Great Terror: A Reassessment*, London: Pimlico.

Davies, N. (1996) *Europe: A History*, Oxford: Oxford University Press.

Dear, I. C. B. and Foot, M. R. D. (eds) (1995) *Oxford Companion to the Second World War*, Oxford: Oxford University Press.

Solzhenitsyn, A. (1974) *The Gulag Archipelago*, London: Collins/Harvill.

Volkogonov, D. (1991) *Stalin: Triumph and Tragedy*, London: Weidenfeld and Nicolson.

GUM (p. 143)

Colton, T. J. (1995) *Moscow: Governing the Socialist Metropolis*, Cambridge, Mass Belknap Press of Harvard University Press.

The Economist (1994) 'After the fall: a fall in Russia's booming stockmarket looks inevitable', 24 September.

Financial Times (1997) 'Property market: modernisers in Moscow', 31 January.

Milner-Gulland, R. (1990) *Cultural Atlas of Russia and the Soviet Union*, Oxford: Equinox (Oxford) Ltd.

Richardson, D. (1995) *Moscow: the Rough Guide*, London: The Rough Guides.

Intelligentsia (p. 73)

Hingley, R. (1978) *The Russian Mind*, London: Bodley Head.

Hosking, G. (1997) *Russia: People and Empire 1552–1917*, London: HarperCollins.

Ozhegov, S. I. (1984) *Slovar' Russkogo Yazyka*, Moscow: Russkii Yazyk.

Wilson, A. and Bachkatov, N. (1992) *Russia Revised: An Alphabetical Key to the Collapse of the Soviet Union*, London: André Deutsch.

KGB (p. 6)

Brown, A., Kaser, M. and Smith, G. (eds) (1994) *Cambridge Encyclopedia of Russia and the Former Soviet Union*, Cambridge: Cambridge University Press.

Conquest, R. (1990) *The Great Terror: A Reassessment*, London: Pimlico.

Moynahan, B. (1997) *The Russian Century: A History of the Last Hundred Years*, London: Pimlico.

Utechin, S. V. (1961) *Everyman's Concise Encyclopaedia of Russia*, London: J. M. Dent.

Kremlin (p. 22)

Colton, T. J. (1995) *Moscow: Governing the Socialist Metropolis*, Cambridge, Mass.: Belknap Press of Harvard University Press.

Gorbachev, M. S. (1996) *Memoirs*, London: Doubleday.

Nagel's Encyclopedia-Guide (1973) *Moscow and its Environs*, Geneva: Nagel.

Richardson, D. (1995) *Moscow: the Rough Guide*. London: The Rough Guides.

Management and marketing: Soviet conceptions (p. 97)

Koziy, V. A. (1990) *Bol'shaya Sovietskaya Entsiklopedia* [Great Soviet Encyclopaedia] (1970–78), vol. 15: *Vyrabotka Strategiya Sistem Upravleniya Stroitelnym Upravleniem*, Leningrad: LIMTU.

Moscow (p. 31)

Baedeker's Moscow (1991) Basingstoke: Automobile Association.

Colton, T. J. (1995) *Moscow: Governing the Socialist Metropolis*, Cambridge, Mass.: Belknap Press of Harvard University Press.

Richardson, D. (1995) *Moscow: the Rough Guide*. London: The Rough Guides.

Nomenklatura (p. 78)

Davies, N. (1986) *Heart of Europe: A Short History of Poland*, Oxford: Oxford University Press.

Papa (p. 180)

Gerhart, G. (1974) *The Russian's World: Life and Language*, New York: Harcourt Bruce Jovanovich, Inc.

Perestroika (p. 88)

Brown, A. (1996) *The Gorbachev Factor*, Oxford: Oxford University Press.

Brown, A., Kaser, M. and Smith, G. (eds) (1994) *Cambridge Encyclopedia of Russia and the Former Soviet Union*, Cambridge: Cambridge University Press.

Golubev, A. (1991) *Istoriya SSSR v Anekdotakh*, Smolensk: Izdatelstvo Smyadyn.

Hosking, G. (1992) *A History of the Soviet Union 1917–1991*, London: Fontana Press.

Russian collective value system. (p. 58)

The extract quoted is a contribution of Dr C. Vlachoutsicos (1996) in C. Vlachoutsicos, E. Bogatova, and N. Holden, 'Final report to the National Training Foundation on the workshop "Grasping the logic to bridge the gap: increasing the professional effectiveness of western consultants and management educators in Russia".' Moscow, 1–6 December 1996.

Russian literature (p. 173)

Baring, M. (1960) *Landmarks in Russian Literature*, London: Methuen.

Field, A. (1971) *The Complexion of Russian Literature*, Harmondsworth: Penguin Books.

Milner-Gulland, R. and Dejevsky, N. (1990) *Cultural Atlas of Russia and the Soviet Union*, Oxford: Equinox (Oxford) Ltd.

Utechin, S. V. (1961) *Everyman's Concise Encyclopaedia of Russia*, London: J. M. Dent.

Siege of Leningrad (p. 222)

Brown, A., Kaser, M. and Smith, G. (eds) (1994) *Cambridge Encyclopedia of Russia and the Former Soviet Union*, Cambridge: Cambridge University Press.

Dear, I. C. B. and Foot, M. R. D. (eds) (1995) *Oxford Companion to the Second World War*, Oxford: Oxford University Press.

Hosking, G. (1992) *A History of the Soviet Union 1917–1991*, London: Fontana Press.

Moynahan, B. (1997) *The Russian Century: A History of the Last Hundred Years*, London: Pimlico.

Salisbury, H. (1969) *The 900 Days: The Siege of Leningrad*, London: Pan Books.

Solzhenitsyn, Alexander (p. 9)

Brown, A., Kaser, M. and Smith, G. (eds) (1994) *Cambridge Encyclopedia of Russia and the Former Soviet Union*, Cambridge: Cambridge University Press.

Hosking, G. (1992) *A History of the Soviet Union 1917–1991*, London: Fontana Press.

Moynahan, B. (1997) *The Russian Century: A History of the Last Hundred Years*, London: Pimlico.

Sputnik (p. 75)

Brown, A., Kaser, M. and Smith, G. (eds) (1994) *Cambridge Encyclopedia of Russia and the Former Soviet Union*, Cambridge: Cambridge University Press.

Graham, L. R. (1993) *Science in Russia and the Soviet Union*, Cambridge: Cambridge University Press.

Keep, J. (1996) *Last of the Empires: A History of the Soviet Union 1945–1991*, Oxford: Oxford University Press.

Milner-Gulland, R. and Dejevsky, N. (1990) *Cultural Atlas of Russia and the Soviet Union*, Oxford: Equinox (Oxford) Ltd.

Moynahan, B. (1997) *The Russian Century: A History of the Last Hundred Years*, London: Pimlico.

Utechin, S. V. (1961) *Everyman's Concise Encyclopaedia of Russia*, London: J. M. Dent.

Stalin (p. 12)

Bullock, A. (1991), *Hitler and Stalin: Parallel Lives*, London: HarperCollins.

Conquest, R. (1993) *Stalin: Breaker of Nations*, London: Weidenfeld and Nicolson.

Davies, N. (1996) *Europe: A History*, Oxford: Oxford University Press.

Volkogonov, D. (1991) *Stalin: Triumph and Tragedy*, London: Weidenfeld and Nicolson.

Zakuski (p. 208)

Brun P. and Le Prat, A. (1990) *Russian Cooking*, London: Hamlyn.

Craig, K. and Novgorodstev, S. (1991) *The Cooking of Russia*, London: J. Sainsbury plc.

Gerhart, G. (1974) *The Russian's World: Life and Language*, New York: Harcourt Bruce Jovanovich, Inc.

Ozhegov, S. I. (1984) *Slovar' Russkogo Yazyka*, Moscow: Russkii Yazyk.

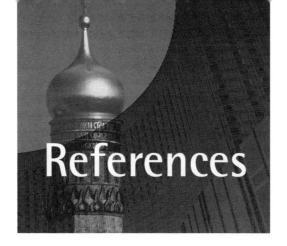

References

1 Coping with a New Russia

Applebaum, A. (1995) *Between East and East: Across the Borderlands of Europe*, London: Papermac.

Berdyayev, N. (1918 [1990]) *Sudba Rossii*, Moscow: MGU.

Conquest, R. (1990) *The Great Terror: A Reassessment*. London: Pimlico.

Davies, N. (1996) *Europe: A History*. Oxford: Oxford University Press.

Dunayeva, D. and Vipperman, C. (1995) 'Similar but different. Why do Russian and American business people, even when they speak the same language, so often seem to be engaging in a dialogue of the deaf?', *Business in Russia*, June.

Dyker, D. (1992)*Restructuring the Soviet Economy*, London: Routledge.

The Economist (1993) 'EC aid to the East'. 10 April.

The Economist (1995a) 'Nag, nag: Russia and the West', 8 April.

The Economist (1995b) 'Survey of Russia's emerging market', 8 April.

The Economist (1996) 'Is Russia different?', 15 June.

Fallowell, D. (1994) *One Hot Summer in St Petersburg*, London: Jonathan Cape.

Financial Times (1993) 'A cross-cultural minefield', 2 August.

Financial Times (1995) 'Moscow suspicion grows: Kremlin factions are at odds over policy', 19 January.

Financial Times (1996a) 'Spy follies', 8 May.

Financial Times (1996b) 'Russia insists it will expel UK "spies"', 15 May.

Financial Times (1996c) 'Survey of Russia: comforts for the well-heeled', 11 April.

Graham, L. R. (1996) *The Ghost of the Executed Engineer: Technology and the Fall of the Soviet Union*, Cambridge, MS: Harvard University Press.

Gunther, J. (1965) *Inside Russia Today*, Harmondsworth: Penguin Books.

Hingley, R. (1978) *The Russian Mind,* London: Bodley Head.

Holden, N. J. (1995) 'Management education in Russia: issues in course design, development and evaluation. A report with special reference to the Russian construction industry', Manchester: Brooke Publications Limited.

Holden, N. J. (1996) 'The reorientation of management learning in Russia and Poland in the transition to the market economy: a neglected perspective', in H. Somers (ed.) *Terminology, LSP and Translation: Studies in Language Engineering in Honour of Juan C. Sager,* Amsterdam: John Benjamins Publishing Company.

Hosking, G. (1997) *Russia: People and Empire 1552–1917,* London: HarperCollins.

Kapuściński, R. (1994) *Imperium,* London: Granta Books.

Keep, J. (1996) *Last of the Empires: A History of the Soviet Union 1945-1991,* Oxford: Oxford University Press.

Kissinger, H. (1994) *Diplomacy,* New York: Touchstone.

Kravchenko, Ye. (1995) 'A land of great expectations/Russian bureaucracy even has the Germans beaten', *Business in Russia,* November, pp. 58-61.

Mikheyev, D. (1996) *Russia Transformed,* Indianapolis: Hudson Institute.

Moynahan, B. (1997) *The Russian Century: A History of the Last Hundred Years,* London: Pimlico.

Poe, R. (1993) *How to Profit from the Coming Russian Boom: The Insider's Guide to Business Opportunities and Survival on the Frontiers of Capitalism,* New York: McGraw-Hill.

Remnick, D. (1994) *Lenin's Tomb,* London: Penguin Books.

Richardson, P. E. (1995) *Russia Survival Guide: The Definitive Guide to Doing Business and Traveling in Russia,* Montpelier, VT: Russian Information Services, Inc.

Sachs, J. (1994) *Poland's Jump to the Market Economy, Cambridge,* MS: MIT Press.

Skurski, R. (1983) *Soviet Marketing and Economic Development,* London: Macmillan.

Sobchak, A. (1992) *For a New Russia: The Mayor of St Petersburg's Own Story of the Struggle for Justice and Democracy,* London: HarperCollins.

Solzhenitsyn, A. (1991) *Rebuilding Russia: Reflections and Tentative Proposals,* London: HarperCollins.

Steele, J. (1994) *Eternal Russia,* London: Faber & Faber.

Utechin, S. V. (1961) *Everyman's Concise Encyclopaedia of Russia,* London: J. M. Dent.

Vlachoutsicos, C. (1995) *Constraints and Opportunities of the Russian Enterprise Manager,* [Work in progress] Athens: Hellenic Foundation for European and Foreign Policy.

Vlachoutsicos, C. and Lawrence, P. (1996) 'How managerial learning can assist economic transformation in Russia', *Organization Studies,* **17** (2) 311–325.

Volkogonov, D. (1991) *Stalin: Triumph and Tragedy,* London: Weidenfeld and

Nicolson.

Wilson, D. and Donaldson, L. (1996) *Russian Etiquette and Ethics in Business,* Lincolnwood, IL: NTC Business Books.

Yergin, D. and Gustafson, T. (1994) *Russia 2010 and What It Means for the World,* London: Nicholas Brealey.

2 *Management cultures in collision*

European Commission (1994) *Dictionary of Economic and Management Terms: English, Russian, German, French,* Brussels: TACIS Information Office.

Massie, R. (1992) *Peter the Great: His Life and World,* London: Abacus.

Wilson, D. and Donaldson, L. (1996.) *Russian Etiquette and Ethics in Business,* Lincolnwood, IL: NTC Business Books.

3 *Technocrats and Tigers*

Boycko, M., Shleifer, A. and Vishny, R. (1995) *Privatizing Russia,* Cambridge, Mass: MIT Press.

Brown, A., Kaser, M. and Smith, G. (eds) (1994) *Cambridge Encyclopedia of Russia and the Former Soviet Union,* Cambridge: Cambridge University Press.

Campbell, R. (1991) *The Socialist Countries in Transition: A Primer on semi-reformed Systems,* Bloomington: Indiana University Press.

Channon, J. and Hudson, R. (1995) *The Penguin Historical Atlas of Russia,* London: Penguin Books.

Conquest, R. (1994) *The Great Terror: A Reassessment,* London: Pimlico.

Cooper, J. (1991) *The Soviet Defence Industry: Conversion and Reform,* London: Royal Institute of International Affairs.

Dyker, D. (1992) *Restructuring the Soviet Economy,* London: Routledge.

Feshbach, M. and Friendly, A. (1992) *Ecocide in the USSR: Health and Nature under Siege,* London: Aurum Press.

Gorbachev, M. S. (1988) *Perestroika i Novoye Myshleniye,* Moscow: Izdatel'stvo Politicheskoi Literatury.

Graham, L. (1993) *Science in Russia and the Soviet Union,* Cambridge: Cambridge University Press.

Graham, L. R. (1996) *The Ghost of the Executed Engineer: Technology and the Fall of the Soviet Union,* Cambridge, MS: Harvard University Press.

Granick, D. (1972) *Managerial Comparisons of Four Developed Countries: France, Britain, United States, and Russia,* Cambridge, MS: MIT Press.

Hickson, D. and Pugh, D. (1995) *Management Worldwide: The Impact of Societal Culture on Organizations Around the Globe,* London: Penguin.

Hosking, G. (1992) *A History of the Soviet Union 1917-1991*, London: Fontana Press.

Hosking, G. (1997) *Russia: People and Empire 1552-1917*, London: HarperCollins.

Kotkin, S. (1991) *Steeltown, USSR: Soviet Society in the Gorbachev Era*, London: Weidenfeld and Nicolson.

Lawrence, P. and Vlachoutsicos, C. (1990) *Behind the Factory Walls: Decision Making in Soviet and US Enterprises*, Boston, MS: Harvard Business School Press.

Liferov, L. A and Dobrusin, D. L. (1969) 'Obuchenie i vospitanie na zanyatiakh v shkolnych masterskikh' in D. Lane, and F. O'Dell (1978) *The Soviet Industrial Worker: Social Class, Education and Control*, Oxford: Martin Robertson.

Mikheyev, D. (1996) *Russia Transformed*, Indianopolis: Hudson Institute.

Moynahan, B. (1994) *The Russian Century: A History of the last Hundred Years*, London: Pimlico.

Nove, A. (1990) *An Economic History of the USSR*, London: Penguin Books.

Read, P. P. (1993) *Ablaze: The Story of Chernobyl*, London: Mandarin.

Rutland, P. (1994) 'The economy: the rocky road from plan to market', in S. White, A. Pravda, and Z. Gitelman (eds) *Developments in Russian and Post-Soviet Politics*, London: Macmillan.

Smith, H. (1991) *The New Russians*, London: Vintage.

Utechin, S. V. (1961) *Everyman's Concise Encyclopaedia of Russia*, London: J. M. Dent.

Volkogonov, D (1991) *Stalin: Triumph and Tragedy*, London: Weidenfeld and Nicolson.

White, S. (1996) *Russia goes Dry: Alcohol, State and Society*, Cambridge: Cambridge University Press.

Wilson, A. and Bachkatov, N. (1992) *Russia Revised: An Alphabetical Key to the Soviet Collapse and the New Republics*, London: André Deutsch.

Zaitsev, A (1996) Comment made in a presentation at the workshop 'Grasping the logic to bridge the gap: Increasing the professional effectiveness of western consultants and management educators in Russia', Moscow, 1–6 December 1996.

4 *The Approach of the Great Feared Unknown*

Abramishvili, G. (1991) 'Filosofiya biznesa', *Ekonomika i Zhizn*, 45:8.

Abramov, L. I. and Manayenkova, E. A. (1990) *Organizatsiya i Planirovaniye Stroitelnogo Proizvodstva*. Moscow: Stroizdat.

Afanasyev, V. A. and Shishkin, A. I. (1989) *Metody Organizatsii Rabot v Stroitelstve*, Petrozavodsk: Petrozavodskiy Gosudarstvenniy Universitet.

British Soviet Business (1991) Magazine of the British-Soviet Chamber of Commerce, winter 1991.

Brown, A. (1996) *The Gorbachev Factor*, Oxford: Oxford University Press.

Brown, A, Kaser, M. and Smith, G. (eds) (1994) *Cambridge Encyclopedia of Russia and the Former Soviet Union*, Cambridge: Cambridge University Press.

Business Week (1990a) 'Crash courses in capitalism for Ivan the globe-trotter', 28 May.

Business Week (1991b) 'From Red Square to Harvard Square: the making of a Soviet MBA', 28 May.

Delovye Svyazy (1990) 'Rynok – zhestokii uchitel', tem i khorosh', 6:12–15.

Dyker, D. (1992) *Restructuring the Soviet Economy*, London: Routledge.

The Economist (1992) 'The wild east', 4–10 January.

Financial Times (1988) 'First Soviet business school open', 30 July.

Financial Times (1990) Special Supplement, 12 March.

Gorbachev, M. S. (1988) *Perestroika i Novoye Myshleniye*, Moscow: Izdatel'stvo Politicheskoi Literatury.

Graham, L. R. (1996) *The Ghost of the Executed Engineer: Technology and the Fall of the Soviet Union*, Cambridge, MS: Harvard University Press.

Hanin, Y. (1991) *Soviet Managers in Transition: Implications for Joint Ventures*. [No other details available.]

Hibbert, N. (1990) 'Training Soviet managers: Coventry Polytechnic's pioneering courses', *Industry and Higher Education*, December.

Hibbert, N. (1991) 'Management development: first principles', *Arguments and Facts* **2** (3): 7–8.

Holden, N. J. (1991) 'Shades of meaning in Soviet business and management'. *European Business Review* **91**(3) 9–14.

Holden, N. J. (1992) 'Creating the new Russian manager: implications for designing a cultural intervention', *Creativity and Innovation Management* **1**(2): 95–101.

Holden, N. J. (1993) 'Making Russian managers: prospects in post-Soviet society', *International Journal of Educational Management* **7** (4):10–16.

Holden, N. J. and Cooper, C. L. (1994) 'Russian managers as learners: implications for theories of management learning', *Management Learning* **25**(4) 503–22.

Hosking, G. (1991) *The Awakening of the Soviet Union*, London: Mandarin.

Kaplan, L. M. (1990) *Ekonomicheskie Problemy Intensifikatsii Stroitelnogo Proizvodstva*. Leningrad: Stroizdat.

Kapuściński. R. (1994) *Imperium*, London: Granta Books.

Keep, J. (1996) *Last of Empires: A History of the Soviet Union 1945–1991*, Oxford: Oxford University Press.

Koziy, V. A. (1990) *Vyrabotka Strategiya Sistem Upravleniya Stroitelnym Upravleniem*, Leningrad: LIMTU.

Kvint, L. V. (1990) 'The bureaucratic but workable Soviet management system', *The International Executive: American Management Association and American Graduate School of International Management*, pp. 3–6.

Lawrence, P. and Vlachoutsicos, C (1990) *Behind the Factory Walls: Decision Making in Soviet and US Enterprises*, Boston, MS: Harvard Business School Press.

McKibbin, L. E. (1992) Introduction in S. Puffer, *The Russian Management Revolution: Preparing Managers for the Market Economy*, Armonk, NY: M. E. Sharpe.

Manoukovsky, A. (1990) 'The outlook for Soviet business school', *European Management Journal* **9** (2): 182–5.

Menshikov, S. (1990) *Katastrofa ili Katarsi*, Moscow: Inter-Verso.

Naylor, T. H. (1988) 'The reeducation of Soviet management', *Across the Board*, February, pp. 28–37.

Nove, A. (1990) *An Economic History of the USSR*, London: Penguin Books.

Puffer, S. (ed.) (1991) 'The status of management education in the USSR.' *Soviet Education* **33** (11): 3–14.

Remnick, D. (1994) *Lenin's Tomb*, London: Penguin Books.

Roxburgh, A. (1991) *The Second Russian Revolution: The Struggle for Power in the Kremlin*, London: BBC Books.

Rutland, P. (1994) 'The economy: the rocky road from plan to market', in S. White, A. Pravda, and Z. Gitelman (eds) *Developments in Russian and Post-Soviet Politics*, London: Macmillan.

Schroeder, G. (1990) 'The "crisis" in the consumer sector', *Soviet Economy* **6**(1) 56–64.

Solzhenitsyn, A. (1991) *Rebuilding Russia*, London: Harvill.

Der Spiegel (1989) 'Vorwärts wie eine Schildkröte', interview with Leonid Abalkin **15**:185–91.

Vikhanskii, O. S. (1991) 'Let's train managers for the market economy', in Puffer, op. cit.

Wall Street Journal (1996) 'Rethinking an empire – the new Russia', 28 May.

Warner, M. (1992) *How Chinese Managers Learn: Management and Industrial Training in China*, Basingstoke: Macmillan.

Wilson, A. and Bachkatov, N. (1992) *Russia Revised: An Alphabetical Key to the Soviet Collapse and the New Republics*, London: André Deutsch.

Yarlinskii, G., Zadornov, M. and Mikhailov, A. (1991) 'Perestroika i peredyshka' *Izvestiya*, 3 January.

5 The post-Soviet manager: the new class struggle

Aguilar, F., Loveman, G. and Vlachoutsicos, C. (1994) 'The managerial challenge in Central and Eastern Europe as viewed from within', working paper 95-041, Harvard Business School.

Åslund, A. (1993) 'The gradual nature of economic change in Russia', in A Åslund and R. Lanyard (eds) *Changing the Economic System in Russia*, London: Pinter.

Åslund, A. and Layard, R. (eds) (1993) *Changing the Economic System in Russia*, London: Pinter.

Baring, M. (1960) *Landmarks in Russian Literature*, London: Methuen.

Belova, L. (1994) 'Economicheskaya voina: mif ili realnost?', *Voprosy Ekonomiki*, **5:** 38–42.

Berelowitch, A. and Wieviorka, M. (1996) *Les Russes den bas: enquête sur la Russie post-communiste*, Paris: Éditions du Seuil.

Boycko, M., Shleifer, A. and Vishny, R. (1995) *Privatizing Russia*, Cambridge, MS: MIT Press.

Cooper, J. (1991) *The Soviet Defence Industry: Conversion and Reform*, London: Pinter.

Dabrowski, M. (1993) 'The first half year of Russian transformation,' in Åslund and Layard, op. cit., pp. 1–18.

Dyker, D. (1992) *Restructuring the Soviet Economy*, London: Routledge.

The Economist (1992) 'A survey of Russia', 5 December.

The Economist (1995) 'A survey of Russia's emerging market', 8 April.

The Economist (1997) 'Russia's new economy tsar', 15 March.

Financial Times (1997) 'Survey: Russia', 9 April.

Hanin, Y. (1991) *Soviet Managers in Transition: Implications for Joint Ventures*. [No further details available.]

Kaplan, F. (1995) in S. Puffer and D. McCarthy 'Finding the common ground in Russian and American business ethics', *California Management Review* **37** (2): 29–46.

Kaplan, L. M. (1992) 'Outline of the Russian/St Petersburg construction industry during the transition to the market economy', unpublished manuscript, translated by N. J. Holden.

Kharkhordin, O. and Gerber, T. (1994) 'Russian directors' business ethic: a study of industrial enterprises in St Petersburg, 1993', *European Studies* **46** (7): 1075–1107.

Löwenhardt, J. (1995) *The Reincarnation of Russia: Struggling with the Legacy of Communism 1990–1994*, Harlow, Essex: Longman.

McCarthy, D. J. and Puffer, S. M. (1994) 'State enterprise managers view the transformation to private enterprise', *Journal of Private Enterprise*, **10** (1): 92–107.

McKinsey & Company, Inc. (1996) *Managing Successfully Beyond Privatization*, (a series of seven management guides) Moscow: Izdatelstvo 'Delo'.

Maslov, V. (1996a) 'Märkte Russlands: fünf nach zwölf für KMU', *Wirtschaften heute*, (3): 59.

Maslov, V. (1996b) 'Rossiya: poisk puti', *Istoricheskaya Gazeta*, 11 November.

Maslov, V. (1996c) 'Rossiya: poisk puti', *Istoricheskaya Gazeta*, 12 December.

Mikheyev, D. (1996) *Russia Transformed*, Indianapolis: Hudson Institute.

Moynahan, B. (1994) *The Russian Century: A History of the Last Hundred Years*, London: Pimlico.

National Training Foundation (1996) 'Barriers on the path of the development of effective management: report of results of a survey', Moscow: National Training Foundation [in Russian].

National Training Foundation: 'Joint conclusions (C) and recommendations (R) on projects 214a "Supply assessment in management development field" and 214b "Demand assessment in management development field" of the National Training Foundation', Moscow: National Training Foundation.

Puffer, S. and McCarthy, D. (1995) 'Finding the common ground in Russian and American business ethics', *California Management Review* **37** (2) 29–46.

Remnick, D. (1994) *Lenin's Tomb*, London: Penguin.

Sachs, J. (1994) 'Economists try to fill the Soviet void with empty words', the *Guardian*, 13 September.

Vasiliev, S. A. (1993) 'Economic reform in Russia: social, political, and institutional aspects', in Åslund and Layard, op. cit., pp. 72–86.

Veiga, J., Yanouza, G. and Buchholtz, A. (1995) 'Emerging cultural values among Russian managers: what will tomorrow bring?', *Business Horizons*, pp. 20–27.

Wilson, A. and Bachkatov, N. (1992) *Russia Revised: An Alphabetical Key to the Soviet Collapse and the New Republics*, London: André Deutsch.

Zhukova, M. and Korotov, K. (1996) 'Distinctive features of organizational change in Russia', paper presented at the workshop 'Grasping the logic to bridge the gap: increasing the professional effectiveness of western consultants and management educators in Russia', Moscow, 1–6 December.

6 Business relationships: asymmetries and anxieties

Åslund, A. (1993) 'The gradual nature of economic change in Russia', in A. Åslund, and R. Layard (eds), *Changing the Economic System in Russia*, London: Pinter.

Business Week (1997) 'The rush to Russia', 24 March.

Chamberlain, L. (1995) *Volga, Volga: A Voyage Down the Great River*, London: Picador.

Conquest, R. (1992) *The Great Terror: A Reassessment*, London: Pimlico.

Dunayeva, D. and Vipperman, C. (1995) 'Similar but different. Why do Russian and American business-people, even when they speak the same language, so often seem to be engaging in a dialogue of the deaf?', *Business in Russia*, June.

The Economist (1994) 'Russia: rights arrive', 18 February.

The Economist (1995) 'Nag, nag: Russia and the West', 8 April.

The Economist (1996a) 'Russia: money kills', 16 November.

The Economist (1997) 'Business Russia' January.

Financial Times (1996a) 'Spy follies', 8 May.

Financial Times (1996b) 'Russia insists it will expel UK "spies"', 15 May.

Financial Times (1997) 'Survey: Russia', 9 April.

Ford, D. (ed.) (1990) *Understanding Business Markets: Interaction, Relationships, Networks*, London: Academic Press.

Graham, L. (1993) *Science in Russia and the Soviet Union*, Cambridge: Cambridge University Press.

Håkansson, H. (ed.) (1982) *International Marketing and Purchasing of Industrial Goods: An Interaction Approach*, Chichester: John Wiley & Sons.

Handelman, S. (1994) *Comrade Criminal: The Theft of the Second Russian Revolution*, London: Michael Joseph.

Hingley, R. (1978) *The Russian Mind*, London: Bodley Head.

Holden, N. J. (1992) 'Creating the new Russian manager: implications for designing a cultural intervention', *Creativity and Innovation Management*. **1** (2) 95–101.

Holden, N. J. (1994) 'Littlewoods in St Petersburg: a major development in UK-Russian retail co-operation', in P. McGoldrick (ed.) *Cases in Retail Management*, London: Pitman.

Holden, N. J. (1995) 'Management education in Russia: issues in course design, development and implementation. A report with special reference to the Russian construction industry, Manchester: Brooke Publications Limited.

Holden, N. J. (1997) 'Coping with Russia as a bad fit', in R. Crane (ed.) *Global Mindsets*, London: Prentice-Hall.

Holden, N. J. and Cooper, C L. (1994) 'Russian managers as learners: implications for theories of management learning', *Management Learning*. **25** (4): 503-522.

Hosking, G. (1997) *Russia: People and Empire 1552–1917*, London: HarperCollins.

Johanson, M. (1994) 'Viking Raps – a case study of joint venture negotiation in the former Soviet Union', in P. Buckley and P. Ghauri (eds) *The Economics of Change in East and Central Europe*, London: Academic Press.

Kappel, G., Rathmayr, R. and Diehl-Zelonkina, N. (1992) *Verhandeln mit Russen: Gesprächs- und Verhaltensstrategien für die interkulturelle Geschäftspraxis*, Vienna: Service Verlag.

Kapuściński, R. (1994) *Imperium*, London: Granta Books.

Kennedy, G. (1985) *Negotiate Anywhere: Doing Business Abroad*, London: Business Books.

Kravchenko, Ye. (1995) 'A land of great expectations/Russia bureaucracy even has the Germans beaten', *Business in Russia*, November, pp. 58–61.

Lyokhin, I. V. and Pertrova, F. N. (eds) (1955) *Slovar' Inostrannykh Slov*, Moscow: Izdatel'stvo Inostrannykh i Natsionalnykh Slovarei.

Massie, R. K. (1992) Peter the Great: *His Life and World*, London: Abacus.

Mejevitch, V. (1993) 'An investigation into the emergence of customer orientation in the construction industry of St Petersburg', unpublished MSc dissertation,

Manchester School of Management, UMIST.

Oxford Russian Dictionary (1993), Oxford: Oxford University Press.

Ozhegov, S. I. (1984) *Slovar' Russkogo Yazyka*, Moscow: Russkii Yazyk.

Poe, R. (1995) *How to Profit from the Coming Russian Boom: The Insiders Guide to Business Opportunities and Survival on the Frontiers of Capitalism*, New York: McGraw-Hill.

Puffer, S. and McCarthy, D. (1995) 'Finding common ground in Russian and American business ethics', *California Management Review* **37** (2): 29–46.

Read, P. P. (1993) *Ablaze: The Story of Chernobyl*, London: Mandarin.

Remnick, D. (1994) *Lenin's Tomb*, London: Penguin Books.

Richardson, P. E. (1995) *Russia Survival Guide: The Definitive Guide to Doing Business and Traveling in Russia*, Montpelier, VT: Russian Information Services, Inc.

Russia Express (1996a) 'Russia remains the final frontier', **183**: 19–20.

Russia Express (1996b) Russia Express Executive Briefing. Supplement to Russia Express (1996a), op. cit.

Russkii Yazyk (1993) *Sovremenniy Slovar' Inostyrannykh Slov*, Moscow: Russkii Yazyk.

Russo-British Chamber of Commerce (1996a) *Bulletin*, Issue 7/96, August/September.

Russo-British Chamber of Commerce (1997a) *Bulletin*, Issue 2/96, February.

Russo-British Chamber of Commerce. Various *Bulletins*, 1996–1997.

Salmi, A. (1996a) 'Exporting of information technology to Russia', monograph: Helsinki School of Economics and Business Administration.

Salmi, A. (1996b) 'Entry of Kemwater, a Finnish company, into the Russian market', monograph, Helsinki School of Economics and Business Administration.

Smith, H. (1991) *The New Russians*, Vintage, London.

Steele, J. (1994) *Eternal Russia*, London: Faber & Faber.

Veiga, J., Yanouzas, J. and Buchholtz, A. (1995) 'Emerging cultural values among Russian managers: what will tomorrow bring?', *Business Horizons*, July–August, pp. 20–26.

Vlachoutsicos, C. (1995) *Constraints and Opportunities of the Russian Enterprise Manager*, [work in progress] Athens: Hellenic Foundation for European and Foreign Policy.

White, S. (1996) *Russia goes Dry: Alcohol, State and Society*, Cambridge: Cambridge University Press.

Wilson, D. and Donaldson, L. (1996) *Russian Etiquette and Ethics in Business*, Lincolnwood, IL: NTC Business Books.

Yergin, D. and Gustafson, T. (1994) *Russia 2010 and What it Means for the World*, London: Nicholas Brealey.

7 Russians, language and communication

Brown, A., Kaser, M. and Smith, G. (eds) (1994) *Cambridge Encyclopedia of Russia and the Former Soviet Union*, Cambridge: Cambridge University Press.

Buxton, C. R. and Jackson, H. S. (1962) *Translation from Russian for Scientists*, London: Blackie.

Comrie, B. (1981) *The Languages of the Soviet Union*, Cambridge: Cambridge University Press.

Comrie, B. and Stone, G. (1978) *The Russian Language since the Revolution*, Oxford: Oxford University Press.

Conquest, R. (1993) *Stalin: Breaker of Nations*, London: Weidenfeld and Nicholson.

Cronin, V. (1989) *Catherine, Empress of all the Russia*, London: Collins Harvill.

De Bray, R. G. A. (1980) *Guide to the East Slavonic Languages*, Columbus, Ohio: Slavica Publishers.

Dunn, J. A. (1996) Presentation on language change in Russia at the Colloquium 'Language and society in Eastern Europe', University of St Andrews, 13 April.

The Economist (1994a) 'I spell, therefore I am', 18 June.

The Economist (1994b) 'What's in a name? Money', 23 July.

Entwistle, W. J. and Morison, W. A (1949) *Russian and the Slavonic Language*, London: Faber & Faber.

Fallowell, D. (1994) *One Hot Summer in St Petersburg*, London: Jonathan Cape.

Filin, F. P. (ed.) (1979) *Encyclopedia of the Russian Language*, Moscow: Russkii Yazyk [in Russian].

Gerhart, G. (1974) *The Russian's World: Life and Language*, New York: Harcourt Brace Jovanovich.

Götz, R. and Halbach, U. (1994) *Politisches Lexikon Russlands*, Munich: C H. Beck Verlag.

Hajdu, P. (1975) *Finno-Ugrian Languages and Peoples*, London: André Deutsch.

Handelman, S. (1994) *Comrade Criminal: The Theft of the Second Russian Revolution*, London: Michael Joseph.

Hingley, R. (1978) *The Russian Mind*, London: Bodley Head.

Holden, N. J. (1996) 'The reorientation of management language in Russia and Poland in the transition to the market economy: a neglected perspective', in H. Somers (ed.) *Terminology, LSP and Translation Studies in Language Engineering in Honour of J. C. Sager*, Amsterdam: John Benjamins Publishing Company.

Hosking, G. (1991) *The Awakening of the Soviet Union*, London: Mandarin.

Hosking, G. (1997) *Russia: People and Empire 1552-1917*, London: HarperCollins.

Isaev, M. I. (1977) *National Languages in the USSR: Problems and Solutions*, Moscow: Progress Publishers.

Kohls, S. (1971) *Business Russian: A Reference and Textbook*, London: Pitman.

Leeming, H. (1994) 'Language: Russian, Ukrainian and Belorussian' in *The Cambridge Encyclopedia of Russia and the Former Soviet Union*, Cambridge: Cambridge University Press.

Matthews, W. K. (1967) *Russian Historical Grammar*, London: Athlone Press.

Mattock, J. (1996) *Russia: The Essential Guide for the Business Traveller*, London: Routledge.

Remnick, D. (1994) *Lenin's Tomb*, London: Penguin Books.

Steele, J. (1994) *Eternal Russia: Yeltsin, Gorbachev and the Mirage of Democracy*, London: Faber & Faber.

Unbegaun, B. O. (1972) *Russian Surnames*, Oxford: Clarendon Press.

Vinokur, G. O. (1971) *The Russian Language: A Brief History*, Cambridge: Cambridge University Press.

Ward, D. (1965) *The Russian Language Today*, London: Hutchinson University Press.

Wilson, D. and Donaldson, L. (1996) *Russian Etiquette and Ethics in Business*, Lincolnwood, IL: NTC Business Books.

Zeldin, T. (1984) *The French*, London: Fontana Paperbacks.

8 The new language barrier

Abramashvili, G. (1991) 'Filosofiya biznesa', in *Ekonomika i Zhizn*, (45) 8.

Åslund, A (1993) in A. Åslund, and R. Layard (eds), *Changing the Economic System in Russia*, London: Pinter.

Åslund, A. and Layard, R. (eds) (1993) *Changing the Economic System in Russia*, London: Pinter.

Baedeker's Leningrad (1991) Basingstoke: Automobile Association.

Brown, A. (1996) *The Gorbachev Factor*, Oxford: Oxford University Press.

Cronin, V. (1989) *Catherine, Empress of all the Russias*, London: Collins Harvill.

Dunn, J. A. (1996) Presentation on language change in Russia at the Colloquium 'Language and society in Eastern Europe', University of St Andrews, 13 April.

The Economist (1993) 'EC aid to the East', 10 April.

Entwistle, W. J. (1974) *The Spanish Language*, London: Faber & Faber.

European Commission TACIS Dictionary of Economic and Management Terms: English, Russian, German, French (1994) Brussels: European Commission.

Hibbert, N. (1990) 'Training Soviet managers', *Industry and Higher Education*, December, 231–7.

Hibbert, N. (1991) 'Management development: first principles', *Arguments and Facts* **1** (3): 7–8.

Hingley, R. (1978) *The Russian Mind*, London: Bodley Head.

Holden, N. J. (1992) 'Management, language and Euro-communication: 1992 and beyond', in M. Berry (ed.) *Cross-cultural Communication in Europe*, Turku: Eurooppa Instituutin.

Holden, N. J. (1995a) 'A diachronic review of Russian misconceptions of marketing: implications for marketing educators and theorists', proceedings of the Second Conference on the Cultural Dimension of International Marketing, Odense University, May.

Holden, N. J. (1995b) 'Management training in Russia: issues in course design, development and evaluation. A report with special reference to the Russian construction industry', Manchester: Brooke Publications Limited.

Holden, N. J. (1996) 'The reorientation of management language in Russia and Poland in the transition to the market economy: a neglected perspective', in H. Somers (ed.) *Terminology, LSP and Translation: Studies in Language Engineering in Honour of J. C. Sager*, Amsterdam: John Benjamins Publishing Company.

Holden, N. J. and Cooper, C. L. (1994) 'Russian managers as learners: implications for theories of management learning', *Management Learning* **25** (4): 503–522.

Holden, N. J. and Gale, A. W. (1993) 'An evaluation of Russian managers' expectations of western-sponsored training programmes', *Leadership and Organizational Development Journal* **14** (6): 24–9.

Holden, N. J. and Yamin, M. (1994)'What *is* the market economy?' in R. Fellowes (ed.) *Distance Learning Course Book for Russian Construction Managers*, Manchester: UMIST.

Kotelova, N. Z. (ed.) (1984) *Novye Slova i Znacheniya: Slovar'-spravochnik po Materialam Pressy i Literatury 70-x godov*, Moscow: Russkii Yazyk.

Lieven, D. (1994) *Nicholas II Tsar of all the Russias*, London: Pimlico.

Lyokhin, I. V. and Petrova, F. N. (1955) *Slovar' Inostrannykh Slov*, Moscow: Gosudarstvennoye Izdatel'stvo Inostrannykh i Natsionalnych Slovarei.

Manoukovsky, A. (1990) 'The outlook for Soviet business schools', *European Management Journal* **9** (2):182–5.

Mikheyev, D. (1996) *Russia Transformed*, Indianapolis: Hudson Institute.

Morrison, J. (1991) *Boris Yeltsin: From Bolshevik to Democrat*, London: Penguin Books.

Ozhegov, S. I. (1984) *Slovar' Russkogo Yazyka*, Moscow: Russkii Yazyk.

Puffer, S. (ed.) (1991) 'Introduction: the Status of Management Education in the USSR, Soviet Education' **33** (1): 3–14.

Puffer, S. (1992) *The Russian Management Revolution: Preparing Managers for the Market Economy*, Armonk, NY: M. E. Sharpe.

Sager, J. C., Dungworth, D. and McDonald, P. (1980) *English Special Languages: Principles and Practice in Science and Technology*, Wiesbaden: Oscar Brandstetter Verlag.

Shapiro, V. and Sheinberg, M. (1993) *Tolkovyi Slovar' po Upravleniyu Proyektami*,

Saint Petersburg: Izdatelskoye Predpriyatiye 'DvaTri'.

Sinelnikov, S. M., Solomonik, T. G. and Yanborisova, R. V. (eds) (1992) *Entsiklopedicheskii Slovar' Predprinimatelya*, Saint Petersburg: SP Alfa-Fond.

Skurski, R. (1983) *Soviet Marketing and Economic Development*, London: Macmillan.

Smith, H. (1991) *The New Russians*, London: Vintage.

Steele, J. (1994) *Eternal Russia*, London: Faber & Faber.

TACIS Training and Management Magazine, No. 1 (1993), Brussels: Commission of the European Communities.

TACIS Training and Management Magazine, No. 2 (1993), Brussels: Commission of the European Communities.

Trubel, E-M. (1994) 'Ungarn: wirtschaftliche Öffnung – sprachliche Neuorientierung', in M. Snell-Hornby, F. Pöchhacker, and K. Kaindl (eds) *Translation Studies: An Interdiscipline*, Amsterdam: John Benjamins Publishing Company.

Utechin, S. V. (1961) *Everyman's Concise Encyclopaedia of Russia*, London: J. M. Dent.

Vlachoutsicos, C. and Lawrence, P. (1990) 'What we don't know about Soviet management', *Harvard Business Review*, November–December, pp. 50–64.

Wilson, A. and Bachkatov, N. (1992) *Russia Revised: An Alphabetical Key to the Soviet Collapse and the New Republics*, London: André Deutsch.

9 *Coping with the green snake: the social side of business*

Bridges, O. (1994) *Business Russian* [Teach Yourself Books], London: Hodder and Stoughton.

Brown, A., Kaser, M. and Smith, G. (eds) (1994) *Cambridge Encyclopedia of Russia and the Former Soviet Union*, Cambridge: Cambridge University Press.

Christian, D. (1990) *'Living Water': Vodka and Russian Society on the Eve of Emancipation*, Oxford: Clarendon Press.

Dostoyevsky, F. M., (1965) *Prestupleniye i Nakazaniye* [Crime and Punishment], Letchworth: Bradda Books Ltd.

Dubyagina, Yu. P. and Bronnikova, A. G. (1991) *Tolkovyi Slovar' Ugolovnykh Zhargonov* [Explanatory dictionary of criminal slang], Moscow: Inter-OMNIS.

The Economist (1995) 'The world this week: politics and current affairs', 26 August.

Encyclopaedia Britannica (1993) 15th edn, Encyclopaedia Britannica, Inc., Chicago: University of Chicago.

Feshbach, M. and Friendly, A. (1992) *Ecocide in the USSR: Health and Nature under Siege*, London: Aurum Press.

Financial Times (1994a) 'Biggest Russian vodka distillery closes', 9 February.

Financial Times (1994b) 'Observer: Hard stuff', 25 July.

Financial Times (1994c) 'Vodka on rocks with bitterness: when the Stolichnaya factory is ailing, what it says about Russia', 20 August.

Financial Times (1994d) 'Russia clamps down on TV advertising', 2 September.

Financial Times (1994e) 'Russia may cut tax to curb vodka deaths', 14 September.

Gorbachov, M. S. (1995) *Erinnerungen*, Berlin: Siedler Verlag.

Hingley, R. (1978) *The Russian Mind*, London: The Bodley Head.

Holden, N. J. (1995) 'Management education in Russia: issues in course design, development and implementation. A report with special reference to the Russian construction industry', Manchester: Brooke Publications Limited.

Kopelev, L. (1994) 'Chem poet zhiv', trans. in A. Brown, M. Kaser, and G. Smith (eds) *Cambridge Encyclopedia of Russia and the Former Soviet Union*, Cambridge: Cambridge University Press.

Massie, R. K. (1992) *Peter the Great: His Life and World* 2 edn., London: Abacus.

Medvedev, R. and Chiesa, G. (1989) *Time of Change: An Insider's View of Russia's Transformation*, New York: Pantheon Books.

Ozhegov, S. I. (1984) *Slovar' Russkogo Yazyka*, Moscow: Russkii Yazyk.

Pokhlebkin, W. (1992) *A History of Vodka*, London: Verso.

Roxburgh, A. (1991) *The Second Russian Revolution*, London: BBC Books.

Smith, H. (1992) *The New Russians*, London: Vintage.

Steele, J. (1994) *Eternal Russia: Yeltsin, Gorbachev and the Mirage of Democracy*, London: Faber & Faber.

The *Times* (1995a) 'Yeltsin orders ban on advertising for drink and tobacco', 20 February.

The *Times* (1995b) 'Russian alcoholism worsens', 10 March.

The *Times* (1995c) 'How an over-the-counter Mickey Finn nearly stopped my heart', 12 December.

The *Times* (1995d) 'Beware Russians aiming to relieve you of blood pressure and wallet', 13 December.

Utechin, S. V. (1961) *Everyman's Concise Encyclopaedia of Russia*, London: J. M. Dent.

White, S. (1996) *Russia goes Dry: Alcohol, State and Society*, Cambridge: Cambridge University Press.

Wilson, A. and Bachkatov, N. (1992) *Russia Revised: An Alphabetical Key to the Soviet Collapse and the New Republics*, London: André Deutsch.

10 *Towards effective relationship management*

Conquest, R. (1994) *The Great Terror*, London: Pimlico.

Conquest, R. (1993) *Stalin: Breaker of Nations*, London: Weidenfeld & Nicolson.

Financial Times (1997) 'Survey: Russia', 9 April.

Gardener, M. (ed.) (1960) *The Annotated Alice: 'Alice's Adverntures in Wonderland and Through the Looking Glass', by Lewis Carroll*, New York: Bramhall House.

Hosking, G. (1997) *Russia: People and Empire 1552–1917*, London: HarperCollins.

Lieven, D. (1994) *Nicholas II: Emperor of all the Russias*, London: Pimlico.

Manager Magasin (1991) 'Trends + Signale Sowjet-Union', July.

Smith, R. E. F. and Christian, D. (1984) *Bread and Salt: A Social and Economic History of Food and Drink in Russia*, Cambridge: Cambridge University Press.

Vlachoutsicos, C. Bogatova, E. and Holden, N. J. (1997) Report to the National Training Foundation, Moscow, on the results of the workshop 'Grasping the logic to bridge the gap', Moscow, December 1996.

White, S. (1996) *Russia goes Dry: Alcohol, State and Society*, Cambridge: Cambridge University Press.

Zaitseva, L. (1994) 'Umom Rossiyu ne ponyat . . .', *Voprosy Ekonomiki*, February, pp. 95–107.

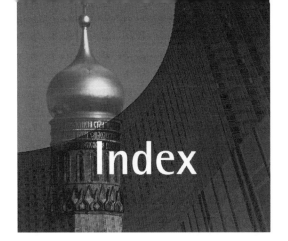

Index

Note: Page references in **bold** refer to information panels

8836